Edible
Wild Plants

THE WILD FOOD ADVENTURE SERIES

Edible Wild Plants

Wild Foods from Dirt to Plate

JOHN KALLAS, PH.D.

GIBBS SMITH

TO ENRICH AND INSPIRE HUMANKIND

To John Kardaras, my grandfather,
who inspired me to learn, work hard, speak my mind, and challenge conventional thinking. He
loved the outdoors and ate wild foods as a normal part of everyday life, just as I do today. There
are a million things I wish I could ask him if he were still with us.

First Edition
24 23 22 21   27 26 25 24

Text & Photographs © 2010 John Kallas, unless otherwise noted
Illustrations © 2010 as noted

Published by
Gibbs Smith
P.O. Box 667
Layton, Utah 84041

1.800.835.4993 orders
www.gibbs-smith.com

Designed and produced by mGraphicDesign
Printed and bound in China
Gibbs Smith books are printed on either recycled, 100% post-consumer waste or on FSC-certified papers, or on paper produced from a 100% certified sustainable forest/controlled wood source.

Cover Photographs—
Front cover photographs by the author (clockwise from the John Kallas photograph by Dana Coffee [1997]: tawny daylily flower, pita sandwich with wild greens, dandelion root crowns, curly dock leaf variations, chickweed tops). Back cover photographs by the author (left to right: curly dock sprout, cut curly dock leaves, wild spinach pizza).

Library of Congress Cataloging-in-Publication Data

Kallas, John, 1952-
  Edible wild plants : wild foods from dirt to plate / John Kallas. — 1st ed.
      p. cm.
  Includes bibliographical references.
  ISBN-13: 978-1-4236-0150-0
  ISBN-10: 1-4236-0150-5
  1. Wild plants, Edible. 2. Cookery (Greens) I. Title.
  QK98.5.A1K35 2010
  581.6'32—dc22
                                          2009040589

Contents

Acknowledgments

There are many people who have inspired and supported me over the years, and that support came in spite of the fact that I was pursuing a nonconventional field and career that few beyond myself took seriously. Dr. John Beaman, the former curator at the Michigan State University Herbarium, was a role model and enabler who gave a young upstart the resources, space, respect, and personal attention to seriously study the world of edible plants.

Drs. Louis Twardzik and Louis Moncrief, the former Chairs of the Department of Park and Recreation Resources at Michigan State, both helped me on my path. It was Dr. Twardzik who encouraged me as young graduate student and provided me with the opportunity to teach wild foods at Michigan State—the start of my professional career. It was Dr Moncrief's challenge for me to do something to genuinely advance the field of wild foods that led me to go on for an advanced degree in nutrition.

Dr. Kathryn Kolasa opened my eyes to the importance of cultural foodways and how much people's behaviors related to food can tell us about food, humans, and human ingenuity. It was Dr. Jenny Bond's unconditional support that helped me complete my doctoral program with style.

Access to land is an important factor in research and teaching about wild foods. I want to thank the grounds crew at Michigan State University, specifically the Beal Botanical Garden, for the unlimited access the staff has given me over the years; my longtime friends Shari and Daniel Raider, for the continuing access to their wonderful Sauvie Island Organics Farm; the Portland Parks Department and the folks at Portland Metro, for helping me actualize our shared mission of educating the public about the region's amazing natural resources, particularly Jim Sjulin, for opening the door for me years ago; Leonard and Therese Tardif, whose swamp is one of my favorite teaching and research areas; my longtime friends Kevin and Deb Howard, whose land in the foothills of Mount Adams is generously offered each year; and all those countless others who have been so kind to offer their land all over North America to a fellow just trying to learn, teach, and make a difference.

I want to thank Dawn Lesley-Carper, who purchased the first copy of this book several years before it was written in a sweet gesture of support. And my brother Dean, who has always been there if and when I needed him.

For thirteen years, Dana Coffee has generously granted me use of the photograph of me holding the wild salad. That relatively candid photograph captured me doing what I love to do—teach. It has served me well over the years and has become my company logo. Thanks, Dana, for being that great photographer.

My approach to the field of wild foods requires that I be a generalist. I observationally study plants in the field; read the botanical, historical, anthropological, nutrition, and food composition literature; interview practitioners; conduct processing and cooking experiments; and teach my findings to the general public. And while I can call upon my skills as a scientist when appropriate, my chosen role is now more of an investigative reporter for the general public. Other than when I have specific questions I am trying to answer, I do not have the time to steep myself in a more global understanding of nutrition research—which is vast and complex, filled with its own controversies. So I turned to my longtime friends and nutrition professionals Ginny Messina and Dr. Mark Messina, who gave me valuable input on the nutrition chapter. This book is better because of their comments and suggestions.

And finally, I want to thank those who have provided me with places to live and work at prices I could afford. Longtime friends Kaj Gyr and Scott Bandoroff and, most recently, Donna Violette have been instrumental in making it possible for me to have this career and to write this book. Without their support, I would not be where I am today. Thank you all.

About the Author

I spent my youth in a quiet suburban midwestern neighborhood. Fascinated with nature, I spent much of this time in nearby woods, riverbanks, and old farm fields. Like many children, I was fascinated with outdoor skills, often building shelters, making bows and arrows from sticks and string, rubbing sticks together to make fire, eating wild berries, and stalking squirrels, rabbits, and frogs. I dreamt of living in the wilderness by using these survival skills.

By the early 1970s, my interests began to focus more specifically on wild foods. Initially, through the study of Bradford Angier's book *How to Stay Alive in the Woods* (1956), and shortly thereafter by Allan Hall's *The Wild Food Trailguide* (1973), and by Euell Gibbons' *Stalking the Wild Asparagus* (1962), I seriously began studying and gathering edible wild plants.

While pursuing a science curriculum at Michigan State University, I organized a six-month vagabonding trip for myself through Europe. I planned to supplement my diet with wild foods, hoping to save some money during my travels. In preparation, I took college courses in wilderness survival, nutrition, and edible wild plants.

John Kallas emerging from a Michigan Swamp with a bundle of cattails. (Photo by Raelle Corliss, 1973.)

I spent my time in the European countryside, traveling on old back roads and through small villages where tourists did not travel. In the mid 1970s, these areas were less affected by modern American culture then they are today. People were still practicing traditional foodways. In the process of traveling, I met locals who invited me for dinner or to stay with them a few days. I routinely asked the food preparers if they knew of and used any wild foods. They almost always did and gladly showed me what they knew. After studying in this way for months, I was getting all of my vegetables from wild plants. Upon returning to the States and with encouragement from administrators and professors, I began teaching senior-level classes in edible wild plants at Michigan State University. That continued from 1978 to 1985.

While teaching and working on my master's and doctorate degrees, I studied botany under Dr. John Beaman, curator of the MSU herbarium. I also took conventional botany and taxonomy courses. Over the years, many wild food research expeditions were conducted, including ones to Washington, D.C., North Carolina, West Virginia, Michigan, Indiana, Illinois, Wisconsin, North Dakota, Montana, Idaho, Utah, Wyoming, Georgia, Nevada, Ohio, Oregon, Washington, California, British Columbia, and Alberta. My PhD in nutrition is helping me achieve my long-term goal of advancing the field of wild foods. My formal academic training has helped me learn about nutrients, human physiology and biochemistry, cultural foodways, anthropology, food preparation, and nutritional toxicology.

I moved to Oregon in 1989, where I continued my research and teaching. Since moving to Portland, I have taught wild food classes at Portland State University, Clackamas Community College, Portland Parks and Recreation, and Wild Food Adventures. As of January 1994, I have been running Wild Food Adventures as a full-time career. It is a teaching and research institution devoted to edible wild plants and other foragables. You can find more information about Wild Food Adventures at http://www.wildfoodadventures.com.

As a result of my experiences, I have a doctorate in nutrition, a master's in education, and degrees in biology and zoology. I'm a trained botanist, nature photographer, writer, researcher, and teacher. Over the years, I have taught and trained thousands of people about wild foods all over North America, given hundreds of wild food presentations to a wide variety of groups, assembled a comprehensive wild food library, and documented hundreds of wild foods in photographs and notes. Between newsletters, magazines, academic periodicals, and the Internet, I have published over 100 articles on edible wild plants.

Disclaimer? Yeah, Right!

If you venture out of your nuclear-proof, earthquake-proof, asteroid-proof bunker into the real world, you might be at risk. Yes, it's true! You may be hit by a bus or get E coli or staphylococcus poisoning from a church potluck. If you kiss someone, you may get herpes, mono, or worse— a tragic relationship. On the golf course, you may be hit by lightning. If you go ice skating, you may break your neck. If you go on a hike, you may trip on loose rocks, fall over a cliff, and die. Or you might be in the World Trade Center at the wrong time.

Look, you can either curl up under your bed covers and live a safe, dull, insulated life reading about other people doing things you wish you were doing. Or you can join the real world. If you venture into the real world, you risk living your life to its fullest. You risk the rush of climbing that mountain, of dancing all night, of scuba diving in reefs of mind-blowing color, of standing in the rain on an ocean viewpoint, watching huge waves crashing against the rocks, of meeting the partner of your dreams. You risk getting exercise and breathing fresh air. You risk making life worth living.

So if you decide to venture into the world of wild foods, you'd better prepare yourself for some fun, adventure, and risk. Yes, there are risks to eating new foods that you've never tried before. You might make some mistakes or have allergies to foods you haven't been exposed to yet. Nature has its own agenda and is not looking out for the safety of humans—and that fact provides some unpredictability in all things wild. But if you are a reasonable student, if you don't just jump haphazardly into eating everything in sight, and if you pay attention to what your body is telling you, your chances of any real danger are slim. For the vast majority of people, getting into wild foods will be nothing but fun. For that rare person who becomes that exception, we may end up talking about your unusual case in future books.

And while your experiences may be different from mine. I have never regretted eating wild foods, which I have done for over thirty-five years. I hope your experiences will be as good as mine. So be a good student, and you will minimize the chance that you will regret living your life to its fullest.

Preface

The field of wild foods, first popularized by Euell Gibbons in the 1960s, has been languishing from neglect. For a field with so much potential, wild foods remain a mystery after almost fifty years of books on the subject. People buy books and try to study the subject but come away with little real understanding or useful knowledge. In addition to lack of information, there is a disconnect between what is said about these plants and what reality seems to serve you, the reader. Pleasant dining experiences are few. Anyone can write a book on wild foods, and almost anyone has.

The effort to aid the reader in plant identification is almost as bad. Cryptic technical descriptions have little meaning for the layperson. Line drawings of plants typically are not useful unless the reader already knows the plant. Photograph-based identification guides are holdovers from wildflower guides. Wildflower guides are concerned with flowers at the neglect of other parts of the plant. Plants are complex organisms that change shape as they grow, often with variable leaves, stems, and overall form. Many species have more than one form, so a single photograph gives you only a fraction, a small clue, to identifying a plant.

Many wild food guides are nothing more than catalogs of plants with no real detail written by authors who have never experienced what they are writing about. The more plants covered in a book results in less useful information per plant. Most books have one to three sentences describing the edibility of a plant. A few rare books take a chapter to describe how a plant is edible and how to make the best use of that knowledge. The handful of great authors are the ones who write based on experience and provide the detail to guide you through all aspects of wild food knowledge— identifying, gathering, transporting, processing, preparing, and serving.

This book was written and designed in every way to serve you, the reader—to overcome directly all the limitations listed above. The goal is to take the mystery, not the romance, out of wild foods, to give you the tools to move forward with confidence, and to have lots of success actually using wild foods. Whole chapters are devoted to single plants. Designed as a pictorial manual, photographs are plentiful, showing you different growth stages from seedling to fully mature plant. All edible stages are shown as well as processing techniques and finished dishes.

To satisfy the need to supply detail, this book represents only the beginning of the plants I will cover over the years. This is the first in an intended series of themed books covering different topics in the area of wild edible plants and other foragables. As the first, I selected easy-to-identify common plants that everyone in North America will be able to find somewhere between their yard and the local neighborhood. Included are important wild greens and vegetables eaten by our European ancestors since the beginning of time. Many of them grow as weeds in the typical garden. The benefit of local plants is that you can have everyday access. If you can grab your salad from the backyard in a matter of minutes, you are more likely to eat these plants than if you have to drive two hours to reach more exotic habitats. That is how our European ancestors ate, from foraged plants growing around their homes.

Historically, people learned about wild foods from their elders. Kids would tag along as parents gathered wild foods. By direct observation and parental guidance, children learned the plants from seedling to seed production. They saw first-hand how to judge when the collectable parts were perfect for picking; how to handle and transfer the take; how to clean it, process it, and prepare it for eating. In lieu of learning from elders today, this book attempts to provide the same content in a different format. You are learning from a career professional who writes from experience.

Some Issues about Content

Botanical names are based on the plants cataloged at the Integrated Taxonomic Information System offered through a partnership between the United States, Canadian, and Mexican federal agencies. Plant names were verified at http://www.itis.gov/index.html.

The maps were generated from several sources, including but not limited to the personal experience of the author, USDA Plants Database (http://plants.usda.gov/), NatureServe Explorer (http://www.natureserve.org/explorer/), Natural Resources Canada (http://www.planthardiness.gc.ca/), the Biology of Canadian Weeds book series—Reprints from the Canadian Journal of Plant Science, and plant distribution maps offered by Web sites of individual states.

Welcome to My World

Whether you are new to wild foods or are well versed in the topic, my intent is that you should find this book personal, practical, and fun to use. I write from personal experience and present information in a way intended to help you learn what you really need to know to be successful. By successful I mean that with time you will be able to identify the plants I cover, understand how to get the most out of them, and have satisfying culinary experiences as a result of your efforts. And that is the point, isn't it? To go from the wild to something your taste buds recognize as good food.

I love wild foods, the whole idea of eating from the wild, the joy of being outdoors and being closer to the earth, and the adventure of the whole experience. Given all that, I do not sugarcoat what you need to know. When something I've read about wild foods is disingenuous or misleading, or doesn't seem to work, I'll let you know. If some taste or texture of something people might have eaten in the distant past is beyond what anyone would find acceptable today, I'll let you know. So if you've been dissatisfied with books you may have read on this topic—those that have too few photographs or not enough information to be useful— then read on. My goal is to make wild foods user-friendly, rewarding, and fun.

This book is designed as a user manual. It is written from the perspective of a career professional in the area of wild foods. Not merely a field guide or a cookbook, it is intended to take you deeper into the secret world of plants. Each plant's clear photographs are used to show you its development at all stages of growth. Captions with each photograph explain what you are looking at. Processing techniques are clearly illustrated. Foundational ways to prepare each food are given within a context that will allow you to improvise recipes. This manual is, in essence, a reverse field guide. It provides the means to learn identification directly from reading the chapters. Therefore, you do not struggle to identify plants when you are in the field; you recognize them and then verify your find by reviewing this book.

Wild Greens, Vegetables, and Their Seeds

Wild greens, vegetables, and their seeds describe the foods offered by the plants in this book. For purposes of discussion, I am labeling leaves as greens (a particular kind of vegetable); three-dimensional parts like shoots, stems, leafy stems, roots, buds, and flowers as vegetables; and fruits with their seeds. I divide the selected plants into the following categories: foundation, tart, pungent, and bitter. In my view, combining elements from these different categories makes the best salads and cooked dishes, and provides a wider array of nutrients and potentially beneficial phytochemicals than eating from any single category alone.

Categorizing plants in distinct groups is difficult. Since the greens and vegetables provided by these plants can have many food applications (eaten raw, boiled, sautéed, creamed, etc.), they may fall under more than one category. So I've tried to place them in groups that make the most overall sense. For example, the pungent greens listed in this book are primarily mustards. So mustards earn their own grouping, even though some of them are also bitter, a different flavor category.

Gourmet quality, of course, depends on gathering the edible parts at their prime stage of growth and using those parts to their best advantage. Likeability depends on your unique array of taste buds and personal preference. For the most part, however, I believe what I call the foundation greens have flavors even the most finicky eaters will enjoy raw or cooked. To be fully enjoyed, the tart, pungent, and bitter greens may require you to pay more attention to detail regarding gathering, preparation, and use.

Newly disturbed soils, where most of the plants in this book grow, are found in gardens, yards, neighborhood lots, and land overturned by construction sites and tilling equipment.

How This Book Is Organized

This book is divided into Parts that have Sections and Chapters:

Part I *Understanding Wild Foods* is filled with practical information you need to know to help you understand and use wild foods and to give context, understanding, and foster success in ways that apply to all edible plants. If you skip this part of the book because you think that going directly to the plant chapters is more efficient, you'll be holding yourself back. Reading Part I will make you a more successful forager.

Part II *The Plants* covers the plants featured in this book. Those plants are separated into the four flavor categories mentioned on page 18. Each plant has its own chapter that follows the plant from emerging seedling to end-of-life seed production, from foraging to food, from preparation to dining.

Part III *The Potential of Wild Foods* takes you beyond the basics, addressing topics like the rationale for eating wild foods, nutrition, and explanations of some additional concepts.

The Value of the Information Within

There are no official certifications or professional degrees that qualify anyone to be a wild foods expert. And there are no expert panels that systematically look at the content of this book to verify its accuracy. As far as I know, the lack of oversight has been true for every book ever written about edible wild plants.

I make great attempts to faithfully report what I have found from my own experiences over the last thirty-eight years. Those experiences are biased/shaped by personal perceptions, previous education and beliefs, food preferences, and my personal complement of taste buds.

Personal experience is further complicated by nature, which is not here for our convenience. Unlike domesticated plants, wild plants are free to mate and mutate and change locally or regionally without consulting us humans. Every plant within a species can have a different genetic makeup. Genetic uniqueness can affect a plant's taste, texture, and chemical composition. Plants are further affected by climatic differences. For example, in order to survive colder winters, a species growing in the north may become hardier than that same species in the south. Hardiness may affect chewability and, hence, the eating experience.

I am one person who is sharing his experiences with you based on the plants I have found and worked with. And while I may be able to provide some guidance, the more you have your own experiences, the more a general understanding develops within you. Your own experience is priceless. The test of the value of any user manual will be on how much the experience the author has facilitates the experiences you have.

The problem with most wild foods books is that authors merely repeat information they've read rather than actually trying things themselves. So when misinformation exists, it gets repeated over and over again by author after author until everyone believes it. Only testing long-held beliefs results in confirming or correcting the record. The more people test and report the results of their personal experiences, the better the picture we have of the real situation for any plant.

Researching and teaching about wild foods has been my life's work. I do it because I'm passionate about the topic, it helps me improve the wild food knowledge base and provides some clear guidance for those that follow. Again, I am but one link in a chain of people who help to keep this knowledge alive.

Summary

This book is designed to help you successfully identify, understand, manage, and enjoy the wild foods covered. It is a user manual and a reverse field guide whose development is based on experience. It is filled with purposeful photographs and the kind of information designed to genuinely serves your learning needs. The plants included are divided into flavor categories to help guide your use.

I take full responsibility for the content of this book. Any mistakes are mine and mine alone. Should you discover a mistake, have an experience fundamentally different from mine, or notice an important omission, please contact me through my Web site at www.wildfood adventures.com. I will seriously consider any advice and make corrections and/or additions in any future editions of this book and on my Web site.

PART I
UNDERSTANDING
WILD FOODS

The first part of this book is filled with things you need to know to help you understand the world of wild foods. If you skip these chapters because you think that going directly to the plant chapters is more efficient, you will be depriving yourself. It provides tools, ideas, context, and perspective that will help you be a more successful forager. It also provides some foundational definitions that the field of wild foods has needed for a long time. These definitions are particularly useful to help keep you safe and to provide a means for teachers to base their instruction on a common foundation.

Plants change as they mature. Look carefully at these four pictures of field mustard. Each shows different leaves, stems, and other structures. They represent only some of the stages and parts of the life story of one plant. Additional variations will occur if the plant is growing under stressful conditions. If you do not learn the life story of this plant—wild mustard—you will only learn a fraction of its usefulness.

Chapter 1

Identifying and Enjoying Wild Foods

This chapter helps you better understand edible plants and offers some guidance to make the most of the information in Part II of this book.

The Life Story of Plants

There are secrets to wild foods—secrets that used to be common knowledge, part of a way of life for people all over the planet. These secrets are revealed when you begin to learn the "life story" of plants, which is composed of two things. First, the phases and forms the plant passes through as it grows from seedling to mature plant is often called a plant's "natural history," sometimes a plant's "life cycle." Second, plant form (what it looks like) is a result of both nature *and* nurture; the conditions under which it is growing affects the expression of those forms.

Each story is unique and gives clues to why a plant and its parts at various stages of growth turn out a certain way—why leaves on one plant are great-tasting while others may be intolerable. Heed these life stories, and you will reap the great rewards that wild foods have to offer. Ignore them, and both your understanding and your success will be limited.

The reason store-bought vegetables are relatively consistent in flavor and texture is because of modern agricultural practices in which farm-raised vegetables grow in similarly prepared land from the same genetically consistent seed, are planted at a similar time in similar climates with similar soil and water conditions, and are harvested at the prime of their lives. In other words, these foods are domesticated. They tend to have relatively consistent flavors and textures, and you typically get what you expect.

Wild plants, on the other hand, do not share this regimented fate. Enlightenment has arrived when you can come upon a wild plant wherever it happens to be and know where it is in its own life story. It "speaks to you" by its appearance, its surroundings, and a myriad of other clues that we'll talk about in this book. It will tell you if and when its plant parts are worth gathering or not.

Due to modern-day preoccupation with general busyness, indoor technology-based entertainment, and the taming of nature for our convenience, there is less and less common knowledge of the natural world. Nature is paved over and built on, and is finding its way farther and farther from our everyday lives. And where it remains, nature is becoming a distant place of postcards and vacations instead of being a comforting friend with whom to commune and interact. Nature has become a shallow relationship.

Because of these trends and the resultant ignorance of nature, there is less and less understanding and appreciation of why anyone needs to know the details of plant life. Even publishers (except mine, obviously) resist including detail from authors who want to give it, because they think readers will just want the summary—just the bottom line. This book takes you where you need to be, because in nature, a summary alone tells you nothing.

Getting on the Path

In lieu of your own personal local wild food expert, this book will get you started on your path to wild food fun. We'll start with plants you can use every day—those that are within walking distance of your kitchen, easy to locate, quick and easy to gather, nutritious, and will provide great-tasting foods with little or no preparation. Yes, you heard me, *great-tasting* with little or no preparation. Perhaps you've heard that before and have been disappointed. This book should change all that—but only if you learn the life stories of the plants we cover.

The principles discussed in this book are just as important as the plants we are focusing on. You may be tempted to take shortcuts—but there are no shortcuts to experience-based wisdom. You have to spend time observing and experimenting with these plants to gain that wisdom. So think of this book as a springboard, a resource that will help you connect to that outdoor world.

Recognize that I am one person with some personal experience with wild foods. And while I think you will have similar experiences to mine under similar conditions and understanding, you may find yourself having a different experience occasionally. Sometimes differences occur because we may have done something in a different way; perhaps we have different taste sensibilities, or we've used plants with different life histories; or perhaps my experiences were too limited and I drew conclusions before the time was right. I make great efforts to speak only from experience and to know the plants well enough to put you on the right track.

This book covers plants I know intimately. A couple of them are relatively new to me, but I am including them because they fit the theme—common, classic wild foods eaten by our European and American ancestors. Most people today know them as weeds. The more experience you have with a plant, the more accurate your perceptions and conclusions are about their uses.

How to Learn the Most

One of my goals for this book is to provide you, the wild food adventurer, with the kind of information that will help you be a successful forager and enjoy what you are doing. To get the most out of this book, consider the following recommendations:

A) If you are unfamiliar with the plants in this book, keep the book handy in a relaxing place. Leaf through the pictures at every opportunity. Go for occasional walks around your house and neighborhood, eyeballing all plants growing in disturbed areas. Become an observer all year long. Sit on the ground with the plants on occasion and study everything around you. Look for interesting and unique characteristics and patterns. At some point you will begin to recognize plants you've

WEED

"What is a weed? A plant whose virtues have not yet been discovered."
—Ralph Waldo Emerson, in *Fortune of the Republic*, 1878

"A weed is a plant that is not only in the wrong place, but intends to stay."
—Sara Bonnett Stein, in *My Weeds: A Gardener's Botany*, 1988

"Man is by definition the first and primary weed under whose influence all other weeds have evolved."
—Jack R. Harlan, in *Crops and Man*, 1992

seen in this book. Once you've verified your iden-tification, follow the steps in part B.

B) If you already know a plant, read the chapter covering it. This will clue you into its life story and its possibilities. Then locate the plant nearby. Once you've found it, study the plant. Try to determine the following:

1) Where is it in its life cycle? Is it a seedling in a rapidly growing phase? Is it in a vegetative form only, or has it begun its reproductive phase by producing buds, flowers, or seeds?

2) What life history (growing conditions) has it experienced? Is it in its ideal habitat or is it under stress? Is it flourishing or is it struggling?

3) What parts, if any, are edible at this stage of growth? What parts are pre-prime, at prime, or post-prime?

4) If any parts are considered edible at this point, predict what the flavors and textures will be like considering where the plant is in its devel-opment, soil conditions, etc.

5) Try the part(s). If your predictions are true, then gather some of the plant. If your predic-tions are wrong, check this book to try to deter-mine why the part was different from what you expected. If your understanding comes out differ-ently than mine, it may be as simple as you and me having different taste or texture sensibilities. It may be that you need to study the plant a little more. Or it may be that my understanding of the plant is inadequate. There is so much more to any plant than I'll ever know. You will gain answers with experience and time.

To get the most out of this book, don't just read the cover pages for each plant; read the entire chapter. If you

Plant forms can vary within the same species. Both of these plants are young miner's lettuce (*Claytonia perfoliata*). They are both at the same stage of growth, just different forms. Their similarities will increase when they are in flower.

go right to the explanations of edibility, skipping the developmental history, you are missing some of the most important parts of understanding the plants you will be eating.

Observe, experiment, and play with plants you find. What you get from this book is only the beginning. You will learn more by being carefully observant in the field and innovative with what you do in the kitchen. Gather, process, and prepare these foods in any way imaginable. A person with enough experience could go beyond the scheme of this book and write a whole book about each plant. I limited what I included in some chapters to get a good representative coverage of plants. Experiment and play. You'll find they are the same thing. DO NOT eat or experiment with plants or plant parts you do not "know" to be edible!

Identifying Plants

Identifying plants is always a wonderful challenge and part of the adventure of wild foods. The same plant can look different not only in this book but in other books, depending on the angle of the photograph, the condition of the plant, and the sensibilities of the photographer. The same plant can also take on several different personalities; that is, you can have several of the same species growing side by side but get the impression that they are different species. This is why it is so difficult to match what you see in nature to what you see in a book. The photograph may only show one version of a plant's personality, while real life may offer another version.

Miner's lettuce, for example, has one form as a sprout, two forms as an adolescent, and two forms as an adult. A novice may only recognize one of these five versions.

As a plant grows, it develops different structures. While moving through different stages of growth, a plant can transform so much that young and old versions look like different species. While I make an effort to familiarize you with all the major developmental stages of each plant, most field guides only show you how a plant looks as a flowering adult. Most edible parts of vegetables are at their prime for eating at young stages of growth—before the flowers appear. So it is essential to know what plants look like in all their developmental stages.

Inedible or poisonous look-alikes

This is one of the most frustrating areas for beginners. There are thousands of plants out there, so how do you begin separating out the edible ones? Make no mistake, this is an important issue. *Inedible* plants are ones not suitable, for one reason or another, to be used as food. Some inedible plants are poisonous. While most inedible plants and their parts are relatively harmless in small quantities, there are certainly a few really bad players out there.

In lieu of becoming a professional botanist, one must take advantage of multiple resources to positively identify plants. I cannot overemphasize the benefits of knowing the natural history of the plants you are interested in eating. If you study the detailed characteristics I will show you, it will be very unlikely that you will accidentally consume a poisonous look-alike. Even so, I make it a point to include some poisonous look-alikes in this book so you can see which common plants to avoid.

Hunting and Gathering Strategy

Plants are found everywhere that has not been paved. It is a great joy to find them clean, in prime condition, in great quantity, and in a form that is easy to gather. Nature and its seasons are relatively predictable, so there are many things we can look forward to. Climatic changes can make things less predictable. One year, chickweed (*Stellaria media*) may be abundant; the next, it may be scarce or stringy. This becomes a problem when you have expectations about what you want to gather. Nature does not always provide exactly what you want.

Once you learn the fundamentals, gathering wild foods

will often be quite easy. There are many times now that I can go into my backyard with an empty bowl and come back with a large, delightfully delicious salad in less time than it would take me to make one from grocery foods in the refrigerator. Some yards may be this way naturally, but others need to be enabled. I'll get into this more later on.

OPPORTUNITY HARVESTING: Since you may not always find the plant parts you want, gather the ones you find. This strategy is very productive. Opportunity harvesting is gathering whatever you find that's worth harvesting. This year the wild spinach may be abundant and in season when you are foraging, so you collect it. The wild lettuce, on the other hand, may be struggling, so you leave it. The greater your knowledge of the life story of plants, the better you will be able to predict what will be available, at what quality, and in what part of the season. The uncertainty is part of the adventure. It is extremely satisfying, however, when your predictions turn out to be right.

PLAY/WORK TO DO: A supermarket is convenient and a restaurant even more convenient. As a forager getting your food directly from nature, you happily take on the following jobs: naturalist, harvester, food transporter, food cleaner, food storer, food processer, recipe designer, cook, waiter, and consumer. This requires very little effort if the food is close to the kitchen and easy to prepare, and if you are creating a simple dish. I am trying to create these *easy* conditions through the content of this book. Proportionately more effort is required if you are working with less-convenient wild foods and/or if you are challenging yourself with an ambitious outcome.

For example, want some dandelion root crowns? The cleaning time required to get out all the soil and creatures wedged in the mass of leaf bases can make these more of a pastime project than a quick meal. But if you are like me, the joy is mostly in the journey.

Aside from nature not providing you with the conveniences offered by modern food systems, there are other things to consider. It is inconvenient that nature generates different species that look alike and that individual plants within a species may have unique genetics affecting flavors and textures. So even if you have everything figured out, sometimes a plant part you eat may just not come out the way you expect it. That's okay. Try again. That is part of the adventure.

Microanalyze This! How to Taste a Wild Food for the First Time

Over a lifetime, the flavors and textures of food you've eaten develop meaning. Food is associated with good times, family, holidays, and other patterns in your life. It is associated with acquired tastes, satisfaction, and comfort, among other things. Because of this, most of us have developed our own comfortable eating patterns. We eat certain foods in certain ways—liking some more than others. We accept their flavors as is and rarely just sit and carefully analyze them. We enjoy our domesticated broccoli. And even if we did do a slow, careful tasting, we can no longer judge it independently from our cumulative experience. Judging broccoli now would result in an expression of how good it is relative to our "idealized" broccoli.

Now propel yourself into a totally new culinary sensation. Every new wild food you try is unknown and mysterious—there is no idealized version of it to compare it to. This results in a much more cautious, deliberate, and focused tasting procedure. You examine each item's flavor and texture more closely than you would any other food in your regular diet. You search for ways to characterize it. You microanalyze it. You can do this from one of three perspectives:

1) You can timidly examine it, hoping you will not come across anything disagreeable like off-

flavors, bitterness, or rankness. This makes you sensitive to and looking for the disagreeable. And if there is any there, you are darned and determined to find it.

2) You can hope that it will taste like a familiar comfort food you already know. How can a new food compete with the old favorites? Or

3) You can view this new sampling as an adventure—looking for the plant's uniqueness, character, and potential. An open-minded anticipation of potential will result in a more pleasurable and useful wild foods kind of experience. And if you are like me, all sorts of culinary options will pop into your mind.

During your microanalysis, you should keep in mind that tasting a raw unadorned food is a very different thing than tasting a food prepared for eating. There are many dandelion dishes that are totally delicious; many without a shred of bitterness—even though the raw dandelions used were tongue torturers. So raw wild foods that are bitter, pungent, or tart, if treated properly, can transform into something pleasing to even the wimpiest palate.

Not that you have to get rid of those interesting flavors. With time, you may learn to like them or learn to use them sparingly to *spice up* dishes rather than *be* the dish. I am not a fan of bitter and strongly pungent flavors eaten alone, but I find that the more I work with these plants and experiment with them in different recipes, the more I enjoy the accents and variety they add to my diet.

Chapter 2

What Is Edible?

I've often heard people say that such and such a plant is "edible." Well, what exactly does "edible" mean in the context of wild foods? If a plant is edible, it's edible—right?

People generally consider blue elderberry to be an edible plant. You might assume that you can eat its flowers, berries, leaves, and stems—right? But wait! My poisonous plant book says that blue elderberry is poisonous! Herein lies the problem. You must "know" a so-called edible plant well before you start eating it. Assuming edibility for a plant or its various parts can be dangerous and even deadly.

Considering the potential confusion, I have created some formal definitions for edible wild plants (also known as wild food plants), poisonous plants, and medicinal plants. These definitions will help you intelligently navigate your way through the world of wild foods.

Edible Wild Plants Defined

Edible wild plants are endowed with one or more parts that can be used for food if gathered at the appropriate stage of growth and properly prepared.

Let's divide this definition into meaningful pieces and discuss the significance of each.

"One or More Parts"

Plants typically have a variety of parts. Stems, leaves, roots, buds, fruits, seeds, and shoots are just a small number of parts that can be found on plants. If a plant is considered edible, that means there is at least *one* part of the plant that you can eat. But the plant may also have poisonous parts, medicinal parts, woody parts, bitter parts, or parts that are too hairy to use. For instance, all but the cooked underground tuber of the potato plant is poisonous! All but the flowers and the ripe fruit of blue elderberry (*Sambucus canadensis* [eastern North America] / *Sambucus cerulea* [western North America]) is poisonous. In reality, potato and elderberry are both edible plants *and* poisonous plants, so one key to the successful and

RAW POTATOES

Raw domesticated potatoes have very small, probably harmless amounts of the toxin that is in the rest of the plant. Cooking destroys most of the remaining toxin and makes the potato more palatable. Green potatoes and those producing buds accumulate harmful concentrations of the toxin that cannot be cooked out.

safe use of wild plants for food is to focus on the part or parts *known* to be edible. Generalizing and improvising by eating unspecified parts of plants can be deadly.

Western blue elderberry (*Sambucus cerulea*). This branchlet has fully ripe edible berries. The plant contains cyanide and other toxins in its leaves, stems, branches, and bark.

"Gathered at the Appropriate Stage of Growth"

Each edible part has its own ideal stage for eating. Knowing that stage not only provides the best food, it can also keep you safe.

Some plant parts become poisonous with maturity. Common milkweed (*Asclepias syriaca*) produces a pod containing seeds. When the pods are young and tender, and the immature seeds are still white, the pod is an excellent cooked vegetable. But once the seeds start maturing (turning brown), the pod is poisonous—and that poison cannot be cooked out. So the bottom line is that if you wish to consume a plant part, gather it at its edible stage. Not paying attention to a plant's various stages of growth can lead to a deadly experience.

"Properly Prepared"

Some "edible" plant parts may not become truly edible or palatable unless they are processed in some way. Processing may involve, among other things, physically removing certain parts of a plant (like the seeds from a fruit or the rind of a root), leaching undesirable water-soluble substances out of a plant part (like soaking tannin out of the acorn), or heating to a certain temperature (like wintercress leaves). Even the edible leaves of dandelion in the raw form carry sesquiterpenes and other substances that, in high enough quantity, can cause excessive urination and diarrhea. Using them sparingly when raw or boiling them helps to minimize these effects.

The biggest and most dangerous mistake that you can make when using wild foods is to eat parts of plants *not* known to be edible. In addition to making a proper identification, you must make sure that only the proper parts are collected at the appropriate stages of growth and properly prepared.

Mature milkweed pods (*Asclepias syriaca*). Fully mature poisonous brown seeds are shown here. Milkweed is considered both an edible and a poisonous plant, depending on the part and its stage of growth. These pods are edible at a younger stage of growth.

Young pokeweed shoots (*Phytolacca americana*). Most people harvest them at the growth stage shown here. Because of the name "poke sallet," which identifies a common cooked dish served in the South, many novices misunderstand *salat* to mean that the greens can be eaten raw. Pokeweed is poisonous raw but becomes edible once cooked properly for that dish.

Poisonous Plants Defined

Poisonous plants are plants endowed with one or more parts having chemical or physical attributes that can cause acute or underlying injury or death upon ingestion, touch, or inhalation. Dosage determines the severity of the damage. Poisons can affect some species differently than others.

POISONS & TOXINS

While having different technical meanings, the words "poison" and "toxin" are used interchangeably in the common plant-related literature. According to my understanding, they can be defined in the following ways:

Poison: a chemical from any source that is harmful, even in small quantities, to living systems.

Toxin: a poison originating from plant or animal sources; that is, a poison synthesized by living things. Toxins are a class or subset of all poisons.

So when talking about poisonous plants, it is not only permissible but also correct to use the two words interchangeably.

Okay, that was a mouthful. But if you take this definition piece by piece, it will be easier to grasp.

Poisonous plants have at least one poisonous part. As I've said, blue elderberry has both edible and poisonous parts. Of course, a whole plant can be poisonous. A plant is considered poisonous even if the poison can be cooked or processed out.

Most people are only familiar with the kind of poison you see in the spy movies, where someone keels over and dies within a few seconds of ingesting that poisoned martini. But toxins found in nature are more clever and diverse than that. Something you've eaten may be causing damage to your liver, kidneys, heart, nervous system, or reproductive system, even if it tasted good and you are feeling fine after eating it.

This hidden toxicity demonstrates the difference between an acute toxin and a more subtle or underlying one. An acute toxin is fast-acting and dramatic. You may not die from it, but you feel symptoms as soon as the toxin starts affecting the body. With an acute toxin, you know that you've been poisoned. Symptoms may include confusion, disorientation, nausea, vomiting, diarrhea, chest pains, arrhythmia, cramps, intense sweating, and even death. You may totally recover from an acute toxic incident, you may retain some permanent damage, or you may die from it.

An underlying toxin is one that works at a less obvious level. The toxin may build up over time to produce more dramatic symptoms later or may continually damage some organ or physiological process, thereby degrading

function. It may also have a temporary effect. That is, your body heals over time if you stop being exposed to it; or the toxin may cause permanent damage even if you stop being exposed to it. An underlying toxin can cause death by damaging vital systems over time. These toxins are the reason you cannot assume that just because a plant part tastes good, it is edible. Many novices and some wild food instructors make this mistake. You must *know* that a plant is edible from a long tradition of use.

Basically, a toxin has to get into your body in order to do damage. Ingestion (eating) is the obvious way to bring a toxin into the body. Certain toxins can enter the body by absorption through the skin, by injection by a plant under the skin, or by inhalation. Poison ivy's toxin urushiol absorbs through the skin. Urushiol can also be inhaled accidentally through smoke when one of these plants is being burned.

(left) Jack-in-the-pulpit (*Arisaema triphyllum*). This plant contains calcium oxalate crystals, a physical and chemical toxin.

(right) Poison ivy (*Toxicodendron radicans*). Urushiol, this plant's toxin, causes a rash on the skin or in the lungs if the smoke from a burning plant is inhaled.

Inhalation of urushiol can be deadly. If inhaled in quantity, poison hemlock pollen can also produce permanent lung damage. This can happen if you are in a field where the plant is in flower. As you walk through, brushing against plants or trying to hack them down, the air can get thick with the pollen. The more you breathe in, the greater your exposure.

Obviously, the more of a toxin you ingest, touch, or inhale, the greater the potential damage. Some toxins are cumulative; that is, they build up over time. That buildup is reduced by the body's ability to remove it. So if you intake the toxin faster than your body can remove it, it builds up. If you are ingesting a toxin at very low levels, your body's ability to remove it may render it harmless. A good example of this is cyanide. The body gets rid of cyanide by exhaling it from the lungs. Many plants you eat contain some cyanide. Eating small amounts is harmless because your body moves it to the lungs where you breathe it out. Ingest too much cyanide, however, and you overwhelm your lungs' ability to clear it, so it builds to harmful levels—harmful enough so that it can kill you.

Medicinal Plants Defined

Medicinal plants are plants endowed with one or more parts having therapeutic effects when gathered at the appropriate stage of growth, properly prepared, and properly administered.

Note the similarity of this definition to the edible plants definition. This definition is relatively self-explanatory. I would like to point out, however, that most medicines are poisons administered in controlled amounts for specific purposes. Self-medication can be dangerous or even deadly without enough knowledge of preparation and administration. Further confusing things, some edible parts like dandelion leaves are also considered medicinal. We'll talk about this in the dandelion chapter.

There are two important things to take away from this

discussion on edible, poisonous, and medicinal plants. First, before you eat anything, learn your plants well enough to know which parts at what stage of growth are edible, poisonous, medicinal, or of unknown status. Knowledge is power and safety. Second, if you are faced with an unknown part, always keep in mind the concept of what I've called "underlying" toxin. Hopefully this will deter you from recklessly experimenting with parts of unknown edibility, because even though they may taste fine, they may cause some underlying damage to you or anyone you feed. Only experiment with and eat plant parts that you know to be edible, that are found at the appropriate stage of growth, and that you know how to prepare. If you do not know *all three* of these things about a plant, you do not know enough to be eating it.

Caution—Uncharted Territory

For the most part, if you learn the basic information you need to know to safely eat wild foods, you can expect to experience many happy dining adventures. Your body will treat these new foods just like any other foods in your diet. For a few people with sensitive digestive tracts, eating a new food for the first time may initiate a temporary laxative effect and possibly some minor flatulence. This is not of concern except to friends breathing nearby. As you eat more of the food, particularly in the context of normal meals, your digestive tract will adjust and behave more in public.

There are a couple of other issues that, on rare occasion, can complicate matters for some people. Your genetic makeup may be sensitive or allergic to certain substances commonly found in certain plants or plant families. For instance, some people are sensitive to edible fruits of the nightshade family (tomato, green pepper), while the rest of us can eat them with impunity. Others are sensitive to peanuts. Some rare individuals are so sensitive that even mild contact can cause anaphylaxis and death. If you have no food sensitivities to conventional foods,

ANAPHYLAXIS
(also known as anaphylactic shock)
A powerful, often life-threatening, allergic reaction caused by a second or third exposure (touch, ingestion, inhalation) to a substance (typically a protein or chemical) that is foreign to the body. This substance is referred to as an antigen. The antigen stimulates a cascade of reactions in the body's defense (immune) systems, causing those systems to go so extreme as to hurt the body they are trying to defend. Mild cases cause hay fever, asthma, and hives. Severe cases can lead to airway constriction and death. The most common food-related causes of anaphylaxis are peanuts, tree nuts, and shellfish. Bee stings are a common nonfood cause.

you will probably have no food sensitivities to wild foods. On the other hand, if you have lots of food sensitivities to conventional foods, your chances are higher that this might also be true for wild foods.

You might also come across a mutant strain of a common wild food that is harmful if eaten. This is rare. One such plant is the tawny daylily. Common to yards and roadside ditches all across North America, it apparently has two forms that differ in their chemistry. The predominant form has buds and flowers that are perfectly edible—a fantastic wild food. A less common, physically identical form has something in it that can cause severe nausea and diarrhea, raw or cooked. Since you cannot tell the difference between these two versions of this species, it is always a bit of a gamble to eat it from an unfamiliar patch.

Tawny daylily (*Hemerocallis fulva*). A small percentage of this plant's population is a mutant strain that causes nausea and diarrhea.

Chapter 3

When Plant Parts Morph into Food

There are certain tendencies that plants have as they develop. The more you know about these tendencies, the better you will be able to make judgments about exactly when an edible part will be at its best. You will also have a better idea of what might have gone wrong if something (taste or texture) does not go as expected.

In this chapter, you will NOT learn how to determine if an unfamiliar plant part is edible. There are no good rules for guessing edibility. What you will gain from this chapter are more insights into plants that are already known to have edible parts. The idea is to improve your chances of success by giving you a basic understanding of how plants change as they go through life and how those changes affect edibility.

In general, vegetative plant parts evolve from being tender to becoming fibrous as they mature. "Rapid growth" and "end size" are important concepts in this chapter. These concepts will give you the best way to determine when a plant part will be at its highest quality for eating. Each plant part will have its own story of growth and size, so let's cover them one by one.

What Makes Plant Parts Tender?

Any plant part undergoes growth until it reaches its end size. Rapid growth results from optimal growing conditions, resulting in larger stems, roots, leaves, etc.

Growth does not happen uniformly across all plant parts. For instance, a lower stem may have solidified into a sturdy nongrowing support structure, but at the same time, it can be transporting nutrients and water to new growth points near the top of a plant. That lower mature stem is fibrous or even woody, while the emerging new growths are tender. The fastest-growing parts are determined by where the emerging new growths are.

Gathering an edible part at the right stage of growth

MORPH

To change gradually from one form to another, like a bud growing/transforming into a leaf or a branch.

PLANT PARTS

Examples of these are root, stem, leaves, flowers, fruits, buds, and shoots. They can be separated into vegetative and reproductive parts: vegetative plant parts include leaves, stems, and shoots; reproductive plant parts include flowers, fruits, nuts, and seeds.

Young bull thistle leaf. There is tenderness underneath all the hairs and spines of young, rapidly growing bull thistle leaf (*Cirsium vulgare*). Most leaves of plants we generally eat do not typically have these barriers (hair and spines) to good mouth feel. If you get a young enough rapidly growing bull thistle leaf, it is completely tender, spines and all, once boiled for a few minutes. When older, the spines remain solid and sharp even after boiling. This is because the spines have reached their end size and stiffen, even though the leaf may still be growing.

is important to maximize flavor and texture. Here we will examine the roles that growth and end size have on various parts of plants

End size

End size can refer to the whole plant once it stops growing. But for the purposes of this book, we are only referring to individual plant parts. Individual plant parts each grow at their own rate and at their own time. The end size of each part is determined by both genetics and how nature has nurtured the plant. The end size of a leaf, for instance, can be large if it has had generous amounts of water, nutrients, and sunlight during its life. The end size is smaller if the plant has been starved of any of these factors.

For most plant parts, chemical and structural changes occur once the end size is reached. Those parts transition from growth to support and maintenance structures. What happens in a maintenance metabolism? Fiber builds to strengthen the leaf, and some of the nutrients that were required for growth travel out to still-growing parts of the plant. Off-flavors often develop as the sun continues to bake a static leaf.

Leaves

As a general rule, leaves (like other plant parts) start out tender and remain reasonably so until they reach their end size. Don't be fooled by small leaf size. Just because a leaf is small does not mean it is young, tender, or tasty. As I've just said, a small leaf might be small because it has been starved of water and nutrients, reaching its end size very early in life. This is often the case in summer, when the soil has been hard and dry for a while. On the other hand, if you find small leaves on a well-watered plant, it is most likely that those leaves are young and still growing. More mature (not so young) plants can have rapidly growing parts that are great for eating.

Some leaves like those found on miner's lettuce (*Claytonia perfoliata*) and wild spinach (*Chenopodium album*) never get "too" fibrous to eat; they just get less choice until they brown, wither, and die. I've enjoyed eating properly prepared dandelion (*Taraxacum officinale*) leaves that were eighteen inches long. These leaves were growing in such excellent conditions that, even at eighteen inches, they had not yet reached their full size. They looked beautiful, like they were found on display in the farmers' market. They were still tender, and their bitterness had not yet had a chance to get intolerably harsh.

In some naturally bitter leaves, the strength of their bitterness is related to slow growth and end size. Plants like dandelions or wild lettuce (*Lactuca serriola*) accumulate bitterness over time. The faster a leaf is growing, the more spread out and less intense that bitterness is. The slower the leaf is growing, or if it has reached its end size, the more bitterness that is concentrated from exposure to the sun. Think of it this way: The longer the leaves bake in the sun, the more bitter they become, and the harder it is to manage that bitterness in the kitchen. So, rapidly growing leaves are not only more tender, they tend to be less bitter in those plants that produce bitter flavors.

Stems

Stems provide structure and support for leaves, flowers, fruits, and seeds. Stems grow to expand the length of a plant, allowing new leaves and other structures to spread out. Depending on the plant, stems can grow upright, along the ground, under the ground, or they can spread outward. Some plants have obvious stems and some do not. All the stems we'll talk about in this book are on herbaceous (nonwoody) plants. Some plants generally called biennials only grow stems in their second year of growth. Stems can be a great source of food if you know the right time to use them in the plant's development.

Just like leaves, stems that are actively growing have more tender parts. It is almost always the tips of stems that are actively growing. Like leaves, the parts of the stem that are not growing serve a support function. The no-longer-growing areas will become more fibrous. The longer the stem gets, the more fiber is laid down to support the weight. Let's talk about the potential edibility of different stages of stem development in plants with edible stems.

Shoots (growing tips of plants)

Let's start at the soil level when a plant is emerging from the ground. Some herbaceous plants like asparagus grow rapidly in the spring from perennial roots. They send up thick shoots that look like the asparagus we buy from the grocery. If you think about it, asparagus is an immature stem that hasn't branched out yet. When it still has that asparagus-sprig look, it is rapidly growing and will be tender enough to eat. We also know that there is a point near the base of that stem that is too fibrous to eat. So we peel it, or snap it off to be discarded. That fibrous part is there to stiffen the stem so it can better support a taller plant.

The asparagus we find in the produce department is typically picked when it is about ten inches long. Rapidly growing asparagus can be eaten as long as the spear can be easily snapped from the elongating stem. I've snapped the tender upper spears of stems up to two feet tall. Even after branching, the growing branchlet tips are tender enough to eat when they are still forming. Asparagus becomes too fibrous to eat once the stem is only supportive and all the leaves have fully grown out. I mention asparagus because most people know this plant—or at least what it looks like in the market or on a dinner plate. But this same principle applies to many wild foods.

Leafy stem

When I was getting started with wild foods, I tried exactly what they said in the books. Since the leaves of wild spinach (*Chenopodium album*) are edible, I would pluck them one by one from the stem. Clearing a stem of leaves can take some time. Once I realized that the whole leafy upper stem was edible, one pluck got me about ten leaves and some tender stem. This makes the job easier and gives you more food. If you just harvest the growing leafy stem tips, your pruning will stimulate growth, providing you with even more food for a later harvest.

Factors Affecting Rapid Growth

Growing conditions

As I've explained, rapid growth is the source of tenderness and choiceness. Many things affect the growth of a plant and its parts. The appropriateness of the soil, the length of daylight, the amount of water available, temperature range, and when the seeds germinate are the main factors. When all of these things are optimal for a

Rapidly growing wild asparagus shoots about 15 inches tall. As long as the upper part of the spears are tender, they are still harvestable. They are tender as long as you can easily snap the stem.

The upper edible leafy stem of young wild spinach. The top of the plant is tender above where the stem snaps cleanly.

(left) Green amaranth (*Amaranthus retroflexus*), **5 feet tall,** mature, and going to seed. This plant germinated early in its season, allowing for a long happy life before that season ended. It had the further benefit of growing in the rich well-watered soil of a garden. This long life in rich conditions allowed lots of tender, edible, rapidly growing stems and leaves (food for us) to be produced prior to seed production. In these conditions, huge amounts of seed (food for us) are eventually produced because the plant was so healthy.

(below) Green amaranth (*Amaranthus retroflexus*), **10 inches tall,** mature, and going to seed. This plant germinated late in its season—not allowing much time to grow before that season ended. The soil was dry and there was a lot of competition from surrounding plants. These conditions forced the plant to mature quickly, using what little energy and water it had to go right to seed—at the expense of leaf and stem growth. So the plant is tiny, almost leafless, and produces only a few seeds. There is not much food to be eaten from plants growing under this kind of stress.

particular plant, the plant grows rapidly, becoming larger and more vigorous. Seed production is delayed so the plant can continue to grow, producing more photosynthesizing machinery (leaves and stems). Then, after achieving vigorous growth, tremendous quantities of seeds are produced.

In contrast, when one or more of these things are restricted, or at least nonoptimal, the plant will change what it does, how big it gets, and how it looks accordingly. This is often called stress. The greater the stress, the more stunted and less productive a plant becomes.

Eating plants stressed by poor growing conditions is one reason why many people give up on wild foods. The first plants they find and experiment with may be growing under harsh conditions. Let's face it, many wild plants survive in severe conditions that would kill other plants. But stressed survival takes its toll. Under stress conditions, instead of putting what little energy, food, and water they have into growth, the plant puts its resources into reproduction. This results in rapid aging rather than rapid growth. Growing slowly but aging quickly results in stunted plants with fewer, smaller, fibrous leaves and shorter stems going to seed. Bitterness and overall rankness also increase in many edible plants with age.

So, if you are sampling wild foods for the first time, tasting leaves from a stressed plant will provide a much less satisfying culinary experience. And from a time perspective, it will take you longer to collect a reasonable amount of food from smaller plants that are near their end size. The leafy stems and leaves will be fewer in quantity, smaller, more fibrous, and less choice.

Germination time

Another factor causing plants to age quickly is late germination. If you are near the end of a plant's growing season but other conditions are right for it to germinate, it will still grow from seed. For some annuals, this can happen if the soil is turned over in late summer and there is just enough moisture to stimulate germination. Since the season is late, the main mission of the plant is to produce seed before it runs out of growing season. Aging accelerates, which results in stunting. The degree of stunting will be greater the closer you are to the end of the season.

Chickweed (*Stellaria media*) surviving winter under the snow. Regular bouts with 20 degree temperatures do not kill chickweed. Colder, harsher conditions and physical damage will kill chickweed.

Overwintering

Many of the plants in this book are winter hardy; that is, in spite of below-freezing temperatures and being covered by snow, they continue to maintain some above-ground greenery. But let's put this in context relative to usability. Winter conditions are harsh. These conditions include temperatures that will crystallize liquid water; very short days, cloudiness, lack of sunshine, or burial by snow; growth-promoting soil organisms hibernating or being compromised; and hardened, regularly frozen soil limiting root growth and restricting water, among other things.

Overwintering plants have to adapt to cold weather in order to survive. In scientific literature, this is called "cold acclimation." This process involves gene expression, special protein production, fluid management, and other things.

How do all these things affect a plant's edibility? Most plants undergo winter changes that make them less desirable as food. They are still edible, just less desirable. Growth seems to stop—old leaves hang on and age in place. Few new leaves develop, if any. Remember that rapid growth improves tenderness and choiceness. Slow or no growth tends to do the opposite. Overwintering plants tend to be fibrous, chewy, and more paper-like. Structural support in the form of increased fiber becomes a physiological priority to prevent damage to the plant. Already-hairy leaves become thicker with additional hairs to insulate them from harsh conditions. Plant parts become less crisp and more dry because crystallizing water is what can do the greatest damage to plant cells. Sugars and alcohols increase to lower the freezing point, allowing the plant to survive lower temperatures.

Four-legged herbivores like deer and rabbits are happy to eat overwintering plants, but they are less picky than humans. Plants that seem to survive with the most vigor include miner's lettuce (*Claytonia perfoliata*), chickweed (*Stellaria media*), and wintercress (*Barbarea vulgaris*). But they still suffer from a quality standpoint. And if you pick what few leaves are there, new ones do not easily grow back.

Another overwintering issue is increased contamination by dirt and mud. Overwintering plants tend to grow closer to the ground, almost flattened. And whether they are fully exposed or growing under the snow, they are immersed in moist grit. So winter plants also require much more cleaning for what you get.

Since there are many fresh supermarket alternatives to wild greens in the winter, I use those. Other than as a curiosity or for recreational survival training, I personally do not do much with aboveground, cold-hardened, over-wintering plants.

In summary, being able to evaluate the growth stage and condition of a plant's parts will tell you whether it is worth gathering and how choice it might be. Understanding how good growing conditions foster rapid growth can lead you to gathering more tender and flavorful parts.

Chapter 4

Foraging Tools

Let's face it. More people will do more things with wild foods if they are having more fun and experiencing less drudgery. If you have to spend half an hour cleaning some part of a plant, only rewarded with tiny pieces of food the size of a thimble, your enthusiasm will go the way of the dinosaur. Any harvest will be easier, less dirt prone, and more productive if accompanied by the right tools. In this chapter, I discuss the tools I use and how I carry them. In addition, this chapter offers concepts involved in food gathering that will help you be more successful.

Different sets of tools and tactics are required for different situations, such as harvesting from trees, shrubs, or vines, and collecting in complicated environments like marshes or the seashore. The tools I'm referring to here are perfect for gathering the wild foods discussed in this book.

Tools are most efficiently and effectively used when they are easily accessible. How do you carry all this stuff around with you? We can all take a lesson from Batman, the comic book hero who is much more effective because of his utility belt. That belt is packed with tools/devices that give him diverse capabilities and advantages over other crime fighters. Modern-day workers have utility belts—police and carpenters, for instance. The handier their tools, the more productive they are. Each of the tools discussed in this chapter have a place on the forager's utility belt.

The simplest tools you can use are your hands, of course. You can always grab a bunch of plant

My fully loaded, wild food utility belt. Left to right: knife, scissors, bag holder, rag, spray mister, and spade-pick. It is not necessary to carry all these tools all the time—just carry what you need to suit the plants you plan to gather.

matter and pull it free from the plant. You can dig with your hands, pinch leaves free with your fingers, and wrap your harvest in that extra shirt or jacket you have with you for transport. Gathering without tools involves pinching, snap-breaking, and jerking parts from the growing plants.

The benefit of this strategy is that you do not have to carry around any tools. The problems, however, can be many—depending on the plants you are gathering and how far you are traveling prior to food preparation. Problems encountered are mostly food-quality issues. If you eat the plants as you pick them rather than transporting them, you have less to worry about. The more you pinch, jerk, and pull plant parts during a harvest, the more you bruise and damage them. Damaged food is harder to clean, has a much shorter shelf life, and does not present as well as it could. And if your hands are dirty (not uncommon while foraging), you grind that dirt right into the plant, making it harder to clean.

What follows are suggested tools to try and the sheaths that hold them. Sheaths are specially designed pockets, often attached to a belt, for holding a tool that hangs off the body; knives are held in sheaths.

Belt

I use three systems, depending on how flexible I need things to be and how many tools I want to take with me—no tool belt, my pants belt, or my utility belt.

In those circumstances where I am on a simple gather in my backyard, I'll just carry the scissors and bags in my hand. A belt is not involved.

On other occasions, I might take scissors, a digging tool, and bags, and loop their sheaths directly to my pants belt. While this may seem like the most efficient way to mount your sheaths, they are stiff solid objects that can restrict movement around your waist. You might have to remove them when getting into cars or sitting on a chair. Threading sheaths on and off your pants belt while simultaneously threading that belt through your pants loops gets a little tedious after a while. Due to this inconvenience, I mostly use a dedicated utility belt.

A dedicated utility belt is strictly for holding the sheathed tools, not for holding up my pants. I can remove it easily and quickly since it rests on top of everything. If I am wearing a coat, a utility belt can easily wrap around the outside of it. That coat would bury/cover/restrict access to tools threaded on a regular belt.

To avoid clutter around your waist, take only the tools you think you will need for the foods you intend to gather.

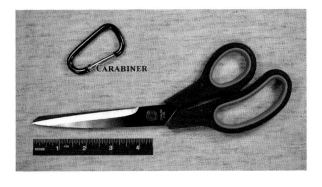

Measuring scissor size. The most useful kind of scissors has a cutting blade that is 4 to 5 inches long from the pivot screw to the tip of the blade. It is helpful to have red or orange markings somewhere on the handle, making it less likely to forget them on the ground as you walk away. Also shown is a carabiner, which is one of many possible ways of attaching a rag to a utility belt.

Scissors

A sharp pair of scissors is probably your most valuable tool. I carry scissors with me whenever I go foraging. If I could only have one tool for the kinds of plants in this book, a pair of scissors would be my choice.

The usefulness of scissors will become apparent once you start using them in the field. Two blades singlehandedly trap what you are cutting, providing their own counterforce and shearing action. Cutting plant parts is simple and precise. Even dull scissors will cut much better than a dull knife. And when the scissors are sharp, they cut through plant matter like butter. A clean cut provides less damage than a jagged edge caused by just pulling with your hands alone, helping to give the plant a longer shelf life.

Scissors are especially useful because they enable mass harvesting of low-to-the-ground, densely growing plants like chickweed. When chickweed is growing in dense mats, you simply grab a handful of the tips, slide your scissors blades below your hand, and snip. You now have a salad in hand that is ready to eat. Try that with a knife, or by pulling or plucking, and you will know immediately the value of the scissors.

In addition to this salad-harvesting technique, cutting stems is a breeze. It's easy, whether you are cutting a tender leafy stem near the top of a plant or cutting whole stems for later leaf extraction.

My favorite pair of scissors has a blade that is almost five inches long, as measured from the hinge screw to the tip of the blade. Ignore the advertised length and measure the blade yourself. A blade of that size is about as big as you can get without special ordering or finding a great hardware or fabric store. And while small scissors are better than none, you will be more productive with a blade that is long. The best selection is found in large craft, specialty hardware, or fabric stores. Some stores are now selling titanium-bladed scissors for extra durability.

Look for heavy-duty scissors with thick, sturdy, stainless steel blades. The cheaper ones have thin bendable blades and brittle plastic handles that will break with outdoor use. If you think that you are paying too much for good scissors, compare the price to what you would pay for a good knife. Good scissors are inexpensive for what you get.

It is also helpful for the handles to have some bright orange or red coloration. You are less likely to accidentally leave them somewhere if you can clearly see that they do not blend in with the mostly green and brown habitat you are harvesting from. It is also not a bad idea to get a scissors sharpener to maintain your blades.

Sheathe your scissors! Carrying scissors in your fanny pack or backpack can work, but the more you have to dig for your tools, the less enjoyable the experience.

I use a knife sheath to hold my scissors. It sits on my belt right next to my knife in its own sheath. That way it is immediately accessible. I call this a scissors sheath. I have yet to find a good scissors sheath on the market, so using a knife sheath is the best alternative. Make sure the sheath is deep enough so that the scissors fits in snugly—you don't want it to pop out accidentally.

Hand Rag

Invariably, your hands will get grimy with soil while harvesting. I do not want that grime on my harvest. This is true whether I am snacking on the spot or if I am gathering for later use. To solve this problem, I like to have a dry absorbent rag handy. Once your hands get dirty, just grab the rag and wipe off the excess. This is not to thoroughly clean your hands; it is intended to get annoying, food-contaminating dirt off them. The rag will get dirty as you use it. Under many circumstances, it will continue to work even when dirty. It is wise to have extra clean rags handy to replace ones getting too dirty.

You have the choice of putting this rag in your pocket and pulling it out as needed, or making it a member of your utility belt. I prefer it being on the belt because of its instant access. This can be hanging from your belt in any number of ways. The simplest way is to just loop it around your belt where it will fit snugly. I personally use an inexpensive carabiner, which used to be the exclusive domain of mountain climbers. These quick, practical, and useful latching devices are now universally available in many sizes in most hardware stores. I see them most often as parts of key chains.

Fasten the carabiner (or other loop of your choosing) on a belt loop and pull the rag through. The size should be such that the rag fits snugly. You want it snug enough so that it does not slide out while you are working. You want it loose enough so that you can pull it out when you are done or need to replace it.

The only problem with hand rags, particularly if they have a thick weave, is that they can collect bur seeds from tall grass and other plants. To reduce this problem, tuck them into the belt when problem plants surround you or if you are kneeling down toward the dirt.

Portable Digging Tool

For many of us outdoorsy types, it is quite pleasurable to dig with our hands. Most of the time, however, the soil is too hard for this to be practical. Pleasure aside, unless all you are going for is roots, digging with your hands not only makes your hands dirty, it infuriates your manicurist. Dirt easily transfers to the greens you are gathering. Dirty greens then take a lot more work to clean. And while this may seem obvious, harvesting enthusiasm can overpower the patience needed to engage in more practical behavior.

It is good practice when harvesting plants to separate the harvesting of greens and roots. I suggest gathering your greens first, placing them in clean bags, then going back to dig the roots last or on a different trip. They should never be put in the same container unless there is no other option. If you are forced to place them in the same container, try to wrap the greens in something, like some large nearby leaves, to protect them from the dirt. No matter the gathering sequence, most people will still want to wash their greens, even if they appear clean. The process, however, will be easier and faster, and you will use less water if you harvest greens first and bag them separately from soil-attached parts.

If your goal is to harvest wild roots in your backyard, it is easy to just grab a shovel, assuming you own one. But what if you live in an apartment, do not own a shovel, or are foraging away from home? You cannot always carry a garden shovel around with you. You need a portable digging tool. Here are some options:

SHOVEL: If you know you are going to do some serious shoveling, like digging large burdock roots (*Arctium lappa*, not covered in this book), just use a regular, heavy-duty, long-handled garden shovel. Any portable digging tool is less practical for roots deeper than a foot. A regular shovel makes sense when you already know where some large-rooted plants are, and you have a harvesting plan. Then make it a special trip focused on gathering that root.

SPADE-PICK: It is impractical, however, to carry a full-sized shovel with you whenever you might be in a foraging situation. In lieu of carrying a large shovel, the best portable digging tool I've found so far is a small spade-pick. This is a hand trowel with a spade (small shovel) on one side and a pick on the other. Here are the two best options I am familiar with:

My preferred option is a gardener's spade-pick, which is typically about fourteen inches long. I find this the best combination of size, utility, and portability. These are lightweight but made of very strong welded steel. They are available in many garden sections of big department stores and nurseries. Skip the ones with blades riveted to the handles—they are less durable than the welded ones. The one I use is made by Lewis Tools under the names of TerraTuff, Terra Planter, or Yard Butler. It is strong enough for most applications and yet light enough to carry with you into the field. Use the pick side for hard and/or rocky soil and the spade side for softer soil.

Spade-picks compared. The one on the left was trimmed with a hacksaw to curve around the body when being worn in its sheath. Unshaped, as seen on the right, these tools have a tendency to stab into the side of the body.

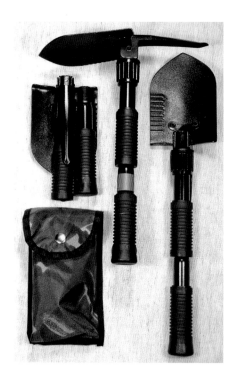

Folding shovel-picks: (left) folded shovel-pick and sheath; (center) assembled shovel-pick positioned for shoveling or picking; (right) assembled shovel-pick positioned for shoveling.

A second option is a camper's mini shovel-pick. This is a folding adjustable multi-position, take-apart gizmo that is similar to the gardener's spade-pick but gives you folding options that the other one does not. This is not your World War II–style folding shovel. Several manufacturers make almost identical versions of this, including Coghlans, Coleman, and Texsport. These are often available in camping stores. The advantages to this kind of shovel-pick are that it can be folded, placed, and carried inside its carrying pouch so that it is less likely to jab you if you fall; the shovel component can be fixed to a straight position, just like a regular shovel, or at a right angle, just like the gardener's spade-pick; and it has a certain prestige factor with guys who love gizmos. The disadvantages are that it is shorter and heavier than the gardening tool (giving less leverage in the digging action), and the folding joints get clogged with dirt. Beware of cheap models whose blade attachments are so weak that they bend at the slightest force.

I prefer and use the non-folding gardener's spade-pick because it is simple and ready to use, is sturdy, and has a reasonable length to feel comfortable while digging. So how does the spade-pick work? It becomes an extension of your arm. Use it like you would a hatchet or a hand ax, only instead of chopping wood, you are chopping into the soil. Unfortunately, due to the shape of this tool, a normal chop splashes dirt toward you. To divert the dirt away from you, learn to chop with your arm slightly angled to the side.

How you carry the spade-pick around with you is a matter of preference. While hiking, you could carry it in a loop on the back of a backpack, much like climbers carry ice picks. But that requires you to remove your pack to retrieve it every time you want to dig. This brings us back to the utility belt idea. The goal is to hang this fourteen-inch-long tool on your belt for convenient access without it getting in the way, hurting, or injuring you. To meet my needs, I've modified the spade's shape so that it does not jab me while attached to the belt. Using a hacksaw, I curved one side to fit the side of my waist. I then sanded the cut edge smooth. (See the spade-pick comparison photo on page 59.) Then I needed a sheath to attach it to my waist and protect my side in case I fell on it. One option that works well is to buy a hammer holder from a hardware store. If you go this route, buy one with a leather loop, not a metal one. Metal clanks against metal, which is annoying, and it does not hold the tool as securely as leather. The hammer holder is made of leather thick enough to prevent the spade-pick head from touching you.

Spade-picks in sheaths. The one on the left is a standard sheath that is designed to hold a hammer (Custom LeatherCraft, Model #426). The spade-pick sheath on the right is one I built myself.

Knife

For the last twenty years, I've been using a fixed-blade hunting knife. Fixed-blade knives are solid and do not fold. For my purposes, the benefits of the size, solidity, and harder edge on the better knives greatly outweigh knives that fold.

For the kinds of plants in this book, a knife has few uses aside from hacking stems and woody material that are too large and solid for scissors. Of course, once you're back in the kitchen, knives play a wonderful food-preparation role. But you have kitchen knives for that. Do I carry my knife when harvesting the plants in this book? Yes, but only because I might find a need for it occasionally. A knife is much more useful for trips into the woods.

Spray misters in belted Catch-Alls. The Catch-All on the left comes with a hook-over-the-belt arrangement. I bent the hook on the Catch-All on the right to circle and fit more snugly on the belt. The shaped hook does not fall off the belt as you move around.

Spray Mister

In the produce department of supermarkets, you might hear the muffled sound of thunder. Then, out of nowhere, sprayers kick on in unison, misting the greens until they are drenched. For years I did not like having to deal with all that wetness in my shopping experience. I thought, isn't there a better way? Do the plants really need to be swimming in all this water?

The answer is YES! Swimming in all that moisture keeps cut greens fresh and alive. Harvested plants wilt because their source of fluid is cut off and because they lose water through their pores (transpiration). Transpiration seems to increase once the stem is cut or when the plant is exposed to sunlight. It's as if the plant knows it's doomed and just gives up. Heat above 40 degrees and direct sunlight will speed up the wilting process. Your goal is not only to prevent harvested greens from drying out but also to give them what they need to stay vital.

A spray mister is one part of the solution. Misting keeps plants hydrated directly. Spray misters are found in supermarkets and department stores offering gardening supplies and cosmetics.

As soon as you harvest leaves and stems of a plant, give them a thorough misting right in your collection bag. This not only prevents transpiration, it also hydrates the plant even further—often making your keep crispier and fresher than when it was still attached to the stem. I'll talk more about maintaining hydration and transporting the greens in the following discussions on bags and water trays.

Spray misters do not come with sheaths. The best sheathe option I've found is something called a "Catch-All" made by Case Logic. It's located in the automotive section of department stores and is intended as a universal holder in your car for cell phones and other odds and ends. It's too small to hold a cup or glass but is good for that small spray mister. It's made of neoprene, which stretches to firmly hold that spray mister. Since a Catch-All is not designed for the rigors of fieldwork, the upper rim can unravel somewhat. This is easily fixed with a needle and thread.

Collecting Bags

Unless you are eating all your wild foods as you pick them, you will need a harvesting strategy, your goal being to keep the pickin's fresh and vital until you get them into more controlled conditions. This is true, even when gathering right out your backdoor, since the sun can bake and wilt your greens in minutes. Heat, sunlight, and dryness are the enemies of fresh produce.

For transporting greens, I recommend reusing those ubiquitous white plastic grocery bags. Plastic maintains moisture, white reflects the heat of the sun, and these bags have built-in handles. Do not use clear or darkly colored plastic bags, particularly on bright-to-sunny days. The sun's rays will go through and get trapped within clear plastic, wilting/cooking the greens. The darker the color of a bag, the more that color will absorb the heat of the sun. If you have a choice, a white bag is your best bet. White double bagging is even better.

I carry my empty bags tightly packed in a pouch on my utility belt for easy access. A small pouch can carry around twelve bags—plenty for most circumstances. Spray-mist

Plant-collecting containers. Water trays and recycled white plastic bags are convenient and keep your greens fresh. Natural material containers (baskets, cloth bags) work great as long as you use techniques to keep your take moist, cool, uncrushed, and out of the sun.

the contents of the bag on regular intervals as it is being filled. Once you have loosely filled the bags with plant material, keep the contents cool and moist. Keep your collecting bag in the shade whenever possible, even in your own body's shade, in the partial shade of a nearby plant, or in your backpack.

If you prefer to use woven bags or baskets made of natural materials, keep them covered with a wet white towel. Spraying a porous container itself will result in some evaporative cooling. If you have a distance to travel, make sure the contents stay cool, moist, and shaded.

Water Trays

Another collecting option is to use water trays. I use the plastic storage containers you find in housewares departments. What I'm calling trays are often called tubs, bins, or storage containers. If you can find white ones to reflect sunlight, that is great, but I can only find semitransparent ones with white tops. Unlike bags and baskets, these trays can hold standing water. That water keeps your harvest hydrated through the stem as well as from your spray mister. The solid structure helps to prevent plants from getting crushed and damaged.

For this to work, the tray's bottom should be filled with cold water. As you collect your leaves, stems, or shoots, stand them in the water, loosely packed against each other. Their cut end is in the water and their tips are up. Spray-mist these to keep the tops moist. When you are done harvesting or if the tray is full, cover it to keep in the moisture and to shield it from the sun. As always, keep it in the shade if you can. If your take is too tall to use its lid, cover it with a white plastic bag and keep it out of the sun.

PART II
THE PLANTS

This part of the book covers just a few of the hundreds of wild plants you could be eating from your yard, garden, neighborhood, woodlot, fallow field, and organic farm. The plants covered are important and common wild foods, and are presented here with the purpose of giving you the detail and photographs necessary to know them well. More plants will be covered in future planned books.

Commonly thought of as weeds, these delectable foods are found anywhere the soil has been disturbed or is soft enough for the seeds to start growing. The better the soil conditions and moisture and the more these plants are growing in their own seasons, the more lush their growth.

There are big differences in flavor and texture between leaves gathered in their prime and ones that are too old. Some can go from delicious and tender to rank and chewy, so pay attention in the following chapters for how to determine when these greens are at their prime.

Plants are grouped into the four sections: foundation, tart, pungent, and bitter. Each plant within these sections has its own chapter, following the plant from emerging seedling to end-of-life seed production, from foraging to food, from preparation to eating. The content runs from basic to advanced, always with an eye on what you really need to know to make good use of these plants. Each chapter starts out with a brief summary of some facts found within. But as you will come to learn, the devil and the angels are in the details.

Foundation Greens

Foundation greens are what I call the mild greens, which are at least mild flavored when they are at their prime stages of development. These greens and vegetables are suitable for almost every occasion and will be accepted by almost anyone who doesn't hate the sight of greens. Their mild flavors can serve as the neutral base for salads containing stronger-tasting greens. They are edible raw and cooked, and most can be used anywhere that lettuce or spinach are appropriate.

Don't let my use of the term *mild* fool you. These greens have their own characteristic flavors and textures. They are delicious by almost any standards. Served fresh, they are excellent in salads, eaten as snacks, added to sandwiches, used as garnishes, and made into pestos and other green-based sauces. Cooked, they can take the place of almost any green in any recipe book you have.

Foundation greens can be nutritional powerhouses, packed with nutrients and phytochemicals. Wild spinach, for instance, is one of the most nutritious leafy greens ever analyzed. The plants covered in this section include wild spinach, chickweed, mallow, and purslane.

Chapter 5

FAMILY: Chenopodiaceae
SPECIES: *Chenopodium album*

Wild Spinach

Wild spinach gives domesticated spinach a run for its money

A rapidly growing wild spinach plant at about 12 inches tall in rich soil.
This is a young plant prior to bud or flower formation.

Estimated Range

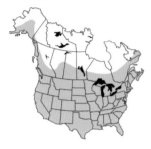

Official Species Name:
- *Chenopodium album* L.

Can be confused with and interbred with
- *Chenopodium berlandieri* Moq.

Common Names:
- Wild spinach
- Lambsquarters
- Goosefoot
- Fat hen
- Pigweed
- Huauzontle, Quelite, Bledo
- Quelite cenizo

Herbaceous weed naturalized from Europe. Widespread and abundant in North America where humans have invaded and where soil has been disturbed.

Edible Parts:
- Growing tips of leafy stems
- Leaves
- Bud Clusters
- Seeds

WILD SPINACH

I prefer to call this plant wild spinach rather than lambsquarters, even though lambsquarters is a more commonly used name. I am not trying to create confusion by calling it wild spinach; rather, I am trying to give this plant the food-related name recognition it deserves.

North America was primarily an agricultural society a hundred years ago. So terms like lambsquarters, fat hen, and pigweed had a little more meaning to the everyday person. The number of people working on farms these days is only a small part of the population, so the old plant names retain little meaning.

What do the terms *lambsquarters, fat hen,* and *pigweed* all have in common? Farm animals. The impression one gets from these names is that this plant was well known for its ability to fatten up livestock. Farmers today use more systematically efficient ways to feed farm animals than bringing them wild plants. Even free-range animals may be systematically fed or not allowed to graze on wild plants.

To modern wild food enthusiasts, the name "pigweed" is more commonly used to refer to green amaranth (*Amaranthus retroflexus*) than to wild spinach. But, according to old-timers in a study I did in the 1980s, many different plants fed to pigs were called pigweed. Since the term *pigweed* can refer to more than one plant, it makes it a poor name.

So why "wild spinach"? Everyone in modern society knows what spinach is, and they know it is good for you. Spinach is a cousin of wild spinach. And while their flavors are different, young wild spinach flavor gives a hint of spinach. Most importantly, you could substitute wild spinach in any cooked recipe for domesticated spinach and, flavorwise, few would notice the difference.

Wild spinach is one of the most nutritious leafy greens ever analyzed, beating out domestic spinach in fiber, beta-carotene (vitamin A), vitamin C, riboflavin, calcium, zinc, copper, and manganese. Domesticated spinach wins in omega-3s, folic acid, and iron. So both are exceptional foods and worthy of being part of a nutritious diet.

According to one study (Bianco, 1998), wild spinach's potassium (K) is as high as 1,286mg/100 grams. That is two to four times higher than spinach, Swiss chard, and broccoli—all good sources. The study also found its magnesium at 117mg/100 grams of fresh material. That is higher than beet greens, which are also an excellent source of magnesium. Wild spinach is also a rich source of lutein and other carotinoids (Raju, 2007).

But nutrient data varies from study to study, particularly for plants growing in variable soils. A study by USDA (Release 18) says wild spinach has a third as much potassium and magnesium as the above study—still respectable amounts, but less. So don't memorize these amounts; they are just here to give you the mind-set that this food is very good for you. Wild spinach is a great food and deserves to be in a complex diet complete with other great foods.

Wild spinach and green amaranth (*Amaranthus retroflexus*) dominating a planting bed on moist fertile farmland. As is common, the wild seed is already in the soil. It just needs to be tilled and watered to grow. None of these wild seeds were introduced by the farmer. They took over a bed planted with some intended crop that never survived the competition from our vigorous wild friends.

The phytochemical and antioxidant potential of this plant have yet to be investigated in depth or in any organized fashion. And even though this plant contains soluble oxalates like cultivated spinach, its widespread use in North America would be a great addition to the array of vegetables we eat. Widespread use already occurs in other parts of the globe.

Wild spinach contains a considerable amount of oxalic acid. Oxalates tend to bind with calcium and other minerals, making them partially unavailable. But in spite of that, wild spinach is still a nutritional powerhouse. Oxalates are not a problem for normal healthy people eating a good diverse diet.

Wild spinach has tremendous potential—as a wild food and as a new crop plant. It already grows with little effort on farmland and on any disturbed soil. Of all the

Wild spinach sprouts compared to green amaranth (*Amaranthus retroflexus*). Upper left and right are wild spinach sprouts. A green amaranth sprout is shown at lower left. Note the blunt to rounded tips on the spinach sprout's leaves. The powder-like white crystals on the wild spinach is characteristic. Except for the first two embryonic leaves (cotyledons), green amaranth leaves have obvious veins and notched (indented) tips. Amaranth does not have a white crystalline powder.

foundational greens covered in this book, wild spinach may be the one most easily adapted by people who have not eaten wild foods before. It is delicious and abundant, produces lots of seeds for next year's growth, is easily harvested, and requires no special preparation to fit into any conventional greens recipe.

Knowing Wild Spinach

Wild spinach seeds last for many years in the soil. When conditions are right, wild spinach will sprout in spring and summer. The sprouting season seems to stretch, depending on local conditions, from mid-May to mid-October. The prime growing season is June through August.

SPROUTS: Wild spinach sprouts are small. By the time they have four leaves, they look a little like tiny green propellers. The cotyledons (first two leaves) are linear and straight with a rounded tip. The second two leaves are more lance-shaped (a little wider at the base) and occasionally show the beginnings of teeth along the margins. They are covered with hundreds of tiny glistening grains.

Sprouts of wild spinach and green amaranth can be confused. They are different in the following ways: amaranth's cotyledons, while strap-like, are less straight along the edges, and their tips are round but show some tapering. Amaranth's first two leaves after the cotyledons are often reddish and more rounded, and have a clear mid vein and a notched (indented) tip.

Wild spinach, narrow version.

LEAVES: One of the reasons that wild spinach is also called goosefoot is because the leaves eventually take on the appearance of web-footed waterfowl. That leaf shape can vary a bit from narrow and pointed to quite rounded. From an overhead view, the leaves are arranged in a starburst pattern, radiating out from the center.

Just like the sprouts, the whole plant is covered with a fine crystalline, waxy-like powder, which is most evident and denser at the growing tips, as can be seen in the center of these photographs.

As the growing tips expand in size, the powder spreads out and becomes less obvious. This powder is an important identifying characteristic for the plant and also renders the plant waterproof. Water droplets bead up and roll right off during a rain. You can use a spray mister to test this in the field.

Wild spinach, rounded version.

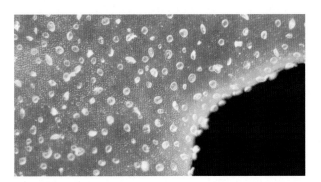

Wild spinach leaf magnified about 50 times. The powder on the leaf is made up of microscopic wax-like crystals. This wax helps make the leaves waterproof and may help repel insects.

Hairy Nightshade / Ground Cherry Nightshade

Solanum physalifolium / Solanum sarracoides / Solanum villosum

Toxic look-alike

Green parts of members of the *Solanum* genus are known to have the chemical solanine, a toxic alkaloid. For our purposes, we will consider hairy nightshade poisonous. A few small leaves in a salad will not hurt you. But avoid eating this plant until we know more. The leaves of hairy nightshade look enough like wild spinach that you should learn to know this plant. Hairy nightshade often intermixes with wild spinach and green amaranth. Like a chameleon, its leaves can mimic both plants.

So what are the differences? Hairy nightshade is hairy while wild spinach is not. Rather, wild spinach has a fine waxy powder covering its surface. The nightshade's white flowers have the characteristic shape of the nightshade family and are larger than those of wild spinach, which are green and inconspicuous. The flowers are a dead giveaway.

Two hairy nightshade plants compared. Even though these two plants are the same species, the leaves of the plant on the left resemble green amaranth; the leaves of the plant on the right resemble wild spinach.

A close-up of hairy nightshade's showy white flowers.

PLANT SIZE AND FORM: The size of the plant can vary from a few inches to seven feet tall, depending on its life story. At the beginning of its growing season in June, a plant sprouting in rich soft soil without competition from other plants and with adequate water throughout its life can grow to six or seven feet tall, looking like a big shrub. A plant sprouting at the end of its growing season in hard dry ground may only grow to a few inches and have a single tiny stem with a few miniature leaves. The first would produce lots of leaves and stems (food for us); the second would not produce enough food to bother with. Most plants will be somewhere in between these two extremes at maturity—two to four feet tall.

Under good conditions, this plant grows fast and mostly upward. The primary stem elongates first, then the side branches grow in later. The stem is roundish but ridged. Leaves grow alternately on the stem.

As the plant grows older in good growing conditions, it takes on a Christmas tree shape. If the stems are clipped (due to harvesting), the side branches start growing out.

(left) Wild spinach—healthy, young, and tall—prior to lateral branch formation. This plant is not quite 20 inches tall, and only the top 10 inches or so are shown.

(right) Wild spinach branching widely following a harvest. Branching eventually occurs in the process of normal development as the plant matures. You can see two places where the stem was cut from harvesting. Each time you trim a tender leafy stem away for food, branching is stimulated, resulting in many new growing tips for harvesting. This plant is almost 3 feet tall.

Wild spinach about 7 feet tall and fully mature. Well-fed wild spinach is well-branched and produces a huge quantity of seeds when mature. The leaves are still edible at this stage but are reduced in quality, taking on a somewhat off-flavor. According to research on other mature plants, the leaves on these older plants retain most of their nutrients and phytochemicals as long as they are still green. (The author stands in for perspective, 2006.)

Young wild spinach buds tightly clustered prior to spreading out. These clusters are analogous to broccoli, which is also a grouping of bud clusters. Note the waxy granules on all the surfaces. This photograph shows the plant tip at about 3 times life-size. When the plant matures (like in the previous photograph), the buds spread out on thin branchlets.

At some point, the plant shifts from making leaves and stems to producing buds, flowers, and seeds. Many things can trigger this: the end of its natural season (cold sets in, shorter days), a lack of moisture, overharvesting, natural aging, etc. Once this seed production begins, there is little you can do to stop it. So if you have wild spinach growing in your yard, feed it, water it, nurture it for as long as you can. All these things help it, and other wild plants grow profusely and delay the onset of seed production. Feed it and it will feed you. If you just leave it, it will age faster with less growth and go to seed. This is why I have rarely seen a seven-foot-tall wild spinach plant outside my garden. Nature does not pamper them like I do.

Wild spinach buds open into tiny green inconspicuous flowers. You will not see them unless you look closely. Once these flowers are fertilized, they produce shiny black seeds that are eventually spread by dropping out of the flower's ovary. If it is late in the season and you happen to brush by a mature wild spinach plant, you will hear thousands of seeds dropping to the ground. They're hard to see easily, but you will definitely hear them hitting leaves as they drop.

Wild spinach seeds in the palm of my hand next to the stem that's dropping them. This enlarged image is actually about 1³/₈ inches wide. In order to show clean seeds, I took great pains to separate its wrapping, or pericarp, which is that part of the ovary directly surrounding the seed. The pericarp is often difficult to remove, particularly if the seeds are not allowed to fully ripen before harvest.

Harvesting and Serving Wild Spinach

I often say that nature is not here for our convenience, but in the case of wild spinach, it is. Insects don't seem to like it, so it does not get eaten before you get there. The plant grows upright and produces plenty of growth, making it convenient to gather. I rarely have to clean it since it seems to reject most dirt. And it does not require any heroic processing procedures to make it edible or palatable—it's delicious right off the plant. I love wild spinach!

Assuming you have a garden in which wild spinach is growing as a weed, you can really make good use of this plant. Whenever the soil is disturbed or turned over and watered within its growing season, wild spinach will sprout. You do not want all the sprouts to grow, so you thin out some of the plants at your convenience.

Thinning allows the remaining plants to grow in stronger. Don't do this at the two- or four-leaf stage; wait until you have six or more leaves. By waiting, you can thin and harvest the "baby greens" at the same time instead of just killing them. Pluck the stems close to the ground where they will still snap cleanly. This should kill the root and gain you the young leafy stem as food. Depending on your land size, you should have enough salad to feed you and several other people. If you want to pull the plant up by its roots, take special care not to mix the dirt of the roots with your baby greens.

Baby greens are particularly susceptible to drying out, so placing them directly in a bowl of water (they will float) for up to fifteen minutes, or in a well-misted bag, will keep them fresh until used. The roots and the lower part of the stem will be too fibrous to eat, so discard those parts. What you are gathering is what I call the leafy stem. Picking off

Wild spinach seedling. At only about 2 inches tall, this form is promising in that it may produce bigger and more densely growing leaves than the taller, thinner sprout seen earlier on page 70.

the individual leaves is unnecessary much of the time since the upper stem is perfectly edible and won't be fibrous unless you clip it too low. You can indeed pluck individual leaves, but why bother at this stage? It is less work to collect them all at once by plucking the whole tender upper stem.

The same is true when the plant gets older. Anywhere you can snap the stem cleanly without it pulling, tearing, or shredding will be tender from that point upward. And as long as there are several branches below the point you are taking, the plant will not only continue to grow, it will be stimulated by your pruning.

The interesting thing about wild spinach leaves is that they never seem to get fibrous. So while you may be snapping off a tender leafy stem tip, you can gather additional leaves from anywhere on the plant, even where the stem is old and woody.

Harvesting Techniques

FOR QUICK SALADS: If I go into my backyard with an empty salad bowl, I'll just clip off the most tender leaves and leafy stem tips, and add them to my bowl along with some salad dressing. That is all there is to it. If you want a more complex salad, add some more plants or other salad fixin's. But a pure wild spinach salad is fine by itself in the same way that some people like a plain lettuce salad, only this salad is way more nutritious and flavorful. Be forewarned that a salad of only wild spinach leaves will be very dense and flat. For a more conventional airy salad, mix them with other greens, leafy stem tips, and bud clusters.

FOR COOKING: If you are gathering from this plant just for cooking and/or preserving, the fresh greens don't have to look presentable. When this is the case, I use what I call the "squeegee method." This works on any relatively straight stem or branch. I grasp the stem down near where it is branching and pull upward or outward, gathering up all its leaves and small tender side stems in one long stroke. This gives me a mass of leaves that are good for chopping and cooking but would look damaged in a salad. If you use this method, gathering is extremely fast, but you will have to pick through the mass of greens to take out any fibrous material that tagged along. Some of the greens will be damaged from this rough method, but since you are cooking them anyway, you won't notice.

FOR MASS-COLLECTING: Mass-collect if you need lots of greens for a big meal or a potluck, or for freezing

Mass collection of upper stems. This mass of greens required about 10 seconds of leafy stems collection and about 5 minutes of kitchen leaf and upper leafy-stem plucking. The fibrous stem remnants were composted.

or canning. Your goal is to gather quickly in the field and do the finishing work in the food-preparation area. To do this, you are either taking whole young aboveground plants anywhere from ten to twenty inches tall or whole upper branches from larger plants. Take care to keep your harvest moist. Note that you are carrying off some of the stiff fibrous stem material, which will not be eaten. It is only serving as a food transport carrier for all the attached leaves.

In less hectic times, food preparers would sit around a table, socializing and peeling potatoes, scoring nuts, or in some way processing food for dinner, for big events, or for food preservation. Here, you and family and friends can sit around plucking leaves from bushels of wild spinach stems. The more stems you gather, the more time it will take. Talk, socialize, learn your kids' names. Once you separate the edible material, you can use it in any way you would use regular spinach, discarding the fibrous stems, of course.

When plucking leaves, I put them directly into a large bowl filled with cold water. This keeps them fresh until use. The leaves will mostly float because the waxy powder repels the water; but contact with the water somehow keeps them hydrated.

As I've said, the leaves remain relatively tender throughout the life of the plant. But older leaves can start taking on a mild off-flavor and even become bitter. My guess is that the off-flavor may be partially due to the buildup of saponins in the aging plant. Current research suggests that some saponins in small quantities are considered potential phytonutrients. And while whatever is causing the bitterness makes the fresh greens a little less desirable to me, most off-flavors go away with boiling. The occasional bitterness of older leaves is less noticeable and often disappears if the greens are included as part of a more complex dish. From a flavor standpoint, as long as they are young, leaves and leafy stems can be used interchangeably in a variety of dishes. They are all delicious.

SAPONINS

Saponins get their name from the soapwort plant (*Saponaria*). The saponin in its roots lathers up and was historically used to make soap. Saponins are found as normal constituents in many edible plants, including spinach, asparagus, oats, soy, and English daisies (*Bellis perennis*). They are typically bitter to the taste. There are many kinds of saponins. There is hope that certain ones in certain small amounts may be beneficial. They are all toxic in high quantity.

Harvesting and processing flower buds and seeds

FLOWER BUD CLUSTERS: I like to call the flower bud clusters *spinach-broccoli*. If you want to enjoy the flower buds, gather them when they first appear at the tips of the upper stems. Your goal is to find tenderness. You can partially gauge the tenderness of the bud clusters by the snap-ability of the stem that supports them. If the stem snaps crisp and clean, then there is a good chance that everything above that point will be tender. If you are tugging, pulling, and finally tearing a fibrous stem, then the buds have already begun maturing into seeds—a whole different food. You might want to taste a sample just to make sure the batch you are collecting is not beyond the bud stage. The flavor should be fresh and leaf-like. If they are bitter, you've arrived too late. To keep your harvest fresh, treat it as you would the leaves.

Young wild spinach bud clusters, as seen on page 74, are packed together and not very defined in shape. Once they start spreading out on thin stems, flowering, and going to seed, they become progressively more bitter.

SEEDS AND SEED CAPSULES: As the bud clusters flower and begin transforming into seed-producing capsules, they get crunchier and the stem stiffens. This stiffness allows you to use the squeegee method to harvest the capsules. These seed-producing capsules include all the flower parts surrounding the seed. As you squeegee, try to get as little stem material as possible.

Wild spinach seed-producing capsules.

The use of these seed capsules or just the seeds as a cooked porridge is complicated by a bitterness. This bitterness makes the seed capsules unpalatable and somewhat toxic in large amounts. If wild spinach is like *Chenopodium quinoa* and *Chenopodium berlandieri*, both with a history of seed processing, the bitterness is due to saponins. I find this very likely, because if you mix uncleaned seeds (those with the chaff still surrounding the seed) in a little water and stir vigorously, a saponin-like foam develops.

I've recently discovered that baking soda (bicarbonate of soda) added to soaking or boiling seed capsules or seeds can remove the bitterness, but I have not yet developed any consistent recipes to do that.

Quinoa (*Chenopodium quinoa*), a close relative of wild spinach, has a long history of use by the Incas and now more and more by modern society. The seeds produced by quinoa are greater than four times the size of wild spinach. They have a shell that is roughly the same light color as the nut meat. That shell is covered with several different saponins. Quinoa is often processed to remove that thin surface layer.

The quote below is part of an interesting account of Bolivian quinoa processing, which may shed some light on the processing of wild spinach seeds:

> *Quinoa seeds are coated with a layer of saponins, exceedingly bitter toxic chemicals. To get rid of this layer, women first toast the seeds on a metal tray over a fire. This helps to loosen the saponin layer and, while it may not be strictly necessary, enhances the flavour of the seeds. Then the hot seeds are tipped into a stone basin and the women tread them with their bare feet. The friction loosens the saponin coat and reduces it to dust. Treading also often gives the women blisters and chronic lower back pain. The saponin powder now has to be cleaned from the seeds, which is done by waiting for a day with the right kind of steady wind and then winnowing the seeds repeatedly so that the wind blows the dust away. Finally the seeds are rinsed in a couple of changes of water and set out to dry.* (Anonymous, 2006.)

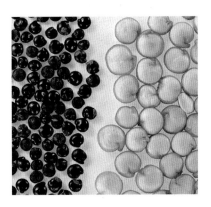

Wild spinach (left) and quinoa seed compared. Wild spinach seeds are about 1mm in diameter. Store-bought quinoa seeds are about 2½mm in diameter. Quinoa comes polished by its manufacturer to remove surface saponins. These are closely related plants that produce copious amounts of seeds. Note that the pericarp (remnants of the ovary) sticks to most of the wild spinach seeds, making some of them dull in appearance.

Wild spinach, used fresh in a cheese-melt fish sandwich and on the side as cooked greens. Since wild spinach is so substantial, the bowl of cooked greens shown here is enough for 3 or 4 servings.

Wild spinach produces copious amounts of seed. Quinoa, its close relative, is known to be a nutritious grain. This raises the hope that wild spinach seed may also be a valuable food.

Serving Techniques

USING LEAFY STEM TIPS: When most people think of salads, they think of light airy collections of greens. In contrast, individual wild spinach leaves are relatively flat in shape. They sort of stack upon each other like playing cards. A salad of just leaves would be very dense, filling, and not very airy. Why is this an issue? The more the food tastes, feels, and reminds them of something they are familiar with, the more likely they will be open-minded about what they are eating.

So how do you make flat wild spinach leaves airy? You mix the leaves that you have with a generous amount of leafy stem tips, which are quite three-dimensional, holding themselves up and creating air spaces. This simulates a more conventional airy salad and prevents stacking. This technique will also work for other greens that we will cover later. Make sure the leafy stem tips are bite-size so they will fit easily on a fork and in the mouth.

COOKING LEAFY STEMS: Tender edible leafy stems can be made into fine cooked dishes. Whenever you have very rapidly growing stems prior to any flower bud development, the part of the stem that is tender can be up to about six inches long. Once the leaves are removed for some other use, that stem becomes analogous to asparagus. So any asparagus recipe will work great with wild spinach stems—except that they taste like wild spinach—and that is a good thing. Like asparagus, fresh stems may seem somewhat fibrous when raw, even if they snap cleanly from the plant; but they will tenderize upon boiling. The longer you steam or boil them, the more tender they get—though six minutes is often enough.

MIXING WITH OTHER GREENS: While a pure wild spinach salad is perfectly great on its own for people like me, there are a couple of considerations to keep in mind—both having to do with those cute little waxy crystals that

Tender Wild Spinach Stems. Steamed upper stems, drizzled in olive oil and red wine vinegar with a pinch of salt, and garnished with an ox-eye daisy flower (*Leucanthemum vulgare*).

Wild Spinach Pizza. Whether starting from scratch or adding to a frozen pizza, wild spinach is a great addition. The key is to steam the greens, then mix them with enough olive oil to coat them before adding them to the pizza. The oil prevents the greens from drying out. If you want more greens in your pizza, put a whole layer of finely chopped wild spinach between the tomato sauce and the cheese.

cover the plant. First, they make wild spinach relatively waterproof. This means that some dressings will bead up and roll right off. This is only a minor nuisance that you will be able to manage with time and experience. The tiny waxy crystals can also give a slightly dry (though not astringent) feeling to the mouth. However, it's only a big issue to those cranky and finicky people in the world. The solution to both is to mix the raw wild spinach with other greens. Even a 50-50 mix goes a long way. Besides, eating a diversity of greens is better for you than just eating one.

BOILING AND STEAMING: Whether you boil or steam wild spinach, it mats down, compacts, and becomes rather dense. This is a feature to be aware of to help you design good dishes. Finely chopping the greens and mixing them with other foods before you cook them will allow them to separate better when serving. Wild spinach is a substantial food; learn to use it wisely. Experience will be your best teacher.

Chapter 6

FAMILY: Caryophyllaceae
SPECIES: *Stellaria media*

Chickweed

A delicious, delicate low-growing plant that will please any palate

A patch of densely growing chickweed plants producing lots of tasty, tender, new flowering tips.

CHICKWEED

Estimated Range

Official Species Name:
• *Stellaria media* (L) Vill.

Synonyms (Historical Names):
• *Alsine media* (L) Love

Common Names:
• Chickweed
• Common chickweed
• Nodding chickweed

An herbaceous weed naturalized from Europe, chickweed is widespread and abundant in North America, primarily where humans have invaded and where soil has been disturbed.

Edible Parts:
• Growing tips of leafy
   stems, including
     Leaves
     Buds
     Flowers

Chickweed is one of my favorite foundational greens. It's often unfairly rejected as fibrous and stringy because most of the wild food literature does not describe precisely how to gather the good stuff. When gathered appropriately, it has one of the freshest, most delicate flavors and textures you'll find. It is an excellent salad green that can be gathered in great quantities when found in the right habitats. In terms of both flavor and texture, fresh young chickweed greens will please just about everyone who eats them. And if you know how to harvest it properly, it will continue to provide new crops for you as it grows back. Knowing the plant and its life story will bring you a delicious treat.

Chickweed is a moisture-loving, cold-tolerant plant that thrives in soft rich soil. It can grow any time of year under the right conditions. Commonly encountered in lawns, landscaped areas, gardens, pastures, and farm fields, it is native to Europe but is found all over the world and enthusiastically followed the pioneers and settlers as they crossed the North American continent. Chickweed prefers neutral to slightly acid soils.

According to our nutrient chart, chickweed is very high in both iron and zinc, higher than any of the domesticated greens. According to one source (Bianco, 1998), chickweed is also very high in potassium (K), second only to wild spinach and higher than domesticated spinach, Swiss chard, and broccoli. It also can be high in oxalates. And while it has been shown to be a strong antioxidant in one study (Pieroni, 2002), the true extent of its phytochemical and antioxidant potential have not been systematically analyzed.

If you are a fan of medicinal plants, you will find chickweed used alone or mixed with marshmallow and other herbs. The most common use, as far as I can gather, is to crush the leaves and stems to use the juice as a soothant for the skin or eyes. There are also internal uses, but I figure food is the best internal use. If you have a rash of any kind and want to try this, juice a bunch of

chickweed, saturate a cloth with the juice, and apply it to the rash. Of course, if you do this around me, I might just start eating the cloth.

Warning: As I will continually remind you, I am not a medicinal plant person and only tell you medicinal uses as interesting side notes. Basically, I understand healthy harvestable chickweed to be a food you can eat with impunity in the context of a well-balanced diet. You do not have to fear that you are medicating yourself unintentionally.

Knowing Chickweed

Chickweed tends to grow in massive spurts when the conditions are right. The most distinctive spurt is in the spring. Chickweed sprouts during the end of winter— when temperatures fluctuate above and below freezing. It is freeze tolerant down to about 20 degrees F, so it can survive downturns in the weather. The new seedlings are so small you don't notice them as you walk by. When the temperature warms into the 40s, chickweed grows like crazy. So, depending on your weather patterns, sometime in early spring, you see all sorts of lushly growing chickweed. It

An early spring planting bed blanketed with chickweed. It's too cold and early in the spring for my neighbor's perennial shrubs to leaf out, but the chickweed is already in flower, spanning the full length of his front yard. Chickweed invades every spring before he tills the bed with fresh manure. This one location can make salads for about 200 people.

A tiny, just-emerging chickweed sprout magnified to about 10 times life-size. This size simulates about how big the mature leaves become on a healthy plant prior to flowering.

grows in dense patches in full flower, just as the daffodils are flowering and the dandelion leaves are starting to come back to life. It surprises me every spring to see, seemingly out of nowhere, big thick patches of chickweed.

Chickweed will continue to grow lushly as long as the weather is cool and there is plenty of moisture. Since each plant only lives about six or seven weeks, dense patches may die off, but the seed dropped by those plants produces new plants. If the area dries out and/or if the temperatures start going into the 90s, chickweed will dry up and no new plants will emerge until weather gets cold and wet again. Cool, shady, well-watered areas can support chickweed growth throughout most of the summer.

The second spurt of growth begins in the fall when temperatures cool and moisture is present. But this spurt is less impressive due to all the competition, not-so-consistent soil moisture, and occasional warm spells. The winter die-off provides the conditions for great growth in the spring.

SPROUTS: These can emerge any time of the year when the soil is moist and the temperature range is roughly somewhere between 36 and 75 degrees F. They will emerge from soft soil or areas where the soil is turned over. Young chickweed sprouts have leaves that are teardrop- to egg-shaped with a pointed tip. The leaves are opposite each other on the stem and small—small, that is, relative to other sprouts.

STEMS: Chickweed stems tend to curve early in life, sending them down along the ground. Once established, they straighten and spread outward. If other plants are around, they will climb them, reaching upward. Mature stems are round and sturdy for their size. Stems in reasonable growing conditions typically reach eighteen inches in length and branch regularly. In large beds of chickweed, all the plants are growing upright because they are all supporting each other. Stems are hollow and very stringy. If you pull a stem apart, you will reveal a strong hollow core, sort of like finding a straw within a straw. That straw-like core is more evident near the base of mature plants.

One of the single most important identifying features of chickweed is the Mohawk-style hairs running along the length of each stem segment. Yes, very peculiar, a single line of hairs. I'm defining a segment as that length of a stem that is found between each set of leaves. As you go from one segment to the next, the line of hairs changes position. I personally know of no other plants that have this characteristic on the stem. Other plants will have a Mohawk, but it's typically found growing along the main vein of a leaf, not on the stem like chickweed.

LEAVES: Leaves are found growing opposite each other along the stem. They arise at what can be thought of as nodes. Nodes are at the end of each segment along the stem. Not only do leaves arise from the nodes, but this is also where the stem branches.

Leaf blades range in shape from elliptical- to oblong- to egg-shaped and all variations in between. Leaves of all those shapes have a pointed tip that is a lighter color or somewhat tan relative to the green leaf blade. The leaf stem

Mouse-Ear Chickweed

Cerastium fontanum (Cerastium vulgatum)

Edible look-alike

Mouse-ear leaves and stem are sturdy and hairy, with flowers growing in dense clusters. Common chickweed stems are sturdy but only have a single line of hairs. Its leaves are delicate, and there are only a few flowers per cluster.

(above) Young mouse-ear chickweed prior to flower formation. The growth and size of mouse-ear chickweed are similar to common chickweed. Though a common plant, it never seems to reach chickweed's abundant growth. The new, young growing tips of mouse-ear chickweed are edible, but the hairs (a texture problem) and sparser growth (a collection problem) make common chickweed much more desirable. Unlike common chickweed, stem hairs on mouse-ear go all the way around the stem and over the leaves—it is completely hairy.

Comparison of chickweed and two look-a-likes. The stem and upper side of the leaves of mouse-ear chickweed (left), chickweed (center), and scarlet pimpernel (right) are shown here. All three have opposite leaves. Note the differences in the arrangement of hairs on each stem. Mouse-ear chickweed has hairs all over. Common chickweed has the single line of hairs along the stem.

Scarlet Pimpernel

Anagallis arvensis

Poisonous look-alike

Scarlet pimpernel grows just like chickweed. It is considered a poisonous plant so try not to mix it in with your common chickweed salad. The square stem, lack of prominent hairs, and reddish flowers distinguish this plant from the chickweeds. Unfortunately, this plant is often found growing intertwined with common chickweed.

Scarlet pimpernel in flower. Many people mistake this plant for chickweed until the reddish flowers appear.

The stem and leaf undersides of chickweed and two look-a-likes. The underside of scarlet pimpernel's leaf (right) has dark spots, clearly distinguishing it from chickweed (center) and mouse-ear chickweed (left). Scarlet pimpernel is the only one with a square stem and no obvious hairs.

A chickweed flower magnified about 16 times life-size. The actual, fully open flowers are about 1/8 inch in diameter. The flower has 5 green sepals and 5 white petals. The petals are so deeply cleft that there appear to be 10 of them.

wraps around (clasps) halfway around the node. It has soft hairs along its edges and back. The hairs are easily seen if you hold the plant up to the light. The leaf stem hairs can continue slightly up the back of the blade.

FLOWERS: Chickweed flowers typically emerge between four and five weeks of germination. They are both distinctive and tiny. Each flower has five bright white petals in the shape of bunny ears. The five petals are so deeply cleft that, at first glance, one would think there are ten. The flower stem and the outside of the sepals are hairy. All the flower parts are tiny. If you cannot see the hairs clearly, hold the plant up to the light.

Gathering and Edibility

Chickweed has four edible parts: the tender leafy stem tips, individual leaves, buds, and flowers. Because this plant and its parts are so small, you really just gather them all together. Plucking individual buds and flowers would require a pair of tweezers, time, and patience. So just stick to tender leafy stem tips with whatever flower parts they happen to have on them.

LEAFY STEM TIPS: Tender young leafy stem tips (the top 1 to 2 inches) are edible and choice, raw or cooked. They have a fresh flavor reminiscent of typical mild greens with a hint of sweet corn. There are no bitter, peppery, tart, pungent or off flavors. Raw, they can be eaten out of hand, enjoyed as a salad unto themselves, mixed with other greens, added to sandwiches, and used to neutralize more powerful greens. Chickweed has no unpleasant aftertaste. Leafy stem tips that have buds and flowers on them are still great to eat as long as the leaves are lush, big, and clustered near the tip. When leaves get tiny and spread out and the flowers have gone to seed, the tips are still edible, just more straw-like in flavor and texture.

Use the tender young leafy stem tips like you would lettuce. Due to the small size of the leafy stem tips, it works nicely anywhere you would use alfalfa sprouts or lettuce. Many of us back-to-the-earth types used to sprout alfalfa seeds in big jars back in the 1970s. It seems like few people do it anymore. According to my sensibilities, chickweed is far superior in flavor and texture to alfalfa sprouts.

Comparison of luxuriant and stressed chickweed plants. Young chickweed growing rapidly in prime conditions yields large delectable leaves (left). Chickweed growing in stressed conditions (summer sun, and/or heat, and/or competition, and/or drying soil) produce tiny leaves, stringy stems, and lots of seeds (right).

A lone chickweed plant spreading/branching outward along the ground. A stand-alone plant takes more time to gather from because its stem tips are more spread out. Compare this photo to the one on page 85, where many plants growing lushly lean on each other to produce tightly packed upright plants.

NOT ALL CHICKWEED IS THE SAME! As I mentioned, many people give up on chickweed because they claim it is too stingy and fibrous—sort of like eating straw. Tastes like straw too. I cannot argue with their assessment. The reason they did not enjoy chickweed is they either picked down past the upper two inches, picked old chickweed, or picked very slow-growing chickweed. After this chapter, you will know how to avoid the unpleasant parts.

While rapid luxuriant growth provides the best eating, slow growth results in reduced quality. Slow growth happens in conjunction with the emergence of reproductive structures—first buds, then flowers, and then seeds. The problem with reproduction is that, once begun, it redirects resources (what limited water and nutrients are available) to seed production and away from leaf and stem growth. This results in leaves getting smaller, stems getting thinner, overall growth slowing down, and stems stiffening to support seed production. Chickweed leaves are small as it is; with seed production, they get absolutely tiny.

If you could, you'd want to keep chickweed in its adolescent stage. Once it hits puberty, quality goes downhill. Sound familiar? If you can find chickweed in the shade and in very moist soil, you can harvest it all summer long. I have some spots in my yard where chickweed is growing in the permanent shade of a wooden fence. That area has all sorts of wild edibles like miner's lettuce, pokeweed, and some blue violets. I water the area regularly to greatly extend the harvestable season.

Harvesting and Serving Chickweed

Even if you have rapidly growing, pre-flowering chickweed, what you harvest from it will determine if it is delectable or straw-like.

Chickweed is a long and regularly branching plant. When novice harvesters find it, they often snap off the upper half of the plant and chop it all into a salad. The result is a food that only a cud-chewing species would love, resulting in a straw-like flavor and texture. Do this and you will need plenty of dental floss. People who know better stick to the tender new growing tips for maximum enjoyment.

Just collect the top one to two inches of each stem—no more than that! The actual take should be determined by you with some testing on the spot. If the texture is tending towards stringy while chewing, only take the top inch. If the full two inches are tending towards tender, take the full two inches.

From a practical standpoint, you don't want to spend

Clipping chickweed tops. Here is a cluster of tips from a densely growing colony of chickweed. Once cut, this handful provides about 1/3 of the greens in a salad. The round leaf mixed in is miner's lettuce (*Claytonia perfoliata*), another edible plant.

the better part of your life plucking individual stem tips. Okay, on a lazy day you might enjoy the Zen of gathering or snacking on lots of separate individual tips for the simple joy that it brings. If, however, you want to gather a substantial quantity to feed a group or to store some in the fridge for later use, you need to find a densely growing colony of many plants packed together and growing upright.

Most of the densely growing colonies I've found are located in unmowed tree-covered city parks, planting beds around my home and neighborhood, and farmland. I scope out these places in the spring (February, March, or April, depending on where you are in North America) so that I have plentiful sources of chickweed. Of course, always ask permission before harvesting from someone else's land. Also, be careful to ask about the treatment of the land. Has it been sprayed with pesticides? Don't snack directly on the plants if it is a high-traffic pet area. You can gather from such an area, but the greens should be cleaned well before you eat them.

Once you've come upon a densely growing colony, find the most evenly growing areas; that is, areas where all the tips are around the same height. With one hand, gather the tips together and snip them from the plant with your scissors. This will give you a small handful of tips. Two to four of these snippings will provide you with a chickweed salad—depending on your skill and hand size. Transfer them to your plastic bag and liberally spray-mist your bounty with water to keep it fresh.

If you want to keep coming back to this site frequently, make sure you remove only the tips. There is a tendency for some enthusiasts to cut farther down the stem. This gives the illusion that you are gathering more food. While the joy of filling the bag faster may initially be satisfying, it has two drawbacks. First, it takes much more work to sort through all the jumbled mix of stems to separate out the

Chickweed salad with julienned carrots and field mustard (*Brassica rapa*) flower clusters. Chickweed laid out on the plate demonstrates the typical size of choice tender leafy stem tips.

Pita bread sandwich with chickweed. This sesame pita includes chickweed, field mustard flower clusters, shredded Swiss cheese, avocado, sweet red peppers, tomato, and purple cabbage.

desired tips later than it does to clip them properly from the beginning. Second, if you clip too far down the plant, it hinders the remaining stem's ability to grow and provide a whole new crop for harvesting later.

Your take should go through two more steps prior to eating: a quick inspection and a good cleaning. For the inspection, lay out the tips and look for unintended tag-alongs and oversized pieces. In the photograph on page 96, there were two tagalongs: grass and miner's lettuce (*Clatonia perfoliata*). This is not unexpected when using the scissors-harvesting technique in densely growing wild areas. The grass was removed and the miner's lettuce was left as another edible with a flavor I wanted to keep. You will also find that some of the chickweed stems will be longer then the desired one to two inches. The excess stem material should be removed.

Soaking them in water for about two minutes will help

to wash and crisp them. Soaking is unnecessary if they are already so fresh and alive that they could sing to you. Drain or spin *gently* to remove the excess water for serving. If you are going to store some in the fridge for later use, just allow them to drain briefly. The trauma of spinning will reduce their shelf life but is fine if you're serving them on the spot, cooking, or otherwise processing them. Store them in loose clear plastic bags. Like any vegetable, the sooner you use them, the fresher they will taste.

As I've said, use chickweed like you would lettuce or alfalfa sprouts. They are mild enough and their texture is delicate enough to make chickweed-only salads. These greens, fresh or cooked, are only limited by your imagination. Recipes in your head or in any cookbook will provide you with years of wonderful salads and other dishes.

As a mild green, chickweed is one of the best foundational greens—one of the greens you can use as a base

Mexican-style tortillas using cooked chickweed. These flour tortillas include chickweed, refried beans, avocado, and salsa. They are garnished with wood sorrel and cilantro.

upon which other greens of diverse character can be added to make a flavorful complex salad. They also work when steamed, boiled, sautéed, or cooked in most other ways. They only need minimal cooking, just enough until they wilt—one or two minutes of boiling, two minutes of steaming. Sautéing without other vegetables is a little tricky and improves with experience.

Chickweed is a delicate plant. Cooking of any kind will greatly reduce its size. One cup of cooked greens requires about seven cups of fresh greens. Since I love these greens fresh and because they reduce so much upon cooking, it seems a pity to cook them. But, if you have plenty and you love their cooked flavor as much as I do, you use them cooked as well. Be aware that cooking does not tenderize the straw-like lower stems.

When gathered properly, chickweed is one of the best-tasting greens you'll ever eat. It is one of my favorites.

Chapter 7

FAMILY: Malvaceae
SPECIES: *Malva neglecta*

Mallow

One of the most diverse and useful plants

A young mallow plant, about 10 inches tall, showing all of its parts: leaves, stems, buds, flowers, and fruits.

Estimated Range

Official Species Name:
- *Malva neglecta* Wallr.

Synonyms (Historical Names):
- *Malva rotundifolia* auct. non L.
- *Malva pusilla* Sm.
- *Malva pusilla* auct. non Sm.

Common Names:
- Mallow
- Common mallow
- Cheeseweed
- Cheese plant
- Buttonweed
- Dwarf mallow
- Roundleaf mallow

Not every time you see *Malva rotundifolia* in field guides will it really be the same plant as *Malva neglecta*. There are two *Malva rotundifolias*. The one listed above with "auct. Non L." after it is *Malva neglecta*. The other

continued

MALLOW

Mallows were fascinating to me the very first time I discovered the little fruits, just hanging there for me to pluck and eat—an easy, great-tasting, and convenient fast food.

Common mallow (*Malva neglecta*) is not your ordinary wild food. It's specialness, however, is often overshadowed by its famous European cousin, the marsh mallow (*Althaea officinalis*). The common mallow is much more abundant in North America than the often domesticated marsh mallow.

Mallow is one of my favorite plants, and it may well be one of yours in short time. Not only does it provide food, it's also lots of fun to experiment with. The kinds of foods it can become are diverse and numerous. Aside from being a regular vegetable green, most parts of the plant contain a thickening agent. With the proper knowledge, one can make excellent greens, soups, stews, gumbos, meringues, and mallowmallows from this plant and its close relatives.

Many members of the mallow family are native to Europe, Eurasia, and North Africa. The most weedy species, the one we are interested in here, has spread across North America. That plant, known as common mallow, is the focus of this chapter.

Malva parviflora (small-flowered mallow) and *Malva rotundifolia* L. (low mallow) are widespread and similar in appearance to, but not as common as, common mallow. And, while their properties and edibility appear to be similar to common mallow, I have not found them in enough abundance to experiment with. These two mallows can be easily distinguished from common mallow. Common mallow has flower petals that are more than twice as long as the surrounding calyx. In contrast, small-flowered and round-leafed mallows have flower petals only slightly longer than their calyx.

The term *malva* originates from Greek, meaning soothing, softening, and generally pleasant to the skin. These characteristics describe the emollient properties of mallow. Common names include mallow, common mallow, and cheeseweed.

"Cheesewood" was inspired by the shape of the fruits, which resemble miniature cheese rounds. Mallow does not have a cheesy flavor or color. From here on, I will refer to common mallow (*Malva neglecta*) as just "mallow."

Mallow is a hardy plant that is a little more habitat-tolerant than many of our wild vegetables. It is abundant in most inhabited areas of North America as well as on farmland. Once you learn to identify it, you will begin to see it all over yards, neighborhoods, disturbed areas, in the cracks of sidewalks, and at home-building sites.

One of the things that makes mallow so hardy is that it grows not only in freshly disturbed ground but also in harder soil that has been softened temporarily by spring moisture. So it is more adventurous than many of the other plants in this book.

Mallow may be an annual, but I have seen the roots overwinter to continue into a second season in the mild Pacific Northwest climate.

I cannot find any reportable information on the nutrient composition of mallow, its phytochemical and antioxidant characteristics. This is surprising considering the worldwide use of this plant. I have no doubt that mallow is wholesome. The fact that it has mucilaginous properties probably bodes well for its potential as a low-glycemic food. But this all has to be studied before we can say anything for sure. Most research in this genus has been done on *Malva sylvestris* (high mallow).

Several sources warn that there is a laxative effect from eating mallows. The mucilage is made of mucopolysaccharides—probably serving as fiber. There have been no documented cases that I can find of mallow causing any health problems for humans. I eat plenty of mallow and have experienced no unusual laxative effects. There is no known risk to the general public. These mucopolysaccharides and other complex carbohydrates are good for digestion and

one, *Malva rotundifolia* "L.", known as low mallow, is the real *Malva rotundifolia*—a brother of *Malva neglecta*. Sometimes the two plants will not be distinguished by their endings—so you will not know which is being referred to. But they will have the same food uses.

An herbaceous weed naturalized from Europe, mallow is widespread and abundant in North America, primarily where humans have inhabited the area and where soil has been disturbed.

Edible Parts:
- Young leaves
- Flowers
- Green fruits
- Brown seeds

CALYX
A term used to describe all the sepals of a flower considered together. The calyx of the mallow is made up of five united sepals.

SEPALS
Typically the green leafy structures that are below and surround the petals.

BRACTS
Typically green leafy structures that are below and sometimes surround the sepals. On the mallow, they are thin and pointed.

A mallow seedling. At this early stage, there are two heart-shaped embryonic leaves (cotyledons) and one tiny adult-shaped leaf. It is about ½ inch from left to right tip.

Top view of a mallow plant growing upright. Flowers are blooming lower on the stem.

elimination. The mucilage is a skin and digestive soothant. Mallows, in general, have been used for many purposes related to treating inflammation and irritation.

Knowing Mallow

Mallow can take various forms depending on its habitat and life history. It can crawl along the ground or grow upright. In poor growing conditions, the leaves can be as small as half an inch in diameter. In good conditions, the leaves can be larger than two inches in diameter.

SPROUTS: Assuming the seeds are already in the soil, and they often are, the young sprouts come up any time you turn over the soil from May through September. Knowing them at this early stage is helpful for garden management. Pull things you don't know or want, and keep just enough mallow sprouts to satisfy your needs.

The sprouts are distinctive. The first two leaves (coty-ledons) that arise from the seed are heart-shaped. The third leaf to appear is the first that is mallow-like—rounded with a toothed margin. As the plant grows, a stem develops. That stem can branch, grow upright, or trail along the ground. The stems are round and sturdy but typically do not get much larger than ¼ inch in diameter.

LEAVES: The overall shape of the leaves is roundish. Close inspection shows them to be lobed, somewhat wavy, and covered with tiny hairs. Some plants have leaves that tend more toward being egg-shaped and pointed rather than round, but the appearance is still mallowish. Mallow has long leaf stems (petioles) relative to the size of the leaves.

FLOWERS: The pinkish-to-white flowers look like miniature versions of its hollyhock and marsh mallow cousins. Most of the white versions have reddish-to-pink veins running through their petals. The petals are notched on their

Common mallow plant with reclining stems. This is shown at about ¼ its actual size.

Mallow flower in full bloom. The flower is shown at about twice its actual size.

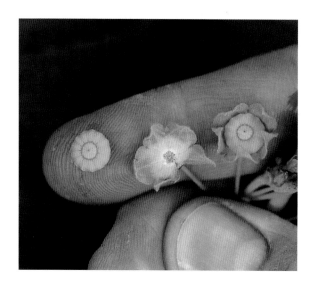

Mallow pea and its surrounding calyx: mallow pea (left), calyx (center), and pea still in its calyx. A calyx refers to the sepals considered as a group. This group of sepals is united into a single structure that encases the fruit.

FRUIT

Botanically, a fruit is a seed-bearing structure of a plant; peas, zucchini, eggplant, and tomatoes are all "fruit."

MALLOW PEAS

The fruits of mallow; previously named cheeses, fairy cheeses, biscuits, amours, and buttons.

ends. The pistil and stamens in the center of the flower cluster together to simulate a water fountain look.

FRUITS: I call them mallow peas. The fruits are small and green flattened vegetables, about ¼ to ⅜ inch in diameter. Hmmm . . . fruits are vegetables? Well, botanically, mallow peas are fruits. We live in a culture that considers fruits that are not sweet to be vegetables. Peas are a reasonable analogy to use here for mallow fruits if you can ignore the fact that mallows have nothing to do with the pea family.

As I've said, the shape of these fruits resembles a tiny cheese round. They also look like tiny tractor tires—a less-appetizing image. These peas are covered with tiny hairs only apparent through a magnifying lens. The sepals are fused into a united calyx, and they surround and curve up over the fruit. Under the sepals are three inconspicuous narrow green bracts.

The edible parts of mallow include the leaves, flowers, and fruits. Mallow produces the most fruit from June through September. Let's look at these items one by one and then discuss the remaining parts of the plant.

MALLOW GREENS: Tender young mallow leaves are edible raw and cooked. They have a mild typical green-leafy flavor. Raw, they are best mixed with other greens and added to salads and sandwiches. Because of their mild flavor, they can be used anywhere that lettuce is appropriate. They are not bitter, pungent, sour, sweet, or strange-flavored. They have no aftertaste.

There are two strategies for gathering the leaves.

Gather directly into a salad bowl with other wild greens for a single serving, rinse, apply salad dressing, and eat. Or you can gather in quantity for a family meal or potluck, which takes a little more care because of the tendency for the leaves to wilt.

For immediate use, grab the leaf blade and pluck it, retaining only about a ½ inch of the long leaf stem, most of which is fibrous and not worth eating raw. Snipping with a pair of scissors is preferable to plucking. Just hold your salad bowl under the leaf, and the leaf falls into your salad.

If you are constructing a salad for later, you will need to "crisp" the leaves (hydrate them) or they will wilt. Drop the leaves directly into a container of clean cold water. After about 15 minutes, drain the water, place the leaves in a plastic bag, and refrigerate. Use as soon as possible for best quality. They will last in the fridge for several days.

There are two practical considerations that will affect mallow leaf use for modern society. First, the leaves are small, delicate, and relatively flat. This means that they will not take up much air space in a salad. Most conventional salads have lots of air because of the irregular shape of their ingredients. Leaving the ½ inch of leaf stem produces a three-dimensional quality, making a lighter, more airy salad—more like people are used to.

How much leaf stem to keep. Here is the underside of a mallow leaf connected to ½ inch of the leaf stem. The physical shape of this leaf plus short-leaf-stem combination is what can be used to help keep salads more airy and three-dimensional. For sandwiches and other uses, this short stem can be left on or off. Never include more than ½ inch of leaf stem, as it is too tough to chew.

Turkey Sandwich with Cooked Greens. Made with provolone cheese, roasted red peppers, and mallow leaves. Mallow greens in the glass bowl are garnished with a marsh mallow flower (*Althaea officinalis*). The mucilaginous texture of the cooked greens takes a little getting used to.

Second, mallow leaves, while tasty, are covered with tiny hairs that you might not notice without close inspection. This affects texture, or "mouth feel," when savoring the raw unadorned leaves. This texture might be annoying to a person with delicate sensibilities. But, fear not, in a mixed salad or in a sandwich, the hairs go unnoticed. Great wild salads can be made of ¼ to ½ mallow leaves.

LEAFY STEMS: On younger, early season plants, the upper one to two inches of leafy stem (the growing tips) are also edible and can be used like the leaves. Tenderness is the limiting factor. If you find yourself eating a stringy or fibrous stem, you are either too far down the stem or eating from a plant that is growing too slow from age or lack of water.

Upon boiling, the character of these greens changes. The flavor is fantastic—a smooth-tasting, mellow cooked green emerges. The other change has to do with mucilage that is released from all parts of this plant. This mucilage serves as a thickener for soups, stews, gumbos, vegetable dishes, and meat dishes. In fact, anywhere that okra is suitable, cooked mallow greens can be substituted.

If you grew up eating unadorned cooked okra, you might love boiled mallow greens just as they are. Look up okra recipes in any cookbook and experiment by replacing it with mallow. This is gobs of mucilaginous fun.

If you are not an experienced okra eater but consider yourself adventurous, try eating just the boiled greens with a pinch of salt. You, like many others, may have a difficult time enjoying the thick and slimy texture. Some love it. The flavor is wonderful.

If you taste the cooked greens first and reject them because of the mucilage, do not make the mistake of stopping there. If you do not try them in recipes as an okra substitute, you will be missing out. When used as a thickener, virtually everyone enjoys them.

MUCILAGE

A viscous or gelatinous material exuding from plants, typically a polysaccharide (a complex sugar).

OKRA

A plant (*Abelmoschus esculentus*) in the mallow family whose immature seedpods are used to thicken soups, stews, and gumbos.

FLOWERS: Mallow flowers are edible and beautiful but small with little flavor. Add them to salads or sprinkle them on a dish as a garnish or on cakes for decoration. Make sure you pluck them fresh, just before eating, otherwise they will shrivel before you can enjoy their beauty. Putting them directly in cold water will help keep the flowers open until use.

If you want the flowers for later, you can cut the whole flowering stem and put it in cold water—like you would a long-stem rose. Keep them out of heat and direct sunlight, and store in a cool location. Spray-mist them regularly. Indirect sunlight during the day opens them; they close at night. Cut mallow stems are fickle and sometimes wilt, no matter what you do.

Like other mallows, the flowers can be used to make a flavorful tea. Steep 3 teaspoons of dried leaves or flowers in a 4-ounce cup. This tea is also used medicinally as a soothant for the throat and digestive tract.

Mallow peas in their clusters of 3 or 4 along a typical stem. This photo is about 1/3 of the plant's actual size.

FRUITS: Mallow peas are great eating, fresh from the plant. Kids love them because they are cute, bite-sized, easily plucked, abundant, nicely flavored, and easy to throw at unsuspecting adults. You can just sit with friends and snack on the fruits of a single, large, well-endowed plant for about twenty minutes before you run out.

Mallow peas are ripe for picking typically from July through September. They are used as a vegetable as long as they are green, no matter their size. They turn brown with age or orange with a spotted plant rust caused by the fungus *Puccinia malvacearum*.

Collecting the fruits is easy. You can pluck them in their clusters by hand, three or four at a time. You can clear (squeegee) the stems rapidly, then select what you want on an open table. Plucking is best done from fresh plants. About half an hour of these techniques yield about one cup of mallow peas. For efficiency, focus on plucking just the larger fruits.

To squeegee the stem, grab it with one hand, then slide the other hand along its length, taking everything but the stem itself. Leaves, flowers, and fruits will collect in your hand as you strip the stem. Spread out what you've gathered on trays and pick out the fruits one by one. The most beautiful fruits make a wonderful edible garnish for any kind of dish you are presenting. They can be spread on top of salads, soups, cooked greens, meats, pasta dishes—you name it.

Cooked mallow peas produce the same mucilage we talked about earlier. So the fruits will work to thicken soups, stews, and sauces, and will make a great substitute for okra in any kind of meat or seafood gumbo. The fruits can also be used to make meringue and what I call mallow-mallows (a version of marshmallows).

Experiment! Everything they are added to will thicken, offering a richer texture. Try mixing them with other vegetables like peas, corn, beans, and the like. Find a creamed corn recipe and use mallow peas in place of the more typical cream or starch thickeners traditionally used. Add them to gravies and meat sauces. There are many wild food adventures to enjoy here.

SPROUTS: Fresh green mallow peas eventually mature into dry brown mallow seeds. Seeds can grow into sprouts in nature or in your kitchen. Some people grow foods like alfalfa sprouts by moistening seeds in glass jars. It is likely that mallow seeds could be used for the same purpose.

ROOTS: Mallow produces one or more ivory-colored taproots. A taproot is one with a carrot-like shape. Mallow taproots are typically thinner and much more fibrous than any carrot you'll ever buy. I have never found mallow roots useful for eating or processing. By the time they are of usable size, they are tough and fibrous, and do not yield any of the mucilage that could make them useful as a thickener.

Marsh mallow (*Althaea officinalis*), a better-known relative of common mallow, is appreciated for its roots. The mucilaginous roots are used as a vegetable and as a thickener. Marsh mallow roots were the original ingredient for the marshmallow confection. Modern marshmallows are no longer commercially made with marsh mallow root.

Mumbo Gumbo

Authentic gumbo is made with okra. Since mallow is related to and has a mucilage like okra, I could not resist seeing how mallow worked in place of it. Since these mallow creations are not true gumbos, I am calling them "mumbo gumbos." Mallows are good in their own right, so we should honor their contribution by giving foods containing mallow their own name. This way we can make "authentic" mumbo gumbo.

Modern recipe books rarely use okra anymore, and it would be hard for you to improvise mallow (mumbo) gumbo without some guidance. So I have done some basic experimenting myself and am passing my successes on to you.

As we have discussed, the leaves, stems, and fruits of mallow, like okra, have thickening properties. This mucilaginous nature goes beyond thickeners like wheat flour or cornstarch. Mallow mucilage adds a richness that is difficult to describe.

Mumbo gumbo can be made from mallow leaves and/or fruits, but in the recipes that follow, I'm just going to be using the fruits.

To invent the following recipes, I modified two recipes I found in the book *Practical Cookery*, published by Kansas State University. I adapted one recipe for gumbo sauce and one for gumbo soup. I changed the original recipes by using olive oil in place of hard fat, mallow fruits in place of okra, and crabmeat in place of crab boil spices. All other changes were minor. The results were superb!

GUMBO & OKRA

The Cajun word for "gumbo" is *okra*. Gumbo is a Cajun soup or sauce typically featuring chicken or seafood, thickened with okra, and flavorfully spiced. Thickener alternatives to okra have been wheat flour, rice flour, and filé (powdered sassafras leaves, pronounced "fee-LAY"). Filé powder is often added to gumbo just before eating for additional flavor.

MALLOW GUMBO

As far as I can tell, the possibility of using mallows for gumbo was first suggested by Ben Charles Harris in his 1961 book *Eat the Weeds*. He proclaimed, "The early leaves are to be included in gumbo soups and stews."

Shrimp Mumbo Gumbo Sauce. Served on a bed of wild rice and leaf lettuce, garnished with a wild sweet pea flower (*Lathyrus latifolius*), and sprinkled with fresh green mallow peas.

Shrimp Mumbo Gumbo Sauce

During this and the following recipe, the mallow fruits turned golden to dark brown and gave off their great thickening property. The flavor and texture were superb—reminiscent of the best gumbo I've had. Due to the dilution factor when the sauce was served over rice, additional salt and pepper were necessary to bring out the flavor. For both recipes, true Cajuns might want to add more spice—ground mustard seed, hot peppers, ground ginger—and some filé powder just before serving. *Makes 3–4 servings.*

INGREDIENTS:

1 tablespoon olive oil
1 tablespoon flour
½ celery rib, chopped
½ green pepper, chopped
½ medium onion, chopped
1 clove garlic, minced
3 cups water
1 small tomato, chopped
½ cup tomato sauce
½ cup mallow peas (or chopped hard-packed greens)
½ cup baby shrimp
½ cup crabmeat
Salt and pepper to taste
Filé powder to taste (optional)

DIRECTIONS:

Heat olive oil, add flour, and brown until dark. Add celery, green pepper, onion, and garlic. Sauté until tender and onion is translucent. Add water, tomato, tomato sauce, and mallow peas. Bring to a boil for 10 minutes. Add shrimp and crab. Simmer for 1 hour covered. Serve over steamed wild rice. Salt and pepper to taste.

Chicken Mumbo Gumbo Soup

Served with some fresh baked bread, this soup would please even the most persnickety Louisianan. Try it yourself! Add a crab boil during the boiling process for more flavor. *Makes 3 hearty or 4 small servings.*

Chicken Mumbo Gumbo Soup. Sprinkled with a few fresh mallow peas and accompanied by mallow pea corn bread.

INGREDIENTS:

$\frac{1}{2}$ cup mallow peas

2 cups water

2 cups chicken stock (salted stock or bouillon)

$\frac{1}{2}$ medium onion, chopped

$\frac{1}{2}$ celery rib, chopped

$\frac{1}{2}$ green pepper, chopped

2 tablespoons extra virgin olive oil

$\frac{1}{2}$ cup shredded cooked chicken

$\frac{1}{2}$ cup chopped tomato

Salt and pepper to taste

DIRECTIONS:

Boil mallow peas in water and chicken stock for 10 minutes. Separately, sauté the onion, celery, and green pepper in the olive oil until soft and transparent. Add the sautéd vegetables, chicken, and tomato to the pot. Simmer for 15 minutes covered. Salt and pepper to taste.

Mallow Confections

Years ago I read with wide-eyed enthusiasm both Euell Gibbons (*Stalking the Healthful Herbs*, 1966) and Alan Hall (*Wild Food Trailguide*, 1973) discussing the idea of making a meringue out of common mallow fruits. Mallow fruit extracts were used in place of marsh mallow root extracts, from which Gibbons had previously made a meringue. Here is the background information:

Euell Gibbons' book contains a chapter on the marsh mallow plant (*Althaea officinalis*). While cooking the root of marsh mallow for food, Euell discovered that the water he poured off was a mucilaginous liquid resembling uncooked egg whites. Being the experimenter that he was and with the goal of making an egg-free chiffon pie for a vegetarian friend, Euell found that he could whip the marsh mallow water into a meringue-style froth. That froth was folded into a mayapple/Irish moss fruit gel and poured onto a graham cracker crust. Hmmm—a mayapple chiffon pie. Leave it to Euell to do it with flair.

Later in that chapter, he reports boiling and trying to eat the roots of dwarf mallow (*Malva rotundifolia*), one of the common mallows. Unlike the marsh mallow root, he found the dwarf mallow root was not an acceptable alternative to marsh mallow root for a vegetable. It was too fibrous, and it did not produce a liquid viscous enough to be useful for whipping into meringue.

Then he tried boiling the mallow peas and came to the following conclusion: "A cupful of these little fruits, boiled in 2 cupfuls of water until the juice was reduced to 1 cupful, yielded a viscous mallow water that seemed almost identical to that prepared from marsh-mallow roots. It would even whip into a stiff froth, like egg whites, and I found I could use this liquid in any preparation that called for mallow water."

In his book, Alan Hall says the following when referring to common mallow (*Malva neglecta*) after talking a little about the marsh mallow: "A substitute for marshmal-

CONFECTION

A food made primarily with sweet ingredients; often, an elaborately made dish or delicacy; a candy or sweet.

low can be prepared from the roots (not so good) or the fruits (better): cover the root or fruit with water and boil until the level is reduced by half. Cool, then beat the resulting viscous liquid into a froth resembling egg white. When beaten with sugar it is a reasonable field confection or it can be used as a substitute for meringue or whipped cream."

At first, I misread "A substitute for marshmallow" to mean that Alan has actually made marshmallows. What he meant was that the juice extract of the common mallow could be used *in place of* the juice extract of the marsh mallow plant to make a meringue or whipping cream. That misinterpretation led me on a 20-year mission to do something that I mistakenly thought had already been done—make a marshmallow (soft, white, fluffy confection that you would use in s'mores) substitute out of common mallow fruits.

Mallow Whites

Mallow whites are created by a process of boiling mallow peas in water. In this boiling, mucilage leaches from the peas, thickening the water. The strained liquid becomes the "mallow whites."

SELECTING MALLOW PEAS: Mallow peas are surrounded by a set of green sepals and bracts. You can leave them on or take them off. For most people, leaving them on will not make a bit of difference. But, if you are persnickety or if you are a professional chef, then the green parts should probably go. Taking them off takes some extra effort. Roughly follow these suggestions:

Pluck full peas at about 1 cup per hour.
Pluck green-free peas at about ¼ cup per hour.

PREPARING MALLOW WHITES: For every ounce of raw "pressed" mallow fruits, use 3 ounces of water. This is a different formula from what Euell had suggested. By

THE SPELLING OF PLANTS VS. THE CONFECTIONS THEY MAKE:

Plants
  Marsh mallow
  Common mallow
Confections
  Marshmallow
  Mallowmallow
  Mallow meringue
  Mallow whipped cream

MALLOW WHITES

A thick viscous or mucilaginous liquid resembling raw egg whites. Using water, mucilage is extracted from either the roots or fruits of various members of the mallow family to make the mallow whites liquid. Mallow whites are a necessary intermediate step to making mallow whip cream, mallow meringue, and mallowmallow. Euell Gibbons' name for what I call mallow whites was "mallow water."

"pressed," I mean to firmly press the mallow peas into the measuring cup to get an accurate measure. You are not mashing here, only pressing to get the air pockets out caused by the sepals and bracts. Green-free peas require no pressing.

Pour the water into a pot that is tall and relatively narrow in diameter. It should be large enough to accommodate the volume of peas and water, with space above to boil. Cover and bring to a rapid boil on high heat.

Remove the cover and add the mallow peas. Leaving the cover off, boil peas vigorously until the total contents reduce by about half. Watch this carefully or the liquid will evaporate and your pan will burn.

As you watch the water boil, you'll know that it is "thickening" because the speed at which the bubbles emerge will slow down. Test the liquid for proper consistency using the spoon test. Try to extract a spoonful of water. If the water pours off the spoon like water, keep boiling. If the water glops or slips off like it doesn't want to be in the spoon, you're done.

Pour the hot contents of the pot through a standard metal kitchen sieve, catching the mallow whites below. "Mild" pressing of the remaining mallow peas is okay if you need more juice. Do not forcefully squeeze the cooked peas for juice or you will get more of a vegetable flavor and fragments of the peas in the juice.

Allow the juice to cool to room temperature before using it in any of the following recipes. Set aside the "spent" peas for later use as a side dish or add them to other foods just as you would add peas. Now that you have mallow whites, you can whip them into mallow foam.

Mallow Foam

Using common mallow, I had little success getting the mallow water from the fruits to whip up into a relatively stable foam—a necessary step for making many confections. I tried making this foam for years with unsatisfactory results.

This is a common problem in the wild food world. One person succeeds in doing something, but you, for some reason, cannot repeat it.

To make whipped mallow, air has to get incorporated into the mallow whites and stay there. The whites are thick, but in my experience, they just don't hold that air as egg whites do. No matter how thin or thick the juice, little air stays, and the foam flattens back to its liquid form.

I decided to "prime" the foam (get it started) using egg whites. Real egg whites whip up every time. So, using my trusty hand blender, I whipped up one egg white to the soft peak stage. I then blended in some cream of tartar, just as egg white recipes demand, to stabilize the now-aerated whites. Then I slowly began adding mallow whites. Lo and behold, the more I added, the higher the foam got. It kept growing and growing. If mallow whites are thick enough, one ounce has roughly the same foaming power as one ounce of egg whites.

I immediately knew I had something. This foam looked exactly like whipped egg whites. But now it was almost all mallow. Over twenty years of disappointment, and now it was really happening. What a joy, what a thrill!

Having a consistent and "relatively" stable foam opens the door to an unlimited number of uses. Even with the egg white starter, however, the foam from mallow is not as stable as foam made from all egg whites. The solution is to work fast. Once the foam is made, use it *quickly*— substitute for fresh whipped cream, fold into chiffon pie, bake into a meringue, dry into mallowmallow, or create your own dish with it.

Mallow Whipped Cream

To make a nonfat whipped cream, just follow the recipes for either mallow meringue (uses less sugar) or mallow-mallow (uses more sugar along with some maple extract). What makes mallow whipped cream different from the other two products is that you are serving this absolutely fresh, right from the blending bowl. You do not follow up by baking or drying this. This fresh foam is a tasty, nonfat, low-calorie alternative to whipped cream. It is not free of sugar or calories.

Be aware that the mallow white mucilage will begin to separate from the foam within fifteen minutes. For most whipped cream applications, a little seeping is not a big issue. If a little sweet mallow juice seeps below into the strawberries or pumpkin pie, no one will notice. But you cannot leave this out for half an hour or there will be a degradation in the look and consistency of foam.

Mallow whites whipped to the stiff peak stage.

Mallow Meringue

Mallow meringue is similar to an egg-based meringue. Taste and texture are so authentic, most people will think they are eating regular meringue. Use mallow meringue in any food that asks for egg-based meringue as an ingredient or a topping—it browns the same as regular meringue. Use mallow meringue to top any pie whose filling holds its shape.

INGREDIENTS:

    1 egg white (at room temperature)

    ¼ teaspoon cream of tartar

    ½ cup mallow whites (at room temperature)

    ½ cup sugar (baker's or ultra-granulated)

    1 teaspoon vanilla extract (or to taste)

DIRECTIONS:

Preheat the oven to 325 degrees F.

Whip egg white at high speed with a hand beater until it is at the soft peak stage. Continue whipping through all the following stages until ready for use.

Sprinkle in cream of tartar.

Gradually pour in small amounts of the mallow whites. Pouring too fast will hinder mixing.

Once all the mallow is incorporated, gradually add the sugar, not too fast, about a tablespoon every 30 seconds. Baker's sugar is best, but regular sugar will work.

Once all the sugar is incorporated (there is no grainy feel between the fingers when you pinch some of the foam), sprinkle in the vanilla extract and continue whipping until foam is stiff but not dry. Total whipping time is longer than for regular meringue.

For pies with precooked contents, spread meringue immediately onto the hot contents, extending it all the way and attaching it to the edges of the baking dish. Bake in the middle of a 325 degree F oven for 20 minutes, or until the meringue has plenty of golden brown areas.

RECOMMENDATIONS:

If the starter egg white does not foam, it means that your bowl or beater blades are not clean.

Once ready, use the mallow foam quickly or re-whip if the mallow whites begin to separate over time.

The sooner the meringue foam is in the oven after whipping, the better.

Huckleberry Mallow Meringue Pie

Once I was successful in making mallow meringue, my first instinct was to make a pie with wild fruit. It's only fitting. So I took some wild mountain huckleberries, cooked them up, poured them into a pie crust and topped them with a huge layer of mallow meringue. I browned it in the oven and marveled at the results.

This is a fantastic pie that everyone will love if you do not eat it all yourself. You will notice lots of tapioca starch (a powder, not beads) in the recipe. This is to firm up the pie. Soft fruit pies will not support the meringue. Tapioca stiffens the fruit and its juice enough to provide that support. If you only have tapioca beads, you can blend or pulverize them into a powder before using. I prefer tapioca to cornstarch or wheat flour as a thickener.

INGREDIENTS:

1 egg white, beaten

1 premade regular or graham cracker pie crust

1 cup sugar

6 tablespoons tapioca starch

4 teaspoons lemon juice

1/8 teaspoon salt

5 cups wild huckleberries (also works with blueberries)

1 recipe mallow meringue (see page 119)

DIRECTIONS:

Preheat oven to 325 degrees F.

Brush egg white onto the pie crust that will come in contact with the filling. This prevents the filling from soaking in.

Stir sugar, tapioca, lemon juice, and salt into a pot containing the huckleberries. Bring to a rapid boil, stirring constantly, then boil for one minute. Pour immediately into the waiting crust.

Apply the meringue to the hot filling immediately. If you are working alone, the meringue will have settled some while you were preparing the filling. If so, whip it again to bring it back to its stiff peaks before applying to the filling.

Place the pie in the oven for 20 minutes. Examine the meringue for proper browning. Remove and let cool. The temptation to eat this immediately is maddening! But you must wait until it cools if you want a perfect result.

Mallowmallow

Mallowmallow is my playful answer to the commercial marshmallow. The original marshmallow was made from the root of the marsh mallow (*Althaea officinalis*) plant and was gummier than what we enjoy today. But that recipe was retired over 150 years ago when the modern marshmallow, made with cornstarch, corn syrup, and gelatin, came into being. Mallowmallows are made from the fruits of common mallow.

As I experimented over the years, my goal was to design a confection that was, at least, reminiscent of the modern Kraft Jet-Puffed Marshmallow—light, airy, and soft. There were many experiments. Keep in mind that accomplishing in your kitchen what food scientists do in a commercial laboratory requires some imagination and patience.

If you are going to embark on this journey, remember that you are doing this for fun, not because you want to save on the cost of commercial marshmallows! This is something you should do to entertain yourself on a casual summer day. Do it with a friend, a date, your family, or with members of an outdoor group.

Making mallowmallows requires more steps, tools, and techniques than your average wild food. If you do your homework here and become successful at making this, you will be able to wow even your local wild food skeptics.

INGREDIENTS:

1 egg white (at room temperature)
¼ teaspoon cream of tartar
½ cup mallow whites (at room temperature)
¾ cup regular or baker's sugar (ultra-granulated)
1 teaspoon vanilla extract (or to taste)
½ teaspoon maple extract

EQUIPMENT:

Hand beater with blades
Large glass bowl

Rubber spatula

2 gallon-size ziplock bags

Food dryer with deep trays (110 degrees F capable)

One or more of the following:

1. Food to dry mallowmallow on
2. Silicone nonstick baking mats
3. Parchment paper

DIRECTIONS:

Directions here have been divided into six sections to give you an idea of the considerations you should keep in mind when making mallowmallows. Read the whole thing before you begin so you can plan ahead for success:

1. Whipping the mallowmallow
2. Using a mallowmallow dispenser
3. Using a food dryer
4. Drying mallowmallows on selected foods
5. Drying mallowmallows on a surface
6. Powdering the mallowmallows

1. Whipping the mallowmallow

Follow the directions for "Mallow Meringue," only now include the mallowmallow ingredients (includes extra sugar and maple extract). Continue whipping until the foam is stiff and offers a bit of resistance. You'll see the foam building up on the beater blades. It will be tougher to move the beater blades around through the foam once you whip it thick enough.

2. Using a mallowmallow dispenser

Use a rubber spatula to scoop up the foam. Pack it into a standard gallon-sized ziplock bag. Remind yourself that the mallow whites will separate if the foam is left out too long. Set up ahead of time so you can do things rapid fire—as soon as the foam gets into the dispenser bag.

Once all the foam is in the bag, get as much air out

Dispensing mallowmallow onto a silicone mat within a food dryer tray.

as you can before sealing the zipper. Once sealed, cut a ⅜-inch piece off one of the lower corners of the bag. You now have a dispensing bag for forming the mallowmallows—just squeeze the foam out the hole.

Try squeezing out about half the thickness of a commercial marshmallow on whatever surface you form them on. If you are putting them on some other food for drying, spread them out in a layer covering that food. If you are putting them directly on a drying surface, give each dollop some space so that if you have to bend the surface to pry the mallowmallow free, the adjacent mallows will not be touched. Touching mallowmallows will permanently glue them to each other. With practice, you can make mallowmallows in the shape of large Hershey's Kisses.

3. Using a food dryer

A food dryer is necessary to transform the mallow foam to mallowmallows. Your goal is to get them to an optimal moisture content—not too moist, not too dry.

DO NOT use an oven to do your drying. Heating the mallow foam somewhere above 118 degrees F will begin to cook it, revealing a mild vegetable flavor. If you can set your oven to 110 degrees F and insert a fan to move the air without risking fire, melting plastic, or electrocution, then go ahead and try an oven.

The most popular food dryer I've seen is the round plastic kind with stackable layers. The American Harvester is a common brand that I use. You can buy them new for about $40 or find them cheap at yard sales.

4. Drying mallowmallows on selected foods

A general reality of drying mallowmallows over a several-hour process is that a small portion of the mallow whites re-liquefy and sink to the base of each drying piece. If the whites sink to a solid surface, the mallow sticks to that surface over most of the drying process. So the most practical drying surface is food. For instance, if you are going to make s'mores, then dry them right on chocolate resting on graham cracker squares. That way, by the end of the drying process, you have a finished product ready to eat. Mmmm . . .

If you are drying them on food, remove them from the dryer after 3 hours. This assures a softer, more delicate product. Eat them fresh for maximum enjoyment. Somewhere between three and five hours of drying, the mallowmallows go from soft and delicate to chewier to dry and crunchy.

5. Drying mallowmallows on a surface

If you want to make mallowmallows that stand alone and can be eaten and used like regular marshmallows, you have the following considerations within a 3- to 4-hour drying time: 3 hours provide superior quality, but the mallowmallows are difficult to pry from the drying surface; 4 hours make a chewier to crunchier quality, with easier removal from the drying surface.

I have tried every conventional and unconventional surface upon which to dry the mallowmallows—most failed because I could not pry the dried mallowmallows free without destroying them. The best surface I've found are the silicon-based baking mats. These begin to work only when the drying time is extended to somewhere between 3½ and 4 hours at 110 degrees F. After that time, the mallowmallow becomes dry enough at its base to begin separating from the mat. These mallowmallows are soft, spongy, and chewy.

Remember that the size of the mallowmallow you are making and the surface area that the base of that mallowmallow takes up will affect the drying time of your finished product. Other considerations are the accuracy of your food dryer's thermostat (check it with a thermometer), how many trays you have stacked in it, how close to the center of the tray (where the air is circulating) the mallow is, and how close the tray is to the top or the bottom of the food dryer (bottom is hotter). These are all things that may affect your final result.

Sorry if your head is spinning at this point. This is not graduate-level biochemistry. I am just trying to alert you to some things to think about if you are having trouble getting that "perfect" mallowmallow.

6. Powdering the mallowmallows

Most people who have tried these confections cannot wait to get their hands on them right out of the dryer. And this is when mallowmallows are at their best. You can pick them up and eat them without any problem and with great enjoyment.

If, however, you are planning on storing them like

regular marshmallow to be eaten later, you have a problem. While they are dry enough not to stick to your fingers, they are still tacky enough to stick to each other. This can become a big gloppy mess unless you do not mind eating one big 30-piece mallowmallow.

To prevent them from sticking to each other, you have to "powder" them. That is, as you pluck them from the dryer, drop them into a bag filled with the following: ¼ cup powdered sugar mixed thoroughly in ¾ cup cornstarch. After you drop some mallowmallows in, close the bag and shake it about. Spoon them out onto a strainer, shake the strainer to remove the excess powder, and your mallowmallows are now ready for bagging. They are best when eaten instantly and are still great within 24 hours. They will be too dried out after 3 days in the bag to be recognized as mallowmallows—still edible and flavorful, but with a texture like Styrofoam.

Mallowmallow S'mores. Take graham crackers or vanilla wafers, cover with chocolate bar pieces, spread with fresh mallowmallow fluff, and eat them as is. Or put it all in a food dryer at 110 degrees F for about 3 hours to give them the consistency of marshmallows, and you have ready-made s'mores. Or use fudge grahams and skip the chocolate bars (see largest s'more at the back of the plate above).

Mallowmallows. Make these into whatever shape you want. Tall narrow ones dry more quickly and are easier to remove from drying surfaces. There are four store-bought marshmallows on this plate for color and shape comparisons.

Follow-Up Notes

Most people will not believe you can do this until they are eating s'mores that you made in front of them. Do it-they'll never look at wild foods in the same way again.

It may take you a few tries to get this perfect because you will be adjusting to your own kitchen, its equipment, and your own way of interpreting my directions. Enjoy your kitchen time—you'll get it right, perhaps even the first time.

From a social perspective, this is a wonderful activity to keep children occupied for four or five hours. They have fun, get a little closer to nature, spend some time with you, and have s'mores to look forward to at the end of the day. What a wonderful time it could be.

Chapter 8

FAMILY: Portulacaceae
SPECIES: *Portulaca oleracea*

Purslane

A low-growing tasty summer succulent

Purslane is a small-leaved plant whose reddish stems look like a network of tiny plumbing laid along the ground with offshoots of small leafy stems. Makes a good edible ground cover.

Estimated Range

Official Species Name:
- *Portulaca oleracea* L.

Synonyms (Historical Names):
- *Portulaca neglecta* Mackenzie & Bush
- *Portulaca retusa* Engelm

Common Names:
- Purslane
- Pursley
- Pusley
- Portulaca
- Little hogweed

An herbaceous annual weed naturalized from Southern Europe, it is widespread and abundant in North America, primarily where humans have invaded and where soil has been disturbed. It loves wet summers and is not found in abundance in cold regions and high elevations.

continued

PURSLANE

I've never been a plumber, though I've dabbled in it as any manly kind of guy would. And while you don't have to be a plumber to eat wild plants, it might help you to recognize purslane. On the ground, purslane looks like a Lilliputian attempt to pipe water along at foot level. Tiny pipes, no; but a plant with succulent stems and leaves, yes.

Purslane is not well known as a food in North America, and this is perplexing because it is a very popular food in the Mediterranean and many other parts of the world. I was recently asked by someone how purslane could be edible when he had heard it was poisonous. Purslane is no more poisonous than spinach. This is a normal food that can be eaten with impunity in the context of a normal diverse diet.

Nutritionally, purslane is a powerhouse. It has more than double the omega-3s that kale has and, as far as I know, more than any other leafy green ever analyzed. It has over four times the vitamin E of turnip leaves, more than any other leafy green ever analyzed. It has glutathione and other antioxidants and about as much iron as spinach. It also has reasonable amounts of other nutrients as well as phytochemicals, like all these leafy greens. So purslane is no slouch, not a poison, and definitely worth eating. (Simopoulos, 1992; 1995.)

Many people studying the Mediterranean diet think that it is foods like purslane and other omega-3 greens that give the Greeks their good balance of fats. Olive oil only contributes some of the omega-3s; the greens, walnuts, oily fish, and a few other foods give them the rest of what they need.

Knowing Purslane

Purslane is a hot-weather plant. It will not sprout until the ground temperature is somewhere between 76 and 90 degrees F. A strong hot sun warming the soil along with good moisture are required for it to sprout below 80 degrees.

Edible Parts
- Growing tips of young leafy stems
- Leaves
- Buds and flowers

The sprouts are green with a reddish tint. The first four leaves look like little rounded propellers surrounding a reddish engine tip. At first, these early leaves are elliptical, but they get a little fatter near the tip very quickly. The tips of these leaves are about as rounded as you can get, not pointed at all.

In general, purslane sprouts and grows best in the hottest four months of the year. Once established, it is very drought resistant. If a young plant is growing in dry conditions, growth will slow and the plant may be tiny. This can be seen often in the cracks of sidewalk cement. The plant starts growing, but the moisture dries up. In these conditions, the plant is so small that it goes unrecognized by most people.

If a healthy more-established plant is exposed to very dry conditions, its stems will pull the moisture from the leaves and drop them. The stems, however, survive longer and can grow new leaves when moisture returns. If conditions continue to dry, even the stems will die.

LILLIPUTIAN
Refers to people of the land of Lilliput, who were about 6 inches tall. These people were characters in the 1726 book *Gulliver's Travels* by Jonathan Swift.

Leaves of young purslane before they start producing much in the way of stems. This is dense growth created by lots of sprouts emerging from a small area. This stage of growth is too young to be producing flowers or seeds.

Purslane sprouts, life-size, relative to my index finger. Note that there are a few mallow sprouts mixed in with the purslane.

Rapidly growing purslane, spreading in the open area of a planting bed in my backyard garden. Purslane branches regularly, trailing along the ground.

As long as the days are long, vegetative growth continues. Great growing conditions will hold off flower and seed development for awhile. I've seen individual stems up to eighteen inches long.

Purslane is a succulent, a plant that retains a lot of water in its leaves and stems. Those leaves and stems appear thick and fleshy relative to their size. This ability to store water is what helps this plant thrive in heat and survive drought.

STEMS: As long as there is direct sunlight, purslane will spread out, with thick primary stems that tend to resemble reddish-green piping. The plant crawls along the ground in huge mats. Sun-exposed open space can be completely

Planting beds at an organic farm. The rubber hoses are supplying plenty of water, and the sun is supplying plenty of—well—sun. Of course, the hoses are not there for the purslane, but the purslane benefits. This growth is about as thick as purslane can tolerate.

A tiny purslane flower, magnified. This flower is a little less than ¼ inch in diameter. The leaves are fairly big here for purslane and appear more flat-tipped than usual.

Bird's-nest-style seed capsule of purslane. Other capsules shown here will pop open as they mature.

covered by purslane. Unlike some other plants that crawl along the ground, purslane does not root at its nodes. If, however, you chop up thriving plants, like when turning over the soil, you may get a surprise. If there is enough moisture in the soil, many of the cut segments may begin rooting and grow new plants. This is particularly troublesome for farmers who want to get rid of purslane. They plow, plant new crops, then water new seeds they've planted during the hottest time of the year. Guess who loves those conditions? Purslane and wild-food enthusiasts.

Purslane has limits on its growth. Shade and competition will kill it. Anything that restricts sunlight can kill it—not necessarily the whole plant, but parts can atrophy and die, leaving the rest of the plant to grow where there is sun. Purslane competes with itself as well as other plants. The earlier that purslane emerges from the soil, the longer it can stay in vegetative growth, continuing to develop its potential. Where you are in North America will determine when temperatures get hot enough and days get long enough for purslane to sprout. Southern climates will be earlier; northern climates will be later—it could be April, May, or June. Individual plants can live for two to four months.

FLOWERS: As purslane reaches a certain age or as growth conditions decline, it starts producing flowers. Individual flowers open only on bright hot days and last for only a day. As long as the plant continues to grow new stems, flower and seed production will be progressive. This means that older stems will flower first, with younger ones flowering later.

SEEDS: Of course, seeds are produced when flowers have been fertilized. When ripe, the top part of the seedpod pops off, revealing what looks like a little miniature bird's nest of black eggs. These seeds quietly sit there until some disturbance forces them out of the nest. This could be an animal knocking the plant as it walks by, a raindrop hitting it, or a strong wind blowing through. The seeds do not travel far from the plant unless they hitchhike on some clothing or digging tool, or if the soil is moved.

Since purslane stores moisture, pulled plants do not stop the seed-ripening process, making eradication difficult. Seeds fall to the ground as the plant is pulled, and seeds continue to mature and drop if you pull the plant and leave it. Even worse (or better).

Harvesting Purslane

While it is perfectly possible to eat the tiny plants growing in cement cracks, I typically only gather purslane when it is growing lushly in more desirable places. Vigorously growing purslane is not hard to find. The best parts are the new, rapidly growing tips before plants go to seed. By "best," I mean that they will work fine in your most delicate salads served to your most-finicky wild-food-fearing friends—and at fine restaurants everywhere.

Gather the leafy stems—*not* just the leaves. Plucking the leaves individually would be the best way to procrastinate from doing anything important in your life. The leaves are too small to pluck except for specific purposes. Some larger individual leaves can be used as a garnish. Kids love plucking the leaves. Lovers who are gambling on their relationship do the "she loves me, she loves me not" thing (daisies are good for that too).

And remember, the stems are part of the food! Say this again to yourself: the stems are part of the food—a great part.

If you plan on using purslane as greens, either fresh or cooked, and you have lots of purslane to choose from, just collect the tips. The last inch or two of the leafy stems will be the most delectable. Why not? You can be choosy.

If you can't find much purslane to gather, either let the plants go to seed for next year or collect whatever you can and use whatever you get.

While gathering, if you are thinning an area to allow something else to grow, pull purslane out by the roots. Be careful to keep all the root material together as you carefully stack them for transport. Doing this will help you in the cleaning process later.

Once collected, purslane travels well. Because it's a succulent, it does not wilt quickly; but it is still helpful to

A healthy, rapidly growing, young purslane plant—roots and all—prior to flowering. The closer the leafy stems are to the tips of these branchlets, the more tender they will be. But this plant provides good eating down most of its stem.

Several minutes of purslane weeding/harvesting from my garden. Whole plants were pulled out by the roots so the tomato plants could spread out. (The author, 1995.)

spray-mist your take unless you collect it with root material. Moistening the dirt on root material just makes a big mess. Keep harvested purslane cool until you can trim and wash it in cold water. Its solid structure makes it easy to clean. Use your harvest fast for the best quality.

Serving Purslane

Purslane is a pleasant-tasting food with a hint of lemoniness, but I do not find it sour. It fits right into the foundational greens category because it is so mild. To most newcomers, the texture is not as familiar as a conventional green. Purslane's succulent three-dimensional form and mildly mucilaginous texture offer a pleasantly unique experience. It transforms into a more conventional green once cooked.

Use the tender leafy stem tips in all fresh-food applications. This will satisfy everyone. The tips (the upper one to two inches of leafy stems) are great in a purslane salad—

Purslane Salad. Contains orange sweet pepper slices, borage flowers (*Borago officinalis*), and a large wild carrot flower head (*Daucus carota*) as a garnish.

a wholesome food all by itself. Most people, however, like to have more complex salads, and mixed salads are better for you. Aside from salads, purslane is great where lettuce, alfalfa sprouts, and any other leafy green are used. Make them into pesto. Experiment.

Since the stems are a major part of this plant, and they have their own unique texture, they can have applications all their own. These are succulent, interestingly crunchy stems that are different from leafy material you are used to. So use them in different ways. Try older, stiffer ones for dipping in fondues or to poke into dipping sauces. Give them to kids as snacks. With experience, you'll learn how to exclude parts that are too close to the root area. I love the stems.

The older leafy stems, below the stem tips and quite far down the stem, are good too. They are crunchier than the tips and have small leafy stems sprouting out of them.

Roasted Lamb Chops. Served with a stir-fry that includes purslane, accompanied by yellow and red sweet peppers, topped with almond shavings, and garnished with purslane leafy-stem tips.

Dill Pickle Experiment. Due to purslane's crunchy texture, it is a natural for pickling. This bunch of purslane leafy-stem tips were placed in the leftover juice of store-bought pickles and then put in the fridge for a few days. Due to a short soaking time, these purslane pickles were understandably weak in flavor and quite limp. To make purslane pickles, use the older, thicker stems—they will stay more solid then the tips used here. And look up a real pickling recipe—it will take more time, but the results will be worth it.

I chop bite-size pieces of the stems into my salads.

Cooking of any type relaxes the greens, making them more like the cooked greens that you are used to. They can be boiled, sautéed, stir-fried, steamed, baked—you name it; you are only limited by your imagination. Cook them into lasagnas, spaghetti sauces, bean casseroles, stews, and anywhere vegetables go.

Cooking reduces the coarseness you might find in some of the older stems, making them more agreeable.

The flowers and seeds of purslane are edible but too tiny to have any use of their own. So go ahead and eat them along with the leafy stems you gather.

Purslane is a wonderful wild food. It is nutritious, with great flavor, and can be eaten raw all by itself. For a leafy green, it is extremely high in omega-3 fatty acid, vitamin E, and glutathione, and will make even the persnickety less so. If you can wait till summer, it will be there for you.

Tart Greens

The greens in this chapter have a pleasant and sometimes striking sour or acidic flavor. They are suitable for occasions where you want to add some mouthwatering character to a dish. Tart greens are often added to milder greens (foundational greens) or complex dishes to add interest and nuance. Like foundational greens, they can also cut the power of pungent and bitter greens but are in no way neutral like foundational greens. They are edible raw and cooked, but their best uses depend on what you are preparing. Tart greens have the potential to greatly improve a dish by using just a little or to dramatically change the character of a dish by adding a lot. People will enjoy them as a flavor enhancer for other foods or eaten on their own.

Each of the greens in this section has its own characteristic flavors and textures. Fresh, they are excellent in combination salads, added to sandwiches, used as garnishes, and made into pestos and other green-based sauces. If you are like me, you will enjoy salads with nothing but sour greens. Cooked, their flavors mellow, often giving the impression of foundational greens when a hefty squirt of lemon juice is added. They go well with other vegetables and any kind of meat, especially fish.

The plants covered in this section include curly dock, broad-leaved dock, sheep sorrel, and wood sorrel. Most of these plants happen to be either in the buckwheat (Polygonaceae) or the oxalis family (Oxalidaceae). The only sour vegetable you will typically find in the supermarket is rhubarb (*Rheum* spp.). French sorrel (*Rumex acetosa*), eaten as a green, is sold in nurseries for planting in your garden. It is as close to the plants in this chapter as you will get from a non-wild perspective. Both rhubarb and French sorrel are in the buckwheat family.

Nutritionally, sour greens tend to be high in iron, zinc, vitamin C, and soluble oxalates. Nutrient values, unfortunately, are often listed under the label "docks" rather than

OXALATES AND SOUR FLAVOR

Oxalates, also known as oxalic acids, are well known to be in the plants in this section. Because of that, people assume that it is the oxalates that are the source of the tart flavor they are sensing. Any acid will probably have a sour taste. But the sour of oxalates in the greens we eat may not be strong enough for us to taste. I say this because both spinach and wild spinach have just as much if not more oxalates than the plants in this section, but neither spinach tastes sour. So how can spinach be so high in oxalates and not be sour? Because plants have more than one acid. Other acids found in plants include ascorbic acid, citric acid, malic acid, formic acid, and many others. Every plant covered in this section has enough combined acid that it will taste sour and turn a dull olive-green when boiled. Wild spinach stays bright green when cooked, even though it has gobs of oxalates. So either wild spinach has chemical components that neutralize oxalate's acidity, or there are other acids in the plants in this section to make them sour to the taste.

the specific dock that they are. So, in truth, the values given in the wild greens nutrient chart listed as *Rumex* spp. could be any of four species: *Rumex crispus* (curly dock), *Rumex obtucifolius* (broad-leaved dock), *Rumex acetosella* (sheep sorrel), or *Rumex acetosa* (French sorrel). The assumed species is curly dock, but we just don't know. Much more nutrient analysis needs to be done.

Phytochemical data is preliminary, but *Rumex crispus* and *Rumex obtucifolius* appear to be high in total phenols, have more myricetin than red wine and black tea, and have more quercetin than onions and black tea. Myricetin and quercetin are flavonoids.

Some books will give warnings about plants with oxalates poisoning sheep, cattle, or chickens. These accounts are real but do not apply to humans. First, these animals have different physiology and digestive processes than humans; they are less able to manage oxalate intake. Second, all animals poisoned were restricted to eating the mass of their total diet from days to weeks of very high oxalate plants. Imagine trying to eat about eight pounds of spinach every day for a week as over 50 percent of your diet. Oxalates are relatively harmless in the context of a normally diverse human diet. (See Oxalates and Nitrates, page 373, for more information on oxalates.)

Flavors offered by sour greens are an excellent addition to the gourmet's arsenal of tastes. Some of the sour greens grow all year long; others are more seasonal. Growing conditions and season greatly affect their quality and availability.

Chapter 9

FAMILY: Polygonaceae
SPECIES: *Rumex crispus*

Curly Dock

A deliciously raw tart green if you can find it young.
A delicious cooked green in spring and fall.

Spring curly dock growing multiple stems from a single large taproot.
Some leaves have curled or wavy margins, others do not.

CURLY DOCK

Estimated Range

Official Species Name:
- *Rumex crispus* L.

Synonyms (Historical Names):
- *Rumex elongatus* Guss.

Common Names:
- Curly dock
- Curley dock
- Curled dock
- Yellow dock
- Narrowleaf dock
- Sour dock

An herbaceous perennial naturalized from Southern Europe and Western Asia, curly dock is widespread and abundant in North America, primarily where humans have invaded and where soil has been disturbed.

Edible Parts:
- Leaf blades
- Growing tips of leafy stems
- Seeds

Most of you will find curly dock when it is a mature plant, either as a cluster of leaves growing from a previous year's root or as a stalked plant. At the stalk stage, it is often towering over grasses and other weeds it is growing within. By the time most people taste the leaves, it seems papery, often astringent, and sometimes bitter. If you have had this experience, it is time to take a new look at curly dock. As with many other plants, good flavor and texture are in the details.

Curly dock and broad-leaved dock (also covered in this chapter) are widely eaten in the old world, particularly broad-leaved dock. The reason I focus on curly dock is that I find its leaves more flavorful for more of its growing season than broad-leaved dock. Both have the same food uses.

The name *crispus* is Latin for "curled, curved, or wavy." This describes the sides or margins of the mature leaves of curly dock.

Curly dock leaves are high in beta-carotene, vitamin C, and zinc. Broad-leaved dock (see page 153) is high in zinc but just about average in other nutrients.

Curly dock seeds are rich in calcium and fiber while low in protein and fat. The limiting amino acid is lycine. (Wiese, 1995.)

Curly dock is rich in phenols, with greater amounts in the seeds than in the leaves. Broad-leaved dock leaves are rich in the flavonoids quercetin and myricetin. They have about twice as much myricetin as broad beans or onions, six times that of red wine, and about eighteen times that of black tea. They have more than twice as much quercetin as onions, about thirty times as much as broad beans, and a hundred times that of red wine or black tea. (Trichopoulou, 2000b; Wiese, 1995; Yıldırım, 2001.) Both are probably high in these phenols, flavonoids, and other phytonutrients, but more research needs to be done to verify this.

Every plant in this section contains soluble oxalates, which are relatively harmless in foods. Eat a wide variety of greens and a wide variety of foods, in general, and the benefits of these greens will far outweigh the small temporary loss of some minerals that oxalates may bind.

Curly dock seeds and vegetation are toxic in quantity to poultry (Royer, 1999). Humans are not affected. We have a different physiology and a more diverse diet than chickens.

Knowing Curly Dock

Curly dock grows readily from seed in the warm part of late spring and early summer. I have not found it germinating in cold spring and fall conditions. That doesn't mean it doesn't germinate at those times of year; I just haven't seen it happening. Germination, of course, depends on the amount of moisture, the softness of the soil, the proximity of the seed to the surface, and sunlight. Turned or disturbed soil brings some seeds to the surface and softens the soil. The seedlings start out with long narrow cotyledons (two developmental leaf-like organs) on long stems. The leaves that follow are more rounded than the cotyledons.

As leaves continue to develop from a growing taproot, the cotyledons wilt away. New leaves begin egg-shaped (ovate) and elliptical, without wavy margins. As more develop, you see them gaining more length, and the margins show more and more curviness.

Curly dock seedling. This shows the two cotyledons (top) that emerged from the seed, with the first true leaf growing towards the bottom of the photograph.

First few leaves of curly dock after the cotyledons have wilted away. From leaf tip to leaf tip, this plant is 2 inches wide.

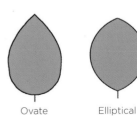

Ovate   Elliptical

Curly dock leaves expanding outward from the taproot. These leaves are just beginning to show more waviness along the margins.

A young, first-year curly dock plant with rounded to elongated leaves coming off the long leaf stems. Basal leaves, particularly of a first-year plant, tend to have less wavy margins than stalked or older leaves. This is the prime stage to gather the leaves of this plant.

There comes a point where the leaves start multiplying and radiating out from the taproot. Like thousands of other plants, including many in this book, a basal rosette is formed. Unfortunately for many people, different species look the same when they are at their basal rosette stage. To help you distinguish, look for a variety of leaf shapes. These shapes tend to look like a wavy serving spoon with a long handle. The spoon part is sort of roundish for some of the leaves. For others, the spoon part starts to elongate. Some leaves are more curly around the edges than others.

This is a second- or third-year plant whose root is large enough to sprout several stems. At the base of these leaves are what looks like several different plants arising from the ground. In fact, all those stems arise from the same root. The leaves are exceptionally curly here.

Curly dock stems. Here we see two of about six stems growing from the same root. Some were cut away to more clearly display the remaining two. This shows young stems prior to flowering. Some tiny flower buds are just forming at the tops. These plants are about one yard tall with the upper 20 inches of the tops showing.

First-year plants (ones growing from seedlings) and early second-year plants tend to have rounder leaf blades in their early basal rosettes than older plants. If conditions are right, lots of leaves will develop. Then, at some point in late spring, something stimulates the plant to bolt (produce a stalk). Once a stalk has developed, the plant starts orienting toward reproduction—the development of flowers and eventually seeds.

Older plants tend to produce long narrow leaves in the spring. Older plants typically skip the rounded leaf blade phase of their youth. You can often spot an older plant by seeing last year's stalk, now dark brown and dried up—usually only a stub sticking one to eight inches up from the root. Another way to identify an older plant is by seeing multiple stems arising from the same taproot. Older plants tend to produce lots of larger leaves much earlier in the spring before they bolt. They can do this because they are living off the stored energy of a large well-developed root.

Because nature is not here for our convenience, curly dock leaf shape varies quite a bit. They range from rounded or spoon-like shapes of the newly formed plant, to small narrow leaves at the top of a stem, to the classic long wavy curly dock leaf. Some are flat and some have curled edges.

The wide leaf variation you will find on curly dock. The five leaves on the upper left are new stem leaves growing at the top of the plant. The remaining leaves all had their long leaf stems trimmed off to neatly fit in the photograph. The three to the right are the more typical stem leaves. The five lower-left leaves are what can be found on first-year or early second-year basal rosettes prior to bolting.

The classic mature curly dock leaf. These leaves are long, narrow, and wavy-margined.

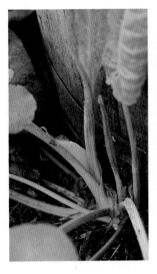

(left) Ocrea on a young, newly forming stalk of broad-leaved dock (*Rumex obtucifolius*). Note the ocrea surrounding the base of the leaf arching to the left, also the ocrea surrounding the base of the newly forming stem that the arching leaf is emerging from. Ocrea can be seen around two other emerging stems as well as several torn, shriveling brown ocrea at the base of the plant.

(right) Curly dock ocrea on a main stem leaf. On the upper stem, the ocrea are smaller and more tight fitting around the stem and leaf base. Note the collar-like enlargement where the leaf meets the stem. This collar is also characteristic of the *Rumex* genus. The ocrea here starts at that collar and travels up the stem. This ocrea's tip has already turned brown.

Leaf stems (petioles) become shorter the higher up they are on the stem. The key is to recognize the plant by its overall characteristics.

One of the characteristics that distinguishes all members of the *Rumex* genus (docks and sheep sorrel of this section) is a thin delicate membranous sheath called an ocrea. It wraps around the nodes of the stem where leaves emerge. Ocrea becomes progressively smaller the higher you find them on the flowering stalk. It is one of the first parts of the plant to dry up and turn brown as the plant ages.

Once curly dock is developing a stem, the plant matures quickly. As the main stem elongates, flower stems arise. This development (as well as when the plant is turning brown) are the stages when most people can easily recognize curly dock.

At first, small whorls of bud clusters develop. Segments of stem can be seen separating each cluster. These buds and the flowers they produce are small and inconspicuous.

As the fruits mature, they turn a dark rust brown. In fact, the whole plant turns brown. Each dry fruit encases one seed. The fruit's three sides are formed by the membranous remnants of the flower's sepals. Each of the sides

Bud clusters of a flowering branch.

A maturing curly dock plant with leaves and fruiting stems.

is topped by a non-seed structure called a tubercle. When I first started processing curly dock seeds, I thought the tubercles were the outer bulge of the seed. In fact, tubercles surround the seed like three pillows surrounding your head. The tubercles add size to the fruit, making the seeds look bigger than they are.

Curly dock fruit differs from broad-leaved dock in that its membranous wings have relatively smooth margins. Broad-leaved dock's margins flare and point outward. Look ahead to page 155 to see how curly dock fruit structure compares to that of broad-leaved dock.

Curly dock has a large fleshy to woody taproot that is yellowish to orange in color.

Whorls of mature curly dock fruits.

Curly dock seeds and tubercles compared. Curly dock seeds (left) are brown, shiny, and three-sided. Tubercles (right) are non-reproductive seed-like structures that surround the seeds. Tubercles remind me of tiny cashews, only with the flavor and texture of a rice cake. I have no idea if they have any nutritional value. To show scale, those are 1mm increments at the bottom of the photograph. Broad-leaved dock seeds and tubercles have a similar appearance.

Curly dock's taproot—possibly from a third-year plant.
Note the multiple stems arising from this one taproot.

FAMILY: Polygonaceae
SPECIES: *Rumex obtusifolius*

Broad-Leaved Dock
Edible brother to curly dock

Estimated Range

Broad-leaved dock parallels the growing habits of curly dock and can be used in many of the same ways. It is more widely used than curly dock around the world. Its seeds and cotyledons (embrionic leaves) look similar, but its true leaves differ almost from the start. The first true leaves of curly dock and broad-leaved dock are similarly egg-shaped. After that, broad-leaved dock's leaves start taking on an arrowhead shape. They remain different from curly dock leaves from that point on.

Once the plant is established and the leaves enlarge, they elongate to a more elliptical shape. The tips can be mildly pointed to rounded. The base lobes are rounded.

Official Species Name:
• *Rumex obtusifolius* L.

Synonyms (Historical Names):
• *Acetosa oblongifolia* (L.) A. & D. Löve

Common Names:
• Broad-leaved dock
• Broad-leaf dock
• Bitter dock
• Blunt-leaved dock

An herbaceous perennial naturalized from Southern Europe and Western Asia, broad-leaved dock is widespread and abundant in North America, primarily where humans have invaded and where soil has been disturbed.

Edible Parts:
• Leaf blades
• Growing tips of leafy stems
• Seeds

Broad-leaved dock prior to stalk development.

Mature curly dock and broad-leaved dock leaves compared. Curly dock leaves are typically over three times longer than they are wide. In contrast, mature broad-leaved dock leaves are typically less than three times as long as they are wide. Broad-leaved dock's margins are flatter than curly dock margins.

Mature broad-leaved dock in the flower bud stage.

A whorl of broad-leaf dock fruits. The flaring pointed edges of the green sepals make these fruits different from curly dock. Once mature, these fruits will turn a rusty dark-brown color, just like curly dock. The brown three-sided seed bound inside each fruit is nearly identical to that of curly dock. The light seed-looking round objects are the tubercles resting on top of and covering the hidden seeds.

Curly dock seeds remain on the stem longer then broad-leaf dock seeds. Late in the season, around the first of September, even though this curly dock plant (left) has died, it holds on to its seeds, while broad-leaved dock (right) under the same growing conditions has dropped most of its upper seeds.

Harvesting Curly Dock

LEAVES: For eating, curly dock leaves come in three qualities. The first is good for eating raw or boiled; the second, in my opinion, is only good boiled; the third is good for compost.

Quality 1

The very best leaves that curly dock produces are the first- or second-year basal rosette of leaves, before the stalk develops. These leaves are somewhat rounder than at any other time in the plant's life. They are also more tender and have a lemony flavor. These are good raw, steamed, or boiled.

Quality 2

Beyond the young basal rosette stage, things get less predictable and downright frustrating. Almost as good though tougher are the rapidly growing leaves of the stem. Good raw flavor has a lot to do with the amount of recent and prolonged rain, cooler temperatures, new leaf growth, and some unknown variables. Even if all the conditions are right, the leaves can still be bitter, astringent, and papery. In the end, you have to taste the leaves to know if they are lemony enough to use raw or need to be cooked. As long as you boil them, rapidly growing leaves are usable even if they are unpalatable raw.

Quality 3

End size caused by hot dry weather and strong prolonged sun can turn curly dock leaves into paper—dry, tough, astringent, and bitter. They may look fine, but weather conditions change them. Even if you boil these leaves, they do not improve enough in flavor to make them worth eating.

The problem here is that Quality 2 (those that improve upon boiling) and Quality 3 (those that don't) are mostly indistinguishable in the raw form. And since weather patterns are variable, your job is not easy. Just keep in mind, a well-hydrated plant that has healthy great-looking leaves is more likely to have leaves that cook into greatness.

Finding curly dock

Young plants often go unnoticed in early summer because they grow low to the ground and can look like a hundred other low-growing basal rosette–style plants. They are often hidden amidst tall grass. The key is to look for basal rosettes or dead stems of last year's plants in the undergrowth. If the seed drops in tilled soil, you are in luck; there they grow in the open.

Choosing leaves

No matter the age of the plant, young, healthy-looking leaves are best. Do not be dismayed when you see reddish spots on the leaves. Wherever a bruise occurs, a reddish coloration results from the high acid content of the leaves. Young healthy leaves spotted with these discolorations are still fine to eat. These spots will not affect the appearance or flavor of cooked greens. They will affect the appearance of raw greens, if that matters to you or your guests. Old, reddish, partially shrivelled leaves are not good to eat.

Curly dock leaf damage. The leaf on the left is undamaged. The leaf on the right is damaged slightly but not enough to cause me to discard this leaf.

Transporting leaves and stems

Collect leaves with their leaf stems (petioles) and keep them well hydrated, out of the sun, and in a plastic bag so they'll stay fresh. Somewhat wilted curly dock leaves will crisp back up if you recut the stem and soak them in cold water. But it is better not to let them wilt in the first place.

A growth tip of a curly dock stem. This tip is no longer edible because the early formation of buds can be seen. The emergence of buds indicates the onset of fibrousness.

The upper rapidly growing tips of curly dock can be eaten as a cooked green if gathered prior to the formation of flower buds. Only a few inches of tender material exists at the top of the otherwise stringy stem. A shorter, stouter, rapidly growing stem will produce more food than one that has elongated.

Seeds

Seed development is complete when the fruit (dry fruit, in this case) turns a rusty brown color. Gathering the dry fruits is easy—just hold the stem and squeegee, or strip, the seed stems of their fruits, which can be used as seed for planting or can be separated from the chaff and used as a grain. Since the seeds are already dry on the plant, there is no need to dry them further. If they are not totally dry, dry them before storing or processing.

Curly dock seeds have great potential. Each plant produces thousands of seeds. And since the dry fruiting bodies stay on the plant when mature, they are easy to harvest. I have started some experiments to remove the chaff (sepal remains and tubercles) but have not yet found a reasonably efficient way to clean them in quantity. For those of you who love sprouts, the seeds easily germinate in warm conditions.

Preparing and Serving Curly Dock

Curly dock leaf stems are tough and stringy, and unless you are working with the very tender, young, first-year leaves, even the leaf blades will be somewhat tough. To get around the toughness, cut off the leaf stem (petiole). Attempting to eat the stem will result in a big spitball, which resembles a hair ball, so your cat will never look at you the same way again.

Even the main vein that extends from the leaf stem to the tip of the leaf blade is often substantial and tough. So if you want to use the stem leaves raw, first make sure the lemony flavor is there, then squeegee the leaf blade from the leaf stem and the main vein.

Do not squeegee the leaf blades until you are ready to use them. Once squeegeed, chop them into bite-size pieces and place them immediately in cold water. This crisps them and prevents discoloration along the edges. After a couple of minutes, drain, spin, and place them where you want them—in a salad, in a sandwich, or wherever.

How to squeegee a leaf blade from its main vein. Hold the leaf stem with one hand. With the other hand, grab the base of the leaf blade on either side of where it is attached to the leaf stem and pull down along the main vein. With practice, most of the leaf blade will separate from main vein.

With a little experimenting, you will come to know how much chewiness suits you. The more tender you want the leaves, the smaller pieces you will want to use.

As a salad ingredient, curly dock provides a wonderful tart punch and can make up anywhere from one-fourth to one-half the content of a salad, depending on how much sour you desire. This green can take the place of a vinegar dressing if enough of it is included. Curly dock also goes well in sandwiches, as a component of fruit salads, and anywhere you use lettuce.

Most of the curly dock I've eaten has been cooked, due to the fact that most of the time I find it, it is astringent

Managing leaf blade chewiness. If curly dock or broad-leaved dock leaves are papery and tough, chopping them into small pieces can reduce or eliminate the perception of chewiness. These pieces can be sprinkled in a salad if they pass the raw taste test, or they can be used for cooking.

and sometimes bitter. Cooking, primarily boiling, for a few minutes transforms the tart raw flavor (or astringent flavor) to a wonderful blend of cooked greens with lemoniness. The texture goes from crisp (or papery) to smooth and creamy. There is a concentration of flavor as the greens reduce to about one-fourth to one-fifth their original size. Once boiled, the natural plant acids that give this plant its sour flavor cause an overall color change. The greens go from a bright green to a dull army green.

All of these characteristics provide a rich source for new recipes—new tastes, new textures, and new colors. As a side dish, the boiled greens can be eaten with a pinch of salt and pepper or served with your favorite salad dressings. The wonderful lemony flavor and creamy texture make a great addition to soups, stews, and sauces. And due to the concentrated flavor, you do not need a huge amount of the leaves to add interesting complexity to combination dishes.

Curly dock leaves can also be sautéed or stir-fried just until the color changes. Cooked like this, it is just as good as it is boiled—a creamy texture, a good lemony flavor with no astringency or bitterness, and some character added by the cooking oil.

Steaming does not work so well for me because it results in greens that are not so creamy, the lemoniness is almost gone, and a mild rankness replaces the original astringent and bitter flavors. So I prefer boiled or sautéed greens.

The higher the concentration of curly dock used in a salad or cooked dish, the more of that roughness you will feel on your teeth when the oxalates temporarily bind with the calcium of your teeth. It is fun to feel this roughness for a minute and to watch others feel the unique sensation the oxalates provide before they dissolve.

Up until now, we have been discarding the leaf stem and the thick main veins. But, like rhubarb, the strongest sour flavors are often found there. While I typically toss them, a potential is there in spite of their fibrousness. My friend Stew Meyers once finely chopped the upper stems of curly dock and cooked them into a rhubarb-like pie. He modified the recipe for Japanese knotweed pie from *Stalking the Wild Asparagus* by Euell Gibbons.

Curly and broad-leaved dock leaves shrink upon cooking. More than 2 cups of finely chopped (1/2 inch) greens boils down to less than 1/2 cup of greens, so volume reduces to less than 1/4 of its original size. Boiling also changes the color from bright green to olive or army green.

Curly Dock Pie Filling

Adapted from Euell Gibbons' Japanese Knotweed Pie Recipe by Stewart Meyers of Eugene, Oregon.

INGREDIENTS:

1½ cups sugar

¼ cup flour

¾ teaspoon nutmeg

4 cups very finely chopped curly dock upper stalks and petioles

3 eggs, beaten

DIRECTIONS:

Preheat oven to 400 degrees F.

Blend dry ingredients together and gradually beat the eggs into the dry mix. Stir in the curly dock until well mixed.

Pour this filling into a prepared pie crust. Top with a top layer of pie crust and poke holes in the top for steam to escape.

Bake for about 50 minutes. Cool before serving

Using the stem tips and leaf refuse (leaf stems and main veins) are one way to get more use out of this plant. This is more than most people will do. But if you are so inclined, these parts can also be used for soup stock, dried for tea, or put through a juicer. However you decide to use them, you must account for their fibrousness. For instance, for soup stock, cook them, then strain the liquid to remove the fibrous stems. Of course, no straining is necessary if you use finely chopped leaf blades for soup stock.

My success with whole stem tips has been mixed. Sometimes the tips have good flavor and sometimes they don't. This is a potentially promising area that needs more study.

Mature stems are hollow except for the joints where leaves emerge, so parts of the stem can be used as a straw for drinking beverages.

Curly Dock Soup

The flavor and texture of this soup are superb. I find it lemony, creamy, and delicious. Experiment. Change the ingredients to suit your tastes. Add more curly dock, add some mallow in place of starch, use broccoli instead of celery, or add sautéed onions. The possibilities are endless. *Serves 6.*

INGREDIENTS:

    4 tablespoons extra virgin olive oil
    3 tablespoons cornstarch or 4 tablespoons
        tapioca starch
    20 ounces chicken broth (salted broth or bouillon)
    16 ounces water
    1½ cups chopped curly dock leaf blades
    1 cup chopped celery
    Salt and pepper, to taste

DIRECTIONS:

Heat olive oil in a large saucepan, stir in cornstarch or tapioca starch, and cook on medium heat until bubbly.

Gradually stir in liquids. Increase heat to high. Bring to a rapid boil, stirring constantly.

Stir in curly dock and celery. Decrease heat and simmer for 5 minutes. Add salt and pepper as desired.

Curly Dock Greens with Raspberries and Cashews

This dish is delicious. The greens are moist, and the combination of the greens, garlic, and raspberries is marvelous and flavorful. The salt and pepper are important for bringing out the flavors. And while I think this dish *looks* beautiful, some think otherwise. You'll have to make it yourself to see what I mean. *Serves 3 huge or 6 standard servings.*

Curly Dock Greens with Raspberries and Cashews. Garnished with raspberries and columbine flower petals.

INGREDIENTS:

1 pound curly dock leaf blades
2 tablespoons extra virgin olive oil
¼ cup chopped or halved cashews
1 or 2 cloves garlic, minced
Salt and pepper to taste
1 cup frozen raspberries

DIRECTIONS:

Boil curly dock greens for 3 minutes, drain, and chop into small pieces. Break those pieces apart so they are not in chopped clumps. In a large skillet, heat olive oil and stir in the cashews. When they turn golden brown, add garlic and stir until thoroughly tempered by the hot oil. Add the cooked curly dock.

Mix and cook for a couple of minutes until the greens are thoroughly heated. Add salt and pepper to taste. Make sure the cooked greens are not sticking together.

Fold ¾ cup raspberries into the greens. Do this gently so they maintain their shape. Remove from heat and serve hot. When ready to serve, sprinkle a few of the remaining fresh raspberries onto the plate as a garnish.

Chapter 10

FAMILY: Polygonaceae
SPECIES: *Rumex acetosella*

Sheep Sorrel

A tart treat for both kids and adults

A cluster of sheep sorrel leaves at the prime of their edible life.

Estimated Range

Official Species Name:
• *Rumex acetosella* L.

Synonyms (Historical Names):
• *Rumex angiocarpus* Murb.
• *Rumex tenuifolius* (Wallr.) A. Löve
• *Acetosella acetosella* (L.) Small
• *Acetosella tenuifolia* (Wallr.) A. Löve
• *Acetosella vulgaris* (Koch) Fourr.

Common Names:
• Sheep sorrel
• Field Sorrel
• Red Sorrel
• Sour Grass
• Sour-weed
• Red-weed
• Gentleman's sorrel
• Surette

An herbaceous weed naturalized from the

continued

SHEEP SORREL

What fun this plant is. A delight for both kids and adults. Pluck the leaves and taste for an instant kick—a spark to the taste buds, a strong sour-apple flavor. When found in quantity, this plant can provide a great addition to salads, soups, and many other dishes. The key is to know how to find it growing in its rapid leaf phase.

Like its relatives curly dock and broad-leaved dock, sheep sorrel is in the buckwheat family (Polygonaceae). It is unrelated to the wood sorrels (Oxalidaceae) that have similar flavor and some similar chemical characteristics.

Sheep sorrel is rather inconspicuous to the average person who passes it every day. In open fields, its flowering stalks give the impression of patches of red-colored grass. Some people spot the cute arrow-shaped leaves.

Average amounts of calcium and iron are all I can find in the scientific literature for sheep sorrel. And there has yet to be any serious study of the phytochemicals it may provide. Both the nutrients and phytochemicals of sheep sorrel need further study.

Sheep sorrel also contains soluble oxalates. This is not of general concern in the context of a normally diverse human diet.

Mediterranean, sheep sorrel is widespread and abundant in North America primarily where humans have invaded and where soil has been disturbed.

Edible Parts:
• Leaf blades

(left) A new sheep sorrel plant whose lobes are just forming. This plant is about 1½ inches tall.

Knowing Sheep Sorrel

Sheep sorrel reproduces in two ways—by seed and by rhizome. A seedling starts out with a pair of oblong cotyledons. Like curly dock, the first few true leaves that appear are egg-shaped and then elliptical; later, you begin to see lobes forming near the base of the leaf blade. Five things happen to the leaves as the plant matures: leaf stems elongate, leaf blades lengthen, and lobes enlarge, lengthen, and flare out to the sides.

Once a seedling establishes itself, the plant produces rhizomes, which are underground stems. Along the length of sheep sorrel rhizomes are buds that give rise to new plants. One rhizome can produce many plants. The photo of sour grass on the facing page shows a bunch of adult plants that could theoretically be connected by rhizomes to a single parent plant. When plants come from the same rhizome, they are considered genetically identical clones.

Sheep sorrel rhizomes are a bane to farmers. Normally they till to soften the soil and to kill weeds. But all tilling does with sheep sorrel is break up and spread its rhizomes. New plants can grow from fragments of the rhizome.

The very first leaves after cotyledons have no lobes, but you can often see pre-lobe angles along the margins.

(facing) Mature sheep sorrel plants in full stem and flower. This plant often grows in clusters in grassy fields and even resembles grass (from a distance) but with a reddish tinge. This resemblance may be how it got one of its common names—*sour grass*.

A young plant's basal rosette of leaves. Individual plants growing alone tend to form a basal rosette prior to stalk development. This plant is about 4 inches in diameter at this stage in its growth.

Sheep sorrel rhizome giving rise to many aboveground plants. These rhizomes are the source of the great clusters of leaves that one occasionally sees.

People often describe sheep sorrel leaves as being arrowhead-shaped. That description typically means that the main part of the leaf blade is pointed one way, while two lobes at the base of the leaf point back in the opposite direction. Sheep sorrel lobes are unique—not so much like arrowheads. While the main part of the leaf blade is how you would expect it to be, the lobes spread out to the sides. If you imagine them as ear lobes being pulled outward and twisted slightly, you get a better picture of how the lobes are shaped. Sometimes the lobes even curve back toward the tip of the main leaf blade.

At some point in the spring, you get a rapid proliferation of leaves from older rhizomatous plants. The leaves look like they are growing in big clumps, or they can carpet a whole area. The healthiest, most luxurious, and abundant growth goes on where the soil is soft, fertile, and well-watered. These conditions also result in the largest leaves. See the photo on page 165 to see some luxurious growth.

When the plants reach a certain maturity, they begin stalk development. In some respects, their overall form mimics a miniature version of curly dock. The base of each leaf is surrounded by an ocrea; the stem eventually branches, and tiny flowers and fruits are arranged along the tips of long stems.

Normally shaped and sized sheep sorrel leaves. They can get much bigger and much smaller than this. I've found leaf blades from 1/2 inch (typically on tall stems in dry ground) to 5 inches long (typically in great soil prior to flower stalk development).

Sheep sorrel leaves compared to morning glory (*Convolvulous spp*) and bittersweet nightshade (*Solanum dulcamara*). Both are considered poisonous to eat. While all these can loosely be called arrowhead-shaped leaves, only sheep sorrel will have a strong sour flavor. The two on the left are sheep sorrel, the four in the center show two varieties of morning glory, and the two on the right are bittersweet nightshade. Across the top are the upper sides of the leaves; across the bottom are the undersides.

Young sheep sorrel whose stem has just started to bolt. This first-year plant is not yet in a rhizome-connected colony. Note the ocrea membranes surrounding the base of each leaf. This shows a tiny version of the same type of ocrea found on curly and broad-leaf docks.

The adult plants can grow up to two feet tall in ideal conditions. In some instances where support is not strong, stalks may fall over and grow in a mishmash of confusion. The picture at left shows the typical upright growth form. Expect to see some variation in nature.

Harvesting and Managing Sheep Sorrel

Sheep sorrel is always a treat to snack on in whatever form you find it. It is famous as a kid's treat and as a walk-by nibble. The leaves always have that great sour flavor regardless of the age of the plant.

For meals, I only collect sheep sorrel when I find large leaves (relatively speaking) growing in abundance. I want my food to be easy: easy to collect, easy to process, and easy to prepare. Sheep sorrel leaves are relatively small and stem leaves are even smaller, so large and abundant make a big difference.

(facing) Several mature sheep sorrel clones growing from the same rhizome system. Stem leaves get smaller and narrower, and sometimes lack lobes toward the upper part of the plant. The seed structures eventually take on a reddish coloration.

The oft-branching stems of sheep sorrel. Not only does it grow multiple plants from its rhizomes, but the stems themselves can also branch quite generously just above ground level. This branching can produce a huge number of leaves prior to bolting.

Leaf-stem removal from the leaf blades. This process reduces the size of your take. Here is the amount of stem material produced by a gallon-size bag of sheep sorrel leaves. The bag was full when the leaf stems were attached. The bag only contains leaf blades now.

I typically gather from healthy patches where the leaves are large and clustered together. This is almost always in the pre-stalk condition, where rhizome-formed clones produce lots of leaves. This growing condition allows me to grab big clusters of leaves with one hand while I snip them with scissors using the other.

Sheep sorrel is of lesser, but still good, edible quality when it is growing in more stressed conditions. Stress in the form of poor dry soils will cause sheep sorrel to bolt quickly into mature stems. In these conditions, sheep sorrel produces fewer and smaller leaves. Only when the soil remains moist throughout its life will sheep sorrel produce large lush leaves in its adult form. Struggling plants are good for snacking but not for gathering on a larger scale.

Like other plants, keep your gathered leaves spray-misted and cool in containers out of the sun until you are ready to use them.

When you are ready to use the leaves, it is time to remove stems. The stems are just as flavorful as the leaves but are too fibrous for polite society. Including stems with the leaves is, of course, the easy way to include sheep sorrel in any dish, but spitballs will ensue, and flossing will be necessary. This is true, raw or cooked. If you are with a bunch of burly survivalists who don't mind smiling with green matter stuck in their teeth, leave the stems on. But if you are feeding these wild greens to your friends who are skeptical of your foraging prowess, you want to give them a pleasant chewing experience, so remove the stems.

Serving Sheep Sorrel, Fresh or Cooked

Sheep sorrel is a wonderful addition to any food where a sour or lemony taste is desired. Fresh, it is an excellent salad green all by itself—though a little strong for some. So, you can make a whole salad out of sheep sorrel, or you can use measured amounts of it in more complex salads where you want a variety of flavors. To me, a good base for a combination salad includes roughly a blend of a third foundational greens, a third pungent greens, and a third sour greens, with shredded bitter greens mixed in to suit your individual tastes. Of course there are a million things you can add to this base, and I'm sure you will.

Fresh sheep sorrel is a great addition to any kind of salad. It goes good with greens as well as fruit, meat, and seafood salads. Put it in sandwiches, add some leaves to a glass of iced tea, or use it in homemade salsa or pesto. Sheep sorrel is similar in flavor and other characteristics to French sorrel (*Rumex acetosa*). Any cookbook recipe you

Sheep Sorrel Salad. Garnished with a wild sweet pea flower and topped with your favorite salad dressing or just olive oil and salt to taste. The leaves shown here are larger than typically found.

Cooked sheep sorrel reduces greatly in size. Four cups of fresh sheep sorrel leaf blades yield only about 3 tablespoons of cooked material. The color also transforms to an army green.

can find that uses French sorrel—also known as garden sorrel—will give you a great guide for inventing recipes for sheep sorrel.

Like curly dock and broad-leaved dock, sheep sorrel reduces greatly upon cooking. For this reason, I typically do not make a side dish of cooked greens from this plant. It is just too much work for whatever little pile of greens you may end up with. So for me, cooking sheep sorrel is limited to the making of soups, sauces, and flavorings—where a little goes a long way. And because of the intensity of sheep sorrel's flavor, this strategy works quite well.

Another change that occurs during cooking is that the greens transform from bright green to a dark olive green. This color change is a feature caused by the high acid content of the greens. You cannot prevent this change under normal cooking circumstances, so learn to love the new color.

Sheep sorrel is a commonly known wild food that is already enjoyed as a mouthwatering snack by many who use it. Knowing the details on its collection and use will help you get the most out of this plant as a real food and as a contributing part of your diet.

The recipes for soup and sauce found at the end of the wood sorrel chapter also work for sheep sorrel.

Sheep Sorrel Pesto

Sheep sorrel pesto (fresh) or sauce (cooked) can be even more varied. Start with this basic pesto recipe and change it to your liking.

INGREDIENTS:

4 cups loosely packed fresh sheep sorrel leaf blades

½ cup grated Parmesan cheese

⅓ cup pine nuts

2 medium cloves garlic, peeled

½ cup extra virgin olive oil

Salt and pepper, to taste

DIRECTIONS:

Process the sheep sorrel, cheese, pine nuts, and garlic into a rough paste in a food processor. With the machine still running, drizzle in the olive oil. If the paste is not liquid enough add more olive oil until it suits you. Add salt and pepper as desired. Serve fresh with pasta and other dishes.

Grilled Fish Sandwich. Adding sheep sorrel leaves gives it a lemony flavor.

Sheep Sorrel Soup and Roasted Chicken with Sheep Sorrel Sauce. The soup is garnished with bull thistle (*Cirsium vulgare*) root slivers and fresh chives. The chicken is garnished with chanterelle mushrooms, red and yellow sweet bell peppers, and potatoes, all drizzled with sheep sorrel sauce (center).

Sheep Sorrel Tea

The lemony flavor of sheep sorrel translates wonderfully into a tea that can be made from the leaves and stems. Dry them as you would any tea you make yourself. I find that a food dryer set at 95 degrees F works best to keep in most of the flavor. Since you only dip the greens into the water and then pull them out again, there is no need to exclude stems. In fact, this is a great use for the stems you have cut from the leaves. The stems require no tea bags; just bundle them with a string. With sweetener added, iced tea made from sheep sorrel makes a lemonade-style drink.

Chapter 11

FAMILY: Oxalidaceae
SPECIES: *Oxalis stricta*

Wood Sorrel

A tart-tasting shamrock of a plant

Wood Sorrel—a non-woody low growing plant that would please any leprechaun.
The fascinating shape of the leaves reveals the identity of this plant.

Estimated Range

Official Species Name:
- *Oxalis stricta* L.

Synonyms (Historical Names):
- *Ceratoxalis coloradensis* (Rydb.) Lunell
- *Ceratoxalis cymosa* (Small) Lunell
- *Oxalis* or *Xanthoxalis brittoniae* Small
- *Oxalis* or *Xanthoxalis bushii* (Small) Small
- *Oxalis* or *Xanthoxalis coloradensis* Rydb.
- *Oxalis* or *Xanthoxalis cymosa* Small
- *Oxalis* or *Xanthoxalis filipes* Small
- *Oxalis* or *Xanthoxalis interior* (Small) Fedde
- *Oxalis* or *Xanthoxalis rufa* Small
- *Oxalis corniculata* var. *dillenii* (Jacq.) Trel.
- *Oxalis dillenii* Jacq.

continued

WOOD SORREL

Most people walk by wood sorrel all their lives, seeing it as clover. Those of us looking closer notice it is unique—sort of a cleaner version of clover with a well-defined leaf. It wasn't until I began studying wild foods that I realized it was also a tasty treat. It is a plant that grows anywhere there is moisture and sunlight bathing the soil. It is common in yards, gardens, sidewalk cracks, and driveways.

Also mistakenly called shamrock, the leaf is the classic shape often seen on display at Irish cultural events—particularly to celebrate St. Patrick's Day. After some research, I discovered that, historically, the true shamrock is believed to be a clover, not wood sorrel—probably *Trifolium dubium* or *Trifolium repens*. No one seems to know for sure, but do a search for shamrock on the Web and you will see all the theories. Larger woodland species of *Oxalis* are often sold as potted plants on St. Patrick's Day, labeled as shamrocks for marketing purposes.

Oxalis stricta and *Oxalis corniculata* are the two most common weedy yellow (flowered) wood sorrels. They are edible, delicious, and easily recognizable—nearly identical. For the purposes of this chapter, all the sorrels can be used in the same ways.

Very tiny seedling of wood sorrel, much enlarged here, soon after germination. It includes two cotyledons, one expanded true leaf at the top, with the second leaf still curled, ready to expand. These seedlings are tiny, about 6mm from left to right—you almost have to have a magnifier to see them.

Wood sorrels are annuals but will struggle and survive into perennial-ness in very moderate winter climates.

Both of the yellow sorrels have high values of iron, calcium, and vitamin C. Even more surprising is the level of iron in *Oxalis corniculata*, which has been found to have three times the iron of spinach. Spinach currently provides the highest source of iron known from a cultivated leafy green.

Aptly named *Oxalis*, this genus and its plant family, the Oxalidaceae, were named after the Greek word for sour: *oxys*. The sourness cannot all be attributed to oxalic acids (oxalates), even though the oxalates are high. The sourness comes from a mixture of acids. In spite of many authors claiming so, oxalates are not a problem for normal healthy humans eating a normally diverse diet.

I couldn't find any phytochemical data on wood sorrel.

Knowing Wood Sorrel

LEAVES/LEAFLETS: Wood sorrel sprouts throughout most of the growing seasons—whenever the soil is disturbed, there is enough moisture, and some sunlight is present to stimulate germination. That is typically in the spring and autumn unless someone is regularly watering the area. The cotyledons and the first true leaves are tiny and difficult to see. The seedlings can be as small as 4mm in diameter.

These plants are very delicate and tiny until the root reaches a critical mass, allowing the leaves to start growing in size. Leaves on a healthy adult plant get to be up to 1 inch in diameter. Leaves grow alternately on delicate stems and give this plant its unique appearance. The leaf is made up of three leaflets, each in the shape of a heart. The three hearts meet at the point where they join the leaf stem.

Each leaflet has a flexible crease along its main vein. The crease gives the leaflets a special talent, an ability to behave differently depending on the whims of nature. During the

- *Oxalis dillenii* ssp. *filipes* (Small) Eiten
- *Oxalis dillenii* var. *radicans* Shinners
- *Oxalis europaea* Jord.
- *Oxalis europaea* var. *bushii* (Small) Wieg.
- *Oxalis europaea* var. *rufa* (Small) Young
- *Oxalis florida* ssp. *prostrata* (Haw.) Lourteig
- *Oxalis fontana* Bunge
- *Oxalis prostrata* Haw.
- *Oxalis rupestris* Raf.
- *Xanthoxalis dillenii* (Jacq.) Holub
- *Xanthoxalis dillenii* var. *piletocarpa* (Wieg.) Holub
- *Xanthoxalis florida* (Salisb.) Moldenke
- *Xanthoxalis stricta* var. *piletocarpa* (Wieg.) Moldenke

Common Names:
- Wood sorrel
- Upright wood sorrel
- Yellow sorrel
- Yellow wood sorrel
- Oxalis
- Shamrock
- Sourgrass
- Toad sorrel

An herbaceous weed thought to be native to North America and Eurasia, wood sorrel is widespread and abundant in North America, primarily near human activity but where the soil is relatively stable, particularly lawns, vacant lots, and landscape beds.

Edible Parts:
- Leaves
- Flowers
- Seedpods

SHAMROCK

A three-leaved (actually
three-leafleted) clover
was used by St. Patrick to
represent the Holy Trinity.

day, the leaflets are generally spread open in shady areas. At sundown, leaflets angle downward toward the stem and fold along their crease, sort of like a collapsible umbrella. During the day, they fold down if the sun gets too intense or if it starts raining. These behaviors seem to protect the delicate leaves from physical damage brought about by sun and rain.

Wood sorrel leaves and stems range in color from pure green to pink to plum to some reddish coloration of green. Sometimes green leaves will have reds darkening the leaves evenly, or there will be red around the edges. Whatever color it is, it will have a dull (not shiny) surface.

(left) Folded wood sorrel leaf with its three folded leaflets.

(right) Plum-colored wood sorrel. Its leaves and stems range in color from bright green to pink, to plum, or red. Sometimes leaves will be green, darkened by a reddish hue.

RHIZOMES: Once established, wood sorrel can grow into big mats. *Oxalis stricta* spreads by rhizomes growing just beneath the surface of the soil, similar to sheep sorrel. *Oxalis corniculata* spreads by aboveground stolons that re-root as they spread. While both wood sorrels develop mats or ground covers, *stricta* tends to grow upward a little more and is capable of reaching about a foot tall. *Corniculata* tends to mat more closely to the ground and spread outward.

FLOWERS AND PODS: Wood sorrel flowers are small with five yellow petals. They are born on small umbels. They, like the leaves, close up in early evening and reopen some time in the morning. The five petals arranged in a circle easily distinguishes this plant from any of the clovers. Clovers have lots of tiny pea-like flowers clustered together on flower heads.

Flowers eventually develop into five-sided seedpods that resemble miniature okra fruits. Those pods arise off the flower stem at a sharp, almost 90-degree angle. This characteristic angle separates the yellow wood sorrels from all the other members of the *Oxalis* genus.

Once the pods mature and dry out, they snap open, ejecting their seeds quite a distance from the parent plant.

RHIZOMES

Underground stems that give rise to new plants. Rhizomes can also be food storage organs for plants.

STOLONS

Aboveground stems that creep along the ground and re-root, giving rise to new plants. The new plants created by both rhizomes and stolons are genetic clones of the original plants.

Wood sorrel flowers and leaves on a young plant.

Wood sorrel's yellow flower, about ³/₈ inch in diameter. Yellow flower clusters arise from the ends of branched stems. Several flowers radiate out from one point in a form that is called an umbel.

Seedpods and flower on a wood sorrel umbel. The pods angle sharply upward from the stems they are attached to. This is different from other members of the same genus (*Oxalis*) that have less-angled seedpod attachments.

Clover and wood sorrel leaves compared. Red clover (*Trifolium pratense*), one of our common clovers (left), is compared to wood sorrel (right). Wood sorrel has three heart-shaped leaflets. Clover leaflets are not heart-shaped.

Wood sorrel or clover?

I am going to generalize here because there are hundreds of clovers. Certain common clovers can *resemble* wood sorrel because their leaves have three leaflets. Also, depending on the species of clover, they can be roughly the same size as and be weak climbers like wood sorrel, and grow somewhat as a mat or ground cover as wood sorrels do.

With a little attention to detail, the differences become obvious. First, wood sorrel leaflets are truly heart-shaped; and while I'm sure I've seen heart-shaped leafleted clover, they are *typically* not heart-shaped. Clover leaflets tend to be round, egg-shaped, or oblong. Their tips are notched

An *Oxalis corniculata* plant that was easy to harvest. I pulled this up as one big plant that took up quite a bit of ground. The tomatoes and coffee mug are there to show relative size.

but do not have that sweeping heart shape of sorrels.

Clovers more often than not have a whitish marking on each leaflet. The design differs somewhat from one clover species to another, but all the leaflets on a particular plant have the same pattern.

The veins on clover leaflets are pinnate (Latin for "feathered"), which means that each leaflet has a main vein with smaller ones branching off it. Wood sorrel leaflets have palmate venation—a main vein plus secondary veins, all originating from its base; smaller tertiary veins branch off the main vein.

The other main difference is that wood sorrel has a wonderful sour flavor, sort of like sour apple, whereas clover taste like, well, clover—a mild green well suited for grazing animals.

Gathering and Cleaning Wood Sorrel

A mouthwatering snack or trail nibble can be in the cards anytime you see wood sorrel. But like sheep sorrel, to start incorporating this plant into meals requires that either you have very little need (mixed in a salad with other ingredients) or you find a large patch of it. Preparing a substantial amount of these greens is a bit labor-intensive even under optimal gathering conditions. So get your Zen on and just enjoy working with the plant.

Assuming you find a patch that's big, healthy, and dense enough to make it worth your while, your strategy will be determined by how you want to leave the plant. If you want it to continue producing leaves for a later harvest, then just clip enough of the upper leaf stems (newest growing tips) to be able to hold them in your hand. To do that, grab the upper parts of a clump of plants and cut the stems with your scissors.

If you do not plan to return to the location and if it's okay to take the whole plant, gently separate it from the ground. Be careful not to mix any dirt with the greens in the uprooting process. You might want to use your scissors to trim off any parts connected to the soil. Try to keep the branched stems relatively intact, keep the greens cool in the shade, preferably in plastic bags, and spray-mist immediately to get them hydrated. Keep them moist until ready for use. The less happy they are (heat, dryness, long time between picking and using), the more they will start to fold up. Folding makes them less visible and less presentable. So keep them happy!

Once back in your kitchen, either transfer the greens to the fridge or begin processing right away. To clean wood sorrel, snip off all but about a half inch of the fibrous stem from the leaf. That half inch of stem should be left on to give the leaves some three-dimensionality. The small amount of fibrousness in the included stem will not interfere with chewing.

What do I mean by three-dimensionality? If you remove all of the leaf stem, wood sorrel leaf blades will stack up like playing cards. This occurs whether they are open or folded. The stems, when left attached, prop them

Wood sorrel leaves and seedpod. Leaf stems are cut to about ½ inch long for ready use. These leaves were flatter than you see here until they were cut and exposed to the intense bright light and heat from my camera setup, causing them to fold up.

About half of what you collect will be fibrous stem material. Stem material (left) has been separated from the edible leaves, flowers, and young seedpods seen in the measuring cup.

up, allowing the leaf blades to stay separated. So why is this important? Conventional salads are very three-dimensional: they contain lots of air. To prevent your friends from asking, "Why are you serving me a flat salad?" leave part of the leaf stems on.

It takes about twelve minutes to separate about a cup of lightly packed greens from the refuse. That comes to about one ounce by weight. Time and weight will vary depending on your efficiency, the leaf size, and your cup-packing prowess. You will find that these light and delicate greens pack a flavorful punch.

Since you are only using the leaves, seed capsules, and flowers, cleaning wood sorrel results in lots of fibrous refuse. Don't throw it out. Make tea bundles (as opposed to tea bags). Make small bundles out of the stem material and tie them with string, leaving about seven inches of string dangling off the tie. Tie the other end to a paper clip. Dry the bundle/string/paper clip creations in a food dryer. Once dry, dip a bundle in your cup of hot water by holding it at the paper clip end. The paper clip's weight will prevent the string from falling in the water. Pull the bundle out by the string when the flavor has transferred to the water, much in the same way one dips tea bags.

Serving Wood Sorrel

While you can make a salad completely composed of wood sorrel leaves, it would be a lot of work to clean all those greens and difficult to spear them with a fork. The flavor would be exceptionally tart, which people like myself really enjoy. Wood sorrel leaves and seedpods are most efficiently used in combination salads with several ingredients. A salad using a third part of wood sorrel has excellent sour overtones. Mix wild sorrel with plants in other sections of this book or with conventional greens.

Wood sorrel flowers are edible and can be included anywhere you use the leaves and pods. Unfortunately, they close up almost as soon as they are picked, making their showiness unusable. So eat them closed.

You can use wood sorrel leaves, seedpods, and flowers any way you can use sheep sorrel—raw or cooked. Due to the acids in wood sorrel, the greens change color as soon as they are heated, becoming a darker army green. Learn to appreciate the color in whatever you make.

Like sheep sorrel, wood sorrel reduces tremendously upon cooking, so just making cooked greens is too much work for most people, unless you like very small portions. The flavor is intense enough to use in soups and sauces with reasonably small amounts of greens. Here are some recipes I created. See if you like them.

Wood Sorrel Soup

Yields 12–13 ounces, enough for 1 large or 2 small servings.

Wood Sorrel Soup. Garnished with red clover flower petals (*Trifolium pratense*) and wood sorrel leaves.

INGREDIENTS:

2 cups chicken stock or vegetable stock or bouillon

¼ cup diced bull thistle root, or potato or celery or broccoli

¼ tablespoon extra virgin olive oil

¼ cup finely chopped onion

⅔ cup packed wood sorrel (roughly = 1⅝ cups loose = 1 ounce by weight)

Salt and pepper, to taste

DIRECTIONS:

Begin heating the chicken broth and bull thistle root (or potato) in a pot.

Heat a saucepan separately until hot; add olive oil and onion; sauté until the onion becomes soft and translucent and then add it to the broth pot. Keep at a mild boil for 10 minutes.

Add wood sorrel, regain boil, and then simmer for 10 minutes.

Use salt and pepper as desired.

Wood Sorrel Sauce.
Poured over whitefish and
a broccoli dish with extra
sauce at upper right.

Wood Sorrel Sauce

The sauce has a good lemony flavor and is great on chicken, fish, veal, potatoes, rice, and quinoa. *Yield: ²⁄₃–¾ cup, enough for 1–3 servings, depending on how much is used per serving.*

INGREDIENTS:

1 tablespoon olive oil
1 tablespoon flour
⅓ cup tiny diced fresh mushrooms
¾ cup salted chicken stock or vegetable stock or bouillon
½ cup packed wood sorrel
½ teaspoon dried dill
½ tablespoon fresh chives
1 tablespoon cooking sherry
⅛ teaspoon salt
Pinch pepper

DIRECTIONS:

Heat saucepan until hot; add olive oil, gradually stir in flour, and cook until medium brown.

Add mushrooms and slowly stir in stock. Bring to a boil and then turn down heat; cook at a low boil for 5 minutes.

Add sorrel, dill, chives, and sherry, and continue cooking at low boil for 3–8 minutes, until the sauce begins to coat the spoon. Season to taste with salt and pepper.

Wood Sorrel Dessert Topping

When used on ice cream, puddings, cakes, and pastries, what you get is a buttery lemon-honey flavor. It is a sweet dessert with mild spinach undertones, genuinely quite good but completely unconventional in its greenish-yellow color and flavor. If you use salted butter (the wrong thing to do), the flavor is more like sweet lemony spinach. There is a mild roughness to the teeth after eating because of the oxalates in the greens. *Makes 1–3 servings, about 3½ ounces.*

INGREDIENTS:

½ cup water
2 cups loosely packed wood sorrel
2 tablespoons honey
2 tablespoons unsalted butter

continued

Wood Sorrel Dessert Topping. Poured over vanilla ice cream and garnished with fresh sorrel leaves.

DIRECTIONS:

Bring water to a boil in a saucepan and add the sorrel leaves; cover and continue boiling, then turn down heat to *just* boiling. Check regularly, stir, and keep leaves from riding up the sides and drying up.

While that's cooking, melt butter in honey in a separate pot, stir, and put aside.

Cook the sorrel for 10 minutes and then uncover. At this point, the sorrel should be moist but not in standing water. (If you tilt the pan, about a tablespoon of water will seep out. That is good. If there is more, keep it on the heat until it gets to the right stage.) While still hot, stir in the butter-honey mixture and mix well.

Pour mixture into a blender and purée until smooth. Use hot, or let cool for a thicker sauce.

So get out there and find your shamrocks—er, I mean wood sorrel—and experiment like you're a kid again. It takes a little work, but your efforts will be rewarded.

Pungent Greens

The greens in this chapter have mildly pungent and/or peppery and/or acrid flavors. These are greens and vegetables that are suitable for occasions where you want to add some character to the dish you are making. Greens with these flavors are often added to milder greens (foundational greens) or complex dishes to add interest and nuance. They are edible raw and cooked, but their best uses depend on your flavor goals for whatever you are preparing. They have the potential to greatly improve a dish by using just the right amount or to destroy it by adding so much that it overpowers. At certain stages of growth, some of these greens are mild enough that you might even be able

Mustard flowers are easily identified. While shape, size, and flower color may vary, the number of petals is always four and the number of stamens is always six. All mustards have four tall and two short stamens. Here you see the four center stamens hugging the pistil, with five and six leaning off to the side.

to make a whole salad with them. But many will prefer to use them as a flavor enhancer for other foods.

Not all mustard family plants taste alike. Each has its own characteristic flavor and texture. When fresh, some are excellent in combination salads, added to sandwiches, used as garnishes, and made into pesto and other green-based sauces. Cooked, their flavors vary tremendously—some remaining pungent, others transforming into foundational flavors.

The plants covered in this section include field mustard, wintercress, garlic mustard, and shepherd's purse. All these plants happen to be in the mustard family (Brassicaceae). Broccoli, cauliflower, brussels sprouts, kale, collards, and cabbage are all mustards. All mustard plants have flowers with four petals, four sepals, and six stamens. The stamens are arranged in such a way that four of them near the pistil are long, and the remaining two near the petals are short.

Flavors offered by mustard greens are an excellent addition to the gourmet's arsenal of tastes. Mustard greens can be nutritional powerhouses packed with nutrients and phytochemicals. Garlic mustard, for instance, is one of the most nutritious leafy greens ever analyzed, according to our nutrient charts. Mustards in general have many phytochemicals in common. Phytochemicals found in mustard family plants include glucosinolates, sinigrin, progoitrin, goitrin, glucobrassicin, indoles, and isothiocyanates. These compounds are thought to fight cancer and heart disease through a variety of mechanisms.

In addition to pungency and pepperiness, garlic mustard and wintercress are typically bitter in the raw state. If you love bitter, that is great; if not, I'll show you ways to prepare these greens that you will enjoy.

The mustards are cold-weather plants—growing most robustly in early spring and autumn. If they are growing in your garden and you nurture them, you can extend their stay somewhat and increase their yield tremendously.

Mustard Seeds

Three of the four plants covered in this section (all but shepherd's purse) produce seed in enough quantity that they can have their own food uses. So a cautionary note is warranted. Mustard seed oils are known to contain relatively high amounts of erucic acid, a natural fatty acid typically found in small quantities of the fats of many foods we eat. All mustard condiments contain them. Who knows, in small quantities it may even have some health benefits we have not yet discovered.

The cautionary note has to do with excessive consumption of erucic acid that you will probably never approach. I mention this only because certain animal studies have raised some concerns. But, for the vast majority of you who will not eat a third cup of prepared wild mustard (the yellow condiment) every day, this may be a nonissue.

Excessive amounts of erucic acid fed over time to certain animals, particularly their newborns, developed fatty deposits in their heart muscles and experienced slower growth rates than controls. So what's new? Excessive amounts of many nutrients and phytochemicals are toxic. When individual food substances are isolated and given in high concentrations, you can often show damaging effects. There is no evidence that reasonable amounts of this oil in the context of a normal diverse diet are harmful in any way to humans. (Mattson, 1973.)

In my opinion, the benefits of the diverse nutrients and potential phytonutrients, which come along with eating the mustard seeds *occasionally* within the context of a healthy diet, outweigh any potential danger from small amounts of erucic acid. Just eat reasonable amounts of the seeds for fun and flavor, on occasion, and stop worrying. I would recommend that you do not feed wild mustard seed preparations or store-bought mustard to newborns. Wait until they are old enough to eat hot dogs with chili. (Boy, talk about fattening the heart muscle!)

GLUCOSINOLATES & ISOTHIOCYANATES

These are mustard compounds and were first thought of as toxins for livestock. Apparently livestock eat mustard plants to excess if that is all that is available to them—particularly mustard plants that have gone to seed. That excess caused a lot of gastroenteritis and other problems. (Kingsbury, 1964.) So, in the late 1960s through the 1970s, there were warnings to humans about eating too much mustard. It was thought that it might cause damage to the digestive tract and potentially lead to cancer. But as we have learned over time, these compounds and their metabolic by-products are now considered possible phytonutrients when consumed in the context of a normally diverse diet. Not only do they not cause cancer, but they may fight cancer and heart disease as well.

Farmland widely covered with adult field mustard. This is in the early spring sometime between early April and early May, depending on where you are in North America. These plants typically get their start in the fall, store energy in their root, overwinter, and bolt into quick growth in the spring.

Chapter 12

FAMILY: Brassicaceae
SPECIES: *Brassica rapa*

Field Mustard

*A fantastic mustard green, better than the one
you can buy in the supermarket*

Field mustard, a prolific, great-tasting plant that is fond of cultivated fields and your garden. It has two forms at different stages of growth: a rosette of leaves at ground level (shown here) and, later, a reproductive stalk producing flowers and seeds.

Estimated Range

Official Species Name:
• *Brassica rapa* L.

Synonyms (Historical Names):
• *Brassica rapa* var. *campestris* (L.) W.D.J. Koch
• *Brassica campestris* L.
• *Brassica campestris* var. *rapa* (L.) Hartman
• *Caulanthus sulfureus* Payson

Common Names:
• Field mustard
• Wild mustard
• Bird's rape
• Rape
• Wild turnip
• Turnip rape

An herbaceous weed naturalized from southern Europe, field mustard is widespread and abundant in North America, primarily where humans have

continued

FIELD MUSTARD

For a plant that is so common, you would think that it would get more attention than it does. In fact, the few times it seems to be mentioned, it is as the less-loved brother of black mustard (*Brassica nigra*), a domesticated plant that grows wild in North America. Black mustard shares field mustard's range.

Brassica rapa has a confusing array of varietal offshoots and cultivated brothers and sisters. They all have the same species name, yet most are dramatically different in appearance and flavor. The reason I bring this up is that if you decide you want to investigate this plant on your own, you had better hope that the papers you read specify exactly which *Brassica rapa* they are talking about. No other wild plant I know of has such a confusing name problem. For instance, if you are looking up nutrient tables and one of the plants covered is *Brassica rapa*, which one are they referring to? Mustard spinach greens? Field mustard greens? Bok choy? Unless they specify which *Brassica rapa*, you may misinterpret whatever they've discovered.

Children (Varieties) of wild *Brassica rapa*

• *Brassica rapa* var. *rapa* L.: birdrape, common mustard, field mustard, rape
• *Brassica rapa* var. *amplexicaulis* Tanaka & Ono: field mustard, rape, rape mustard
• *Brassica rapa* var. *dichotoma* (Roxb. ex Fleming) Kitam: toria
• *Brassica rapa* var. *silvestris* (Lam.) Briggs: Colza
• *Brassica rapa* var. *trilocularis* (Roxb.) Kitam: Yellow sarson

invaded and where soil
has been disturbed.

Edible Parts:
- Leaves
- Growing tips of leafy stems
- Buds
- Flowers
- Seeds
- Pre-stalk root

Cultivars of the *Brassica rapa* species

Members of these groups are all named *Brassica rapa*. One example of each is given on the right.

- Chinensis Group: Bok choy
- Pekinensis Group: Napa cabbage
- Perviridis Group: Mustard-spinach (tendergreen)
- Rapifera Group: Cultivated turnips
- Ruvo Group: Broccoli raab

Other common large-leaved wild mustards you might find are charlock (*Sinapis arvensis*), black mustard (*Brassica nigra*), and brown mustard (*Brassica juncea*). Brown mustard and black mustard are cultivated for their seed. In addition, brown mustard is cultivated for greens. Cultivation helps expand the wild spread of seeds beyond the farmland they are planted in. Field mustard, black mustard, and charlock are more common than brown and share similar ranges.

Brassica napus, the source of canola or rapeseed oil, is nearly identical in appearance to field mustard. It is less widespread than the other wild mustards. We'll talk about *napus* later in this chapter.

I believe the greens in the produce section of the supermarket are probably brown mustard (*Brassica juncea*). Of course, the packaging never specifies the species or variety used. Whatever they are, the mustard greens I've purchased can have a harsh flavor relative to field mustard. You can also buy turnip greens, another mustard that, confusingly, is one of the cultivated forms of *Brassica rapa*. Turnip greens have a stronger pepperiness than field mustard.

As far as I can tell, the nutritional value of field mustard is unknown. The USDA has values for two different mustard greens: mustard spinach (a Japanese cultivar of *Brassica rapa*) and domesticated brown mustard (*Brassica juncea*). Because of their close relationship, field mustard might be somewhat comparable to mustard spinach, brown mustard, or turnip greens for conventional nutrients. Those three have their nutrients listed in the USDA nutrient database. In addition, because it is in the mustard family, field mustard is likely to have indols, isothiocyanates, glucosinolates and other phytochemicals.

Field mustard is commonly found along roadside embankments, waste areas, farmland (growing amongst crops), and anywhere else the soil has been disturbed. Being a cold-weather plant, it is possible that field mustard could be found anywhere within the range of the maps I've designed. The range I've shown does not account for deserts and mountain ranges—which will have little field mustard only because humans aren't bringing it in and making the habitat (gardens, farms, etc.) for it.

The mustards, in general, have a rich history and a variety of uses. While I focus on greens, mustards are most known for their seed, which is made into the yellow or brown condiment that people squirt on their hot dogs. For an interesting and comprehensive overview of the uses of mustard plants, check out Cheatham, Johnston, and Marshall's book, *The Useful Wild Plants of Texas*, Volume 2. They cover many of the uses as foods, spices, food additives, preservatives, medicines, effects on livestock, weaponry, use as cover crops, spiritual uses, history, and more—a fascinating read.

The major use of field mustard is to add varying degrees of pungency to a dish of other foods. Some people might like it enough to make it the featured food of a dish.

Knowing Field Mustard

The first sighting you'll have of field mustard will probably be from your car in the spring. In a field, by the roadside, or on farmland, you'll see bright yellow flowers towering above the grass, crops, or other weeds. These are the flower stalks of the adult plants.

If the plants you locate are indeed field mustard, try some, take some home, experiment with it. If it is already producing seed, throw some in your garden.

As an annual

Field mustard that germinates in spring or summer can grow a stalk and go to seed within a couple of months, which makes field mustard an annual. The summer heat and/or the long days cause mustard to bolt (grow a stem). This is likely to happen in a garden or on a farm, where the soil is turned over throughout the year and watered. Field mustard can only germinate in the summer if the ground is disturbed and enough sustained water is available.

As a biennial

Without summer watering, field mustard seed will wait in the soil until the fall rains begin. By that time in the year, the days are shorter and the temperature is cooler. Field mustard will then sprout and grow its basal leaves but will not bolt. Winter's arrival has several effects on the plant. First, the leaves stop growing and eventually die from the cold. Second, its root goes through physiological changes to survive winter's freezing temperatures. These plants will come alive again in the spring.

Field mustard seedling with its two fat embryonic leaves (cotyledons). The first two true leaves are just beginning to emerge. Outside of a frozen winter, field mustard seeds germinate anytime where the soil is turned and watered.

Germination and life patterns

LEAVES: As with most plants, the first two leaves that emerge from within the seed (embryonic leaves = cotyledons) do not appear like the older leaves. The first two

Young field mustard. Here, the first true leaves have overtaken the cotyledons in size and are still growing.

Young field mustard. The largest leaves here are about 5 inches. Note how the later leaves are different from the first and second pair. More character is expressed from the fifth leaf onward. At this point, the leaves start to show their dimples—bumps on the surface that are characteristic of field mustard.

leaves of all members of the *Brassica* genus, including field mustard, tend to look like a person's posterior pressed against a pane of glass. (Sorry for the image, but if you can come up with a better description, let me know.)

Field mustard grows quickly after germination. The first true leaves differ from the cotyledons in both shape and size. They begin taking on characteristics of the leaves that follow.

As more leaves develop, they begin to show much more character. The margins are irregular and often wavy. Leaves start dividing into lobes. Bumps occur all over the leaves.

Taking on a decidedly mustard family appearance, the leaves eventually crowd around the growth point of the root in what is called a basal rosette (*basal* referring to base or ground level and *rosette* referring to all the leaves radiating out from a single point, like petals on a rose).

Once the plant is established, its leaves can be anywhere from eight to twenty inches long, depending on soil moisture and competition from other plants. The photos here only represent good healthy growth. Stunted growth produces smaller, fewer, less-luxurious, slower-growing leaves.

TAPROOT AND CORM: As the leaves develop, so do the taproot and the corm. A corm is an enlarged base of the stem just below the ground and above the taproot. The corm is barely noticeable most of the time, barely thickening at all. But, at other times, it can get rather fat. Whatever size the corm and root are, they store energy and provide support for the plant.

If the plant germinated early enough in the year, it will send up a flower stalk within the same growing season. If it germinated in the fall, the plant will overwinter.

As winter ends and spring arrives, the root and corm use their stored energy to produce a new basal rosette of leaves. This new set will not be as grand as those from the previous autumn, perhaps only about fifteen inches long as opposed to twenty in great conditions and as small as six inches in poor conditions.

STEM: As the days lengthen and temperatures warm, a stem emerges. That stem grows quickly, producing three types of leaves. At the base are the larger, deeply lobed leaves—so deeply lobed that they appear to be compound leaves with leaflets. Farther up the stem are unlobed irregular leaves. Near the top are teardrop-shaped leaves.

All three of these leaf types clasp the stem where they are attached; that is, they wrap around the stem, or embrace the stem. That embracing part has the additional feature of being shaped like earlobes.

The stem itself is round and covered with a fine, almost imperceptible powder that can be rubbed off. New stems (branches) can form anywhere a leaf is attached.

Field mustard plants can vary in color from a pale cyan-green to a dark green.

As with the first-year plants, if there is a lot of competition or if the ground dries up, wild mustard's growth will be

Stalk development. Shown here is the upper 15 inches of a plant that is about 20 inches tall. This plant is growing in good soil conditions. It's too young to have formed the upper teardrop-shaped leaves.

(left) The top 8 inches of a young, but rapidly growing, 30-inch-tall stem. Teardrop-shaped leaves only grow near the top of the stem. The closer to the top of the plant, the more pointed the teardrop-shaped leaves are. Flower buds top this stem.

(right) Three kinds of leaves on adult field mustard plants: (left to right) large bottom leaves, unlobed leaves midway up the stem, and smaller, upper teardrop-shaped leaves. All of these leaf types wrap around (clasp) the stem.

stunted. This second-year plant can grow anywhere from only a foot to six feet tall, depending on soil conditions.

If field mustard is growing in dense undergrowth with competition from other plants, the leaves at ground level will deteriorate and wither away, leaving only stem leaves. In the open, those basal leaves will last well into flowering.

BUDS AND FLOWERS: Field mustard buds form in clusters at the tip of each stem. As new baby buds continue to form at the tip (the center of the cluster), older enlarging buds get pushed to the side. By the time the buds blossom into flowers, they are at the edge of the cluster of buds. As the stem elongates to form new buds, the flowers move down the stem. As the flowers are fertilized, the petals fall away, allowing the seedpod to form, enlarge, and elongate. Once a plant starts flowering, the better the growing conditions, the more it branches. Every branch will produce a new flower cluster at its tip.

Adult field mustard in April. The upper older stems have blossoming flowers. Younger stem branches have still-developing flower buds at their tips.

Field mustard flower cluster with unopened buds at the center.

A flowering stem with pod development. As the stem continues to grow from the tip and elongate, seed pods (called siliques) mature down the stem. These stems can get very long, typically supporting 20 to over 100 pods.

Field mustard flowers, like other mustard family flowers, have four petals, four sepals, and six stamens (pollen-holding structures). Four of those six stamens are tall and two are short. The flowers on this particular mustard are yellow.

The newly opened flowers of field mustard reach up and over the newest (center) buds. This becomes more obvious as the flowering stems elongate. After a while, new buds become hidden under overtopping flowers. This is one feature that makes field mustard distinguishable from canola (*Brassica napus*). Canola flowers do not overtop their buds but grow to the sides. *Brassica rapa* and *Brassica napus* are easily confused. The good thing is that both are used as food in similar ways.

(above) Reddish-brown seeds of field mustard. Each of these seeds is about 1½mm in diameter.

Mature seed pods are brown. Each holds 36 to 46 seeds. A papery membrane holds the seeds in the center of the pod.

Harvesting Field Mustard

All harvested greens and stems of field mustard dry out very quickly. So before you do any collecting, make sure you have the tools to make and keep the greens moist until you use them. In fact, the best thing you can do is crisp them right away; that is, immerse the greens in a tub of very cold water as soon as you pick them. Let them absorb the water until they are as firm as they can get. Drain well, wrap them in a paper towel, place all that in a plastic bag, and put it in your fridge. Short of that, the spray-mist technique works well. Keep your take out of the sun.

SPROUTS: If you have access to thousands of sprouts in newly disturbed soil, you can wait till they are a perfect size, then harvest the tops with scissors for use as baby greens. This means you are taking the whole aboveground plant when it is young enough to fit in your mouth. It may have anywhere from two to four leaves. You pinch it somewhere along the stem to extract it. This, of course, kills the remaining plant (lower stem and root). Typically this is okay because you are thinning the population. You leave the remaining sprouts to grow and produce plants that can be harvested later.

LEAVES: From the basal rosette to the adult flowering plant, field mustard is continually producing leaves. Any leaf on this plant that looks beautiful enough to display in the produce section of your supermarket is good to use.

GROWING TIPS: Any growth tip will be tender enough for eating. On healthy plants, that includes the top four to six inches of leafy stem, new branches, and bud tips. You can go as far down the stem as will easily snap free. If you are pulling and/or tugging, and there is no clean "snap," then you've gone too far down the stem. And while growing tips are not as fragile as the leaves, it is still important to keep these parts moist before using. On occasion, the stem will snap but will still be fibrous when you cook it, so experiment a little to get the hang of it.

Growing tips of field mustard in bud. Of the 12 inches of plant stem here, only the top 4 to 6 inches will be tender enough to use. All you have to discard here is the fibrous lower 6 to 8 inches of that stem. All of the leaves coming off the stem are tender and delicious.

FLOWER CLUSTERS: These are great for food and are a wonderful garnish for salads and dinner plates. You can take part of the stem below the clusters, but once these plants are in flower, the stem begins to toughen up. So instead of harvesting the flowers with four inches of stem, you might be able to take one or two inches. Flowers do not take so well to submerging in water, so freshen them by spray-misting.

Young flower stems produce great-tasting flower heads. Once the flower stems are really long with lots of seedpods, the flower clusters lose some flavor and develop a paperiness, and their bases get tougher. So, younger flower clusters with buds still on them are the best.

SEED PODS: Only the very upper immature seedpods are tender enough to use as food. The older ones get tough and stringy. I use the few immature pods that come along for the ride with the flower clusters but usually not more than that.

ROOTS: While many biennials typically have tender first-year roots, I do not remember ever doing much with field mustard root. So I leave it to you to make some new discoveries here. By the time the stalk has begun to form, the root becomes too tough for any practical use.

SEEDS: The best way I've found to harvest seeds is to take the whole pod-bearing stems indoors where they can continue to mature in controlled conditions. Mustard seedpods mature progressively from the bottom of a stem to the top. Maturing pods are tan in color, and immature ones are still green. They are not all ripe at the same time.

Take whole stems that are already dropping seeds from their lowest pods. If the lowest pods are dropping seeds, this means that many more pods just above those are almost mature enough to drop their seeds. If you take stems that are too green or young (not dropping any seeds), the pods on it will not be able to mature, and you will not get many seeds.

Lay the stems directly on a clean old bedsheet in a dry, well-ventilated location. As the stems dry, seeds will

When field mustard growth is lush, the seedpods weigh down the stalks and arch over. The browning pods here are mature enough for their stems to be harvested for seed collection. The still-green pod-laden stems are too immature to collect.

continue to mature inside the pods. Once the stems are totally dry, compress them into a tight bundle and wrap them in the sheet they were resting upon. Use fasteners to tightly and securely seal the sheet closed. Use your weight to crush the sheet-enclosed stems. Take out your frustrations: dance on them, hit them with your broom, mash them to smithereens. This causes the pods to break open and release the seeds inside the sheet casing.

Once the pods are sufficiently smashed, open the sheet and pour out the seeds. There will be plenty of chaff and pod remains mixed with the seeds. To get rid of the large debris, pour the seeds through a sieve with holes just big enough for the seeds to pass through. To get rid of the dirt and small particles, pour the seeds into a sieve with holes smaller than the seeds. Pour the seeds into a big bowl and shake it until the seeds settle to the bottom, allowing you to physically pick off or blow away much of the remaining chaff. To finish clearing the chaff from the seeds, winnow the rest.

Winnowing is the process of using the movement of air to blow away the light chaff and debris while the heavy seeds drop down into a collection container. On a day with consistent wind speed, you can throw the mixed material up into the air from a big bowl with the intent of catching the seeds. As you do so, the chaff gets blown away in the wind. Another option is to pour the seeds and chaff from one container into another—varying the drop distance so that most of the chaff gets blown away. To control wind speed in the drop method, you can use an electric fan. All of these methods take practice and a mild, controlled wind speed.

Processing Field Mustard

Young first-year leaves and upper stem leaves are small and tender enough to put in a salad as is. Mid-level leaves need to be chopped or torn into bite-size pieces. Large basal leaves have a main vein and leaf stem that are too fibrous to use as is. To remove them, pluck the lobes off the central vein into bite-size pieces, slice out the vein, or squeegee (pull and strip) the blade from the vein. Discard the veins or juice them. This is really no different from what one would do with kale or collard greens bought from the store. Kale and collards are also in the mustard family.

Cooking and Serving Field Mustard

Fresh greens

Field mustard is the source of one of my favorite flavors. I love adding the leaves to salads and sandwiches as well as to cold vegetable and fruit dishes. Remember that anywhere you are adding mustard greens, you are adding mild pepperiness and pungency, so here are some general tips to better eating:

Generally make mustard greens only about a third to a fourth of the mass of a salad. You want to add character, not overpower the salad. Since everyone is different, you may find yourself adding more or less than this over time. My culinary preference is to make bite-size pieces. Don't grab a whole large leaf on a fork unless you've got some really

Wild Greens Salad. Includes field mustard baby greens, green amaranth leaves (*Amaranthus retroflexus*), wood sorrel, borage leaves (*Borago officinalis*), wild sweet pea flowers (*Lathyrus latifolius*), and marsh mallow flowers (*Althaea officinalis*). Absolutely delicious. Cut pieces of the leaves from older plants would work just as well as the baby greens; they would just have more of a pungent bite.

mild greens or you really love the pungency. The exception to this is the baby greens and leaves from the really young plants, which are always mild and bite-size.

Sandwiches heavy with other ingredients, particularly meat, cheese, and sauces, will welcome mustard greens. Use the mustard in place of lettuce.

Cooked greens

The pungency in field mustard can sometimes get overpowering if that is all you are eating. This is true of both fresh greens and cooked greens. In fact, when you cook greens, you concentrate them physically, concentrating the pungent and sometimes acrid flavor.

BOILED: If you just want fine-tasting, good-for-you, regular cooked greens, then use the boiling method. Preheat a pot of boiling water. To save energy, keep the top on while bringing the water to a boil. Use enough water so that the greens can freely move around—you do not want them to be tightly packed in the pot. Once the greens are added, boil with the top off. The acrid flavor that sometimes haunts mustard when cooked will partially escape into the air. Fresh leaves should be boiled for two to six minutes. This range takes into account that each plant may have different amounts of acridness. Once done, drain and serve as is, or add salt and a little olive oil, or use your favorite dressing. You can add these cooked greens anywhere you would use cooked spinach.

You can boil the buds, their stems, or the flower clusters in the same way. Sometimes the flowers take a minute or two more than the leaves; sometimes they don't. The key is to taste the greens or flowers or buds as you go along. To make them delicious, do not boil any of these foods any longer than you have to. If they are good in one minute, take them out of the water. If you want them to stop cooking, dunk them in cold water for later use or to serve them cold. The cooking water of any of these boiling techniques works fine as a soup base.

STIR-FRIED: If you are going to cook fresh greens in stir-fries or stews, gauge carefully how much you use. Start conservatively and add more or less as you develop your recipes and your taste for mustard. Try mustard green recipes you find in your cookbooks.

If you like strong greens, try stir-frying them. They will retain some pungency and a little acridness, but the hot oil you cook them in will both temper the acridness and add some character to the greens. You might enjoy eating them like this or using them as an ingredient in an omelette or a stir-fry. Mustard greens cooked this way might be too strong for some unless used as a minor ingredient in a larger dish.

If you want milder mustard greens in a stir-fry, boil them first for a few minutes before adding them. After boiling, drain and dry them on a towel or they will spatter when placed in the hot oil.

STEAMED: I have never enjoyed any mustard parts steamed. Steaming just retains and concentrates too much of the acridness. Due to the flavor, I find the steamed greens difficult to work with. But don't give up on my account. Experiment on your own. You might love them steamed.

Mustard flower bud stems, ready for eating. These stem tips were boiled for about three minutes, drizzled with olive oil and balsamic vinegar, seasoned with salt and pepper, and garnished with sautéed mushrooms and a mustard flower cluster.

Field mustard seeds

Mustard seeds, in general, are used as a spice, for pickling, to make mustard (the condiment), and for much more. Commercially, seeds mostly from black (*Brassica nigra*), brown (*Brassica juncea*), and white (*Brassica hirta*) mustard plants have a long history of use and well-documented recipes for making the condiment we know as mustard. Commercially, mustard seeds are mixed in different proportions to create certain unique mustard flavors. Search the Internet or any number of old cookbooks, and you will find recipes for mixing ground mustard seeds with vinegar and other ingredients to make a variety of condiments. In fact, there are hundreds of recipes. Field mustard seed is typically not an ingredient in those recipes but is certainly worthy of kitchen experimentation.

One fun option is to put the seeds into a clean pepper mill and grind them into foods of your liking. Mustard seeds are about a sixth the size of peppercorns, so if you do this, make sure the grinder can take the smaller seeds.

Mustards and Mustard Sauces

Here are a few mustard recipes I found with little effort. If they are too runny for your liking, you can add a thickener like flour, tapioca, or cornstarch. If they are too pasty, you can add a mixture of 50 percent water and 50 percent white wine vinegar until it meets your needs. Add these dry or liquid ingredients in tiny amounts—slowly and cautiously. Additions may not be necessary, as some recipes will thicken as they set, and others will thicken when refrigerated. Some sauces work better for certain uses because they flow more easily than the mustard paste you are used to. All of these preparations should be refrigerated.

Be aware that field mustard seed produces *hot* mustard, so a little goes a long way. Some may want to dilute it with regular yellow mustard or mayonnaise, or to soften its kick with sweetener. Be aware that trying these prepared mustards in a sandwich or somewhere else that mustard is appropriate is a whole different experience from tasting these *strong* condiments directly. If you want a yellower color, add turmeric.

Euell Gibbons' Prepared Mustard

From his book *Stalking the Wild Asparagus.*

"Put some flour in a pan and toast it in the oven, stirring occasionally until it is evenly browned. . . . Mix this browned flour, half and half, with ground mustard and moisten with a mixture of half vinegar and half water until it is the right consistency . . . vary the amounts of mustard and flour to suit your taste."

Simple Prepared Mustard

Adapted from various sources.

INGREDIENTS:

1 cup field mustard seeds

⅓ cup water

⅓ cup white vinegar

⅓ cup brown sugar (optional)

DIRECTIONS:

Grind mustard seeds in a well-cleaned coffee grinder or a compact small-capacity food processor. Pour into a bowl and add water. Let stand for 15 minutes so the enzymes in the mustard can develop their flavors. Then stir in the wine vinegar and brown sugar (omitting the sugar will make the mustard hotter).

Fancy Mustard Sauce

Adapted from Chef Michael Smith's Homemade Mustard Recipe.

INGREDIENTS:

¾ cup field mustard seeds

½ cup white wine vinegar

½ cup extra virgin olive oil

½ cup chardonnay

1 tablespoon ground turmeric

Juice and zest of two lemons

Salt and pepper, to taste

DIRECTIONS:

Use a coffee grinder to grind the seeds until they resemble coarse meal. Pour the meal and remaining ingredients into a food processor and blend until mixture is smooth. Use salt and pepper as desired. Let this age a few days; it will become smoother and less sharp to the tongue.

Mango Mustard Seed Sauce

Adapted from *The 1997 Joy of Cooking*. This sauce is designed to go with grilled chicken or fish.

INGREDIENTS:

- 1½ tablespoons field mustard seeds
- 2 ripe mangos, peeled and cut into small cubes
- 1 medium ripe banana, chopped
- 2 tablespoons peeled and finely minced fresh ginger
- 1 teaspoon finely minced garlic
- ½ teaspoon curry powder
- ½ cup grapefruit juice
- 2 teaspoons sherry vinegar
- 1½ teaspoons hot chili oil
- 1 teaspoon honey, or to taste
- Salt and ground black pepper, to taste

DIRECTIONS:

Place mustard seeds in a small dry skillet over medium heat and toast until they just begin to pop. Remove from heat and combine with remaining ingredients in a blender; process briefly to produce a smooth sauce. Serve immediately, or cover and store in the refrigerator for up to 3 days.

Field mustard flower bud
clusters, boiled and served
as a side dish to a stir-fry
and garnished with a fresh
mustard flower cluster.

Chapter 13

FAMILY: Brassicaceae
SPECIES: *Barbarea vulgaris*

Wintercress

A versatile spring succulent

Several wintercress plants in basal rosettes just prior to bolting. It's a cold, hardy, rubbery-looking plant that produces greens throughout the spring and flowers soon after field mustard.

Estimated Range

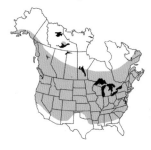

Official Species Name:
- *Barbarea vulgaris* Ait. f.

Synonyms (Historical Names):
- *Barbarea arcuata* (Opiz ex J.& K. Presl) Reichenb.
- *Barbarea stricta* auct. non Andrz.
- *Campe barbarea* (L.) W. Wight ex Piper
- *Campe stricta* auct. non (Andrz.) W. Wight ex Piper

Common Names:
- Wintercress
- Yellow rocket
- Garden yellow rocket
- Bittercress
- Creasy greens

An herbaceous weed naturalized from southern Europe, wintercress is widespread and abundant in North America, primarily where humans have invaded and where soil has been disturbed.

continued

WINTERCRESS

The first time I saw wintercress, I was on a research farm on the Michigan State University campus. It was late winter, patches of melting snow were still around, and I was walking through a pasture that was quite muddy from lots of farm animal traffic. One green plant was growing all over the place. The recent freezes had not killed it; the leaves had overwintered. In Michigan, the winters get pretty cold—down to 15 degrees below zero on occasion. Yet here was this plant—not looking great, but alive. I had found my first wintercress.

So wintercress is a good name. It is a cress (a member of the mustard family), and it survives the winters. Like other overwintering plants, it prepares for freezing temperatures by decreasing the amount of water it retains, producing alcohols and sugars, and undergoing other changes. The added chemistry allows wintercress to get super cold without forming the ice crystals that would ordinarily destroy plant cells. It does not grow during the harsh parts of the winter; it mostly sits there, trying not to die. So as long as the frozen-looking greens are not damaged physically, the plant survives to photosynthesize (provide food for the rest of the plant) when temperatures rise in the late winter or early spring. Overwintering leaves like this are not worthy of eating. Let these old tattered leaves remain for the local deer and rabbit populations.

Wintercress can be a biennial or a short-lived perennial. If the seeds sprout in the fall, the plant gets its start, overwinters, and produces flowers the next spring—making it a biennial (sometimes this is called a winter annual). No matter when it gets its start, if conditions are right, wintercress can live for three years—making it a short-lived perennial. Favorable conditions are shade, good soil, and reasonable moisture throughout the year.

The first time you see it, it might be growing in a moist field or along a sidewalk, often as a colony of flowering plants. If it is off in a field, then all you'll see is a cluster of yellow flowers barely overtopping all the surrounding green plants. Wintercress is only about a half to a third the height of field mustard, given the same growing conditions.

There has not been a lot of research on the nutritional value of wintercress. We know it is very high in vitamin C, has reasonable amounts of beta-carotene, and contains the phytochemical glucosinolate. The seeds have been analyzed for macronutrients. When the moisture has been removed, the seeds are 40 percent fiber, 34 percent fat, 19 percent protein, and 7 percent ash. There is virtually no starch in wintercress seed. Of the total fat in the seeds, 28 percent is erucic acid, 23 percent is oleic acid, 21 percent is linoleic acid, and 10 percent is linolenic acid. (Andersson, 1999.)

As I stated in the introduction to this section, the seeds of any mustard plant will contain erucic acid. Eating them occasionally as a wild food treat in mustard preparations or as a spice in meals in the context of a diverse and healthy diet is likely to make you healthier than if you did not. But do not overdo it.

Healthy flowering wintercress plants in great growing conditions.

Wintercress seedling. The cotyledons are the smallest leaves at the mid-upper and mid-lower left of the photograph. The three larger leaves are the first true leaves. These seedlings can be mistaken for bitter cress (*Cardamine oligosperma*), another edible mustard.

Young wintercress growing in good moist shady conditions. This plant is in my garden, where it gets watered regularly. The leaves here are about 7 inches long from center to tip. Plants in the wild are smaller and struggle in the warm months because I am not pampering them. New leaves emerge from the center and then recline to the side as newer leaves replace them.

I believe watercress to be a good food. If you search the Internet, however, you will find the following warning: "Wintercress could cause kidney malfunction." The first source I could find to state this was Foster and Duke's *A Field Guide to Medicinal Plants* (Houghton Mifflin Co., 1990), and then repeated in Dr. James Duke's *Handbook of Edible Weeds* (CRC press, 1992). Unfortunately, neither book offered the original source of the warning. After searching the literature and e-mailing Dr. Duke (personal communication, January 13, 2006), I have been unable to substantiate this kidney problem. I have not found any recorded incidents of humans being harmed by eating wintercress. Both Dr. Duke and I eat wintercress.

A good testament to the value of wintercress is that it was eaten by the Greeks, Italians, Russians, many people in the southeastern United States, and probably additional southern European cultures. Even my mom knew this plant as "creasy greens" from her father picking them in Ohio. Creasy greens more commonly refers to upland cress (*Barbarea verna*), an edible plant similarly used throughout the southeastern United States (see page 225).

Wintercress greens are a great springtime food. Let's get to know it a little better.

Knowing Wintercress

Wintercress seeds germinate any time the conditions are right: regular moisture, disturbed soil or seeds near or at the surface, longer days, and the beginning of warmer temperatures. The seeds may also have to overwinter once before they have the capability to germinate.

Wintercress is very adaptive and quite hardy. It can grow in almost any kind of ground, from rich topsoil to gravel to sand; it can grow in open sun or deep shade; and it thrives in temperatures anywhere from 35 to 70 degrees F. With enough moisture, it grows modestly in higher temperatures of summer. The seeds can survive in the ground for years, waiting for the right conditions.

Wintercress can take over areas, outcompeting other plants, due to high seed production, good winter survival (giving it a head start on competitors), strong growth, development of a sturdy taproot, and adaptation to whatever soil it is growing in.

All leaves of the first-year plant are relatively the same shape. They have a terminal or end lobe that is larger than all the other lobes. Down the leaf stem are typically two to four pairs of smaller lobes. All these leaves originate from a short stem above the root and radiate outward. This

Basal leaves displayed. These are the ones growing closest to the ground. All the leaves from a first-year wintercress plant look like this and radiate out from the root at ground level. The second-year plant that has grown a stalk has leaves that change shape as they go up the stem. At the base of the second-year plant, the leaves still have this shape.

(left) Bolted wintercress showing bud clusters spreading out prior to flowering. This plant was never watered, and it is growing in hard soil. So its growth and end size are less than you would see from pampered garden plants—less leaves, less dense growth, fewer stems.

(right) Younger, tightly clustered buds and upper stems. The buds are shown prior to spreading out.

arrangement is called a *basal rosette*. Many of the plants in this book, including dandelions, field mustard, and cat's ear, have a basal rosette stage.

Wintercress has two growing periods when it thrives— spring and autumn. The cooler temperatures and the moisture of these two seasons support better growth. It grows slowly in summer and just survives in winter.

In most of North America, where winters are severe, wintercress stops growing and goes into a hibernation mode. In temperate areas like the Pacific Northwest and the Deep South, it will continue to grow very slowly throughout the winter. If you attempt to harvest some of its leaves in the winter, no new leaves grow back to replace them until spring.

As spring arrives, wintercress comes back to life, forming thick leafy growth particularly wherever it has no real competition. When it is crowded with grass or other densely rooted plants, growth will be less—making the plant smaller.

Wintercress bolts when the days get longer and temperatures begin to reach into the 50s F. At first, the basal rosette starts to look a little different, sort of like there are green starbursts emanating from the center of the basal leaves. The photograph on page 217 shows this stage clearly.

The plants begin to send up one or more stems from each root. The more rigorous the first year's growth, the larger the root, the greater the number of stems the plant produces, and the more luxuriant the growth.

Bolting is a quick process. Flower buds begin forming while the stems are still short. They are found at the tip of each stem and look like miniature broccoli heads. At first, the buds are tightly clustered; then, as the stem elongates further, the buds begin separating into several smaller clusters.

At this point, the plant's full diversity of leaf shapes appear. All the leaves, regardless of shape, clasp the stem; that is, they wrap around the stem. At the base of the second-year plant are the same-shaped leaves we've seen on the first-year plants. As you follow the stem upward, the lobes on the sides of the leaves become narrower, and the terminal lobe takes on an interesting arrowhead-like design.

A winter cress stem is ridged along its length. Sometimes called eight-sided (a poor description), the ridges are

(left) The mid stem showing leaves that are changing from bottom to top. Lower leaves look more like the basal leaves. Top leaves look more like the unlobed upper leaves. The bases of all these leaves clasp the stem.

(right) Wintercress stems are ridged along their length. Leaves and branches have been removed from these stems to reveal the ridges.

(above) Bolted wintercress showing open flowers. These plants were never watered and are growing in hard soil, so they are smaller and less lush than they might be. They had to compete with grass, some of which I pulled to get this view. Grass roots compete with wintercress for both water and nutrients.

(above right) The top of an adult wintercress plant. Here are terminal buds, flowers, and the tiny beginnings of seedpods down the stem where the first flowers used to be.

Wintercress flower heads and their bud clusters. Some of the older side buds have blossomed into flowers. Like all other mustard family plants, wintercress has four petals and six stamens—four long and two short.

(left) Upland cress (*Barbarea verna*)—a close relative to wintercress. This view shows the extra numbers of lobes that leaves have for this species. (Printed with permission from "A Photo Flora": www.aphotofauna.com.)

(right) Seedpods growing along the lower flower stem. The seedpods are long, thin, and angled up and outward. They have a short thin neck (peduncle) and a small beak at their tip. The beak is nothing more than a small area that is not fattened by seeds.

angular in shape. The tip of each major ridge supports a leaf and a branch of the stem.

Flowers begin blossoming sometime in April or May, depending on where you are in North America. They open to the side of the newly formed central buds. As the stems elongate, buds continue to form at the tips, and flowers spread down that stem. At this point, wintercress becomes visible from a distance. Patches of it are seen here and there. Whenever you find a field with patches of yellow flowers, it is likely a mustard family plant of some sort. You should investigate to see if you can determine which one it is.

Upland cress (*Barbarea verna*) is a less-common relative of wintercress. It grows throughout eastern North America, particularly in the Southeast and along the Pacific coast, west of the coastal mountain range. Note the longer, more lobed leaves. It is purported to have the same uses as wintercress. I do not have any direct experience or knowledge about it. It is shown here for comparison.

The flower stalks, which become pod stalks, can get very long, producing thousands of seeds. The pods transform from green to brown as they mature. When dry, they break open, releasing seeds within a few feet of the original plant.

Wintercress seeds and open pods in hand. This photo shows about a 1¼-inch-wide section of my hand.

Harvesting Wintercress

LEAVES: The leaves of wintercress can be gathered anytime they look fresh and clean. First-year or second-year plant leaves are good. The earliest spring leaves are only slightly less bitter than the leaves at any other time of the year, so getting them earlier is no great benefit.

Since there is a thickness to wintercress leaves, they do not tend to dry out as easily as field mustard leaves. But, whenever possible, you should always spray-mist them to keep them fresh. Due to the smaller leaf size, gathering from this plant can be a little more time-consuming than collecting field mustard. If you have lush growth, gathering is easy and you'll get what you need in no time.

BUD CLUSTERS: To gather the broccoli-like buds, snap the stem about an inch or two below the buds. Wintercress bud stems are fibrous almost as soon as they are formed, so only that still-growing upper inch or two will be tender enough to chew. If you are not going to use them right away, cut the stems longer and place them in water like you would do for flowers. Cover loosely with a plastic bag and place them in the fridge. They will keep fresh for several days. When ready to use, cut off and discard all but the upper inch or two of stem.

A collection of flower bud clusters. This mass of buds is from the tops of about 15 plants held together to resemble a large head of broccoli.

FLOWERS: The flowers are small, so the best way to collect them is to clip whole flower-laden stems. Put the stems in water, as you would ornamental flowers, until ready for use. Just before serving that wild salad garnished with wintercress flowers, pluck them from the stem, which is too fibrous to include with the flowers. If you just want the petals, place vases of these flowering stems over newspaper or plastic. As the flowers mature, their petals will drop. When enough have fallen onto your collecting surface, you can gather and use them for tea.

PODS: Only the young, newly formed pods are tender enough to eat. They are too small for me to enjoy. If you want them, either eat them off the plant or collect the stems, holding them as you would collect the flowers. Keep the stems alive in water. Pluck the pods free when you are ready to use them. The stem attached to any pod is too fibrous for use.

SEEDS: Trying to gather seeds directly from a mature plant is difficult. If you want the seeds, your goal is to remove the plant from its natural environment and continue the ripening process in a controlled situation. For directions, refer to the field mustard chapter and follow its seed-harvesting technique.

Cooking and Serving Wintercress

LEAVES, FRESH: Wintercress leaves are bitter and pungent in the raw form, and they can leave a strong bitter aftertaste. If you love bitter, enjoy them raw. I need to mix wintercress leaves with other foods in order to enjoy them. This allows the bitterness to add character to what I'm eating rather than overpowering the dish. I love adding the leaves to salads and sandwiches as well as cold vegetable and fruit dishes. Remember that anywhere you are adding wintercress greens, you are adding bitterness and pungency. Here are some general tips to enjoy its flavors:

Wintercress Greens. Boiled and served with a little olive oil and a squeeze of lemon, and topped with columbine flower petals (*Aquilegia chrysantha*).

Make wintercress greens only about a fourth to a fifth of the mass of a salad. Always make bite-size pieces to avoid grabbing a large whole leaf on a fork unless you really love the bitterness.

Sandwiches heavy with other ingredients, particularly meat, cheese, and sauces, will welcome wintercress greens just as they are, in place of lettuce. Those other ingredients will mute the bitterness. You are the best judge about just how much is enough.

LEAVES, COOKED: There are thousands of bitter substances in foods. Humans have thousands of different taste buds to sense different bitters. To me, the bitters in raw wintercress are particularly strong. If you want to reduce that bitterness and eat wintercress like a regular vegetable, it's time to grab a pot. Boiling will greatly expand your ability to eat more wintercress in different ways.

In my experience, the bitterness in wintercress evaporates when heat is applied, and the best medium to make that happen is through boiling without a lid so the bitterness can escape into the air. The underlying non-bitter flavors are superb. After just a few minutes of boiling, wintercress goes from a bitter green to a foundational green that can be used anywhere spinach is eaten.

To make boiled wintercress, preheat a pot of water to a rapid boil (with the lid on to conserve energy). Remove the lid and add chopped wintercress leaves. There should be enough water for the greens to move about freely while they are boiling. After three minutes, taste a sample. If it is to your liking, remove the greens, drain, and use immediately; or immerse in cold water to stop the cooking process. If still bitter after sampling, continue boiling the greens until they meet your taste needs. I suggest boiling them as little as necessary. Save the cooking broth for soup stock.

Steaming does not always remove all the bitterness. This is probably because the pot lid, necessary for steaming, prevents some of the bitter from escaping. Steaming is also not as successful as boiling because there is no agitation from the water to massage out all the bitter. After about five minutes of steaming, the greens retain some bitterness. When wintercress is dressed or added to other foods, that bitterness becomes an interesting character of the greens. If you are still not a fan, then just use the boiling method.

Sautéing in oil removes even less of the bitterness. But the oil blended with the greens is interesting and enjoyable, particularly if lots of herbs and seasonings are added. Again, if you are bitter-intolerant, you might want to stick to boiling.

BUDS, FRESH: The buds are just as bitter as the leaves. Since they are more three-dimensional than the leaves, you will get big mouthfuls of bitterness with every bud cluster you bite into unless you chop them up. So, raw buds are for the creative food preparer who knows how to use protein, fat, and carbohydrate foods to mask the bitterness. For people who love this kind of bitter or who have no bitter taste buds, use the fresh wintercress buds any way you want.

BUDS, COOKED: Cook the buds as you would the leaves. But because the bud clusters are three-dimensional, they will be more bitter than the leaves when steamed or sautéed—everything else being equal.

FLOWERS, FRESH: Whole flowers are mildly bitter, much less bitter than the greens or buds. That bitterness goes unnoticed if those flowers are used as a garnish to add color to a salad or dinner plate.

The flower petals can be used to make a tea. The petals by themselves are sweet in flavor. Place a teaspoon of dried petals in a tea bag and steep in previously boiled water until the flavor has emerged. Drink as is or add your favorite sweetener.

Wintercress for dinner. Bud clusters are boiled for three minutes, presented carefully on a plate, and garnished with thin carrot slices. Serve with your favorite sauce.

SEEDS: Like other mustard plants, the seeds might be ground to season foods or to make condiments.

Chapter 14

FAMILY: Brassicaceae
SPECIES: *Alliaria petiolata*

Garlic Mustard

A nutritious wild green—eat it to control its spread.

Young garlic mustard plants flourishing in the spring before stalk development becomes obvious.

GARLIC MUSTARD

Estimated Range

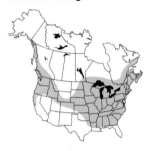

Official Species Name:
- *Alliaria petiolata* (Bieb.) Cavara & Grande

Synonyms (Historical Names):
- *Alliaria alliaria* (L.) Britt.
- *Alliaria officinalis* Andrz. ex Bieb.
- *Erysimum alliaria* L.
- *Sisymbrium alliaria* (L.) Scop.

Common Names:
- Garlic Mustard
- Hedge Garlic
- Jack-by-the-Hedge
- Sauce Alone

An herbaceous weed naturalized throughout Europe, garlic mustard is widespread and abundant in North America, primarily where humans have invaded, and is spreading fast. It loves partially shaded

continued

This is a mustard family plant with the smell of garlic, so garlic mustard is a good name. The genus *Alliaria* is a reference to the genus *Allium*, which contains the true garlics and onions. *Petiolata* refers to the long leaf stem. A leaf stem to botanists is known as a petiole.

Garlic mustard is beloved by many rural people in Europe, where it has natural predators that keep its populations in check. It is considered a noxious weed in North America. A search for garlic mustard on the Internet brings up a noxious weed alert and informational piece from nearly every state and province. Why is this weedy vegetable such a problem here? The big answer is that we are not eating enough of it. If we ate more of this plant, its spread would be severely limited.

But what makes this one special? It has phytochemical weapons. Here's the scoop: Garlic mustard, like any other weed, spreads by seeds. Unlike dandelion with its paratroopers (seeds floating around on parachute-like fluff, which can travel long distances), garlic mustard seeds typically fall within a few feet of a plant. On its own, it moves very slowly. With the help of passing animals and humans, it hitchhikes a little farther each season—on shoes, animal fur and paws, car tires along roadsides, and bicycles.

In their first year, garlic mustard plants often go unnoticed. They are small with inconspicuous leaves, mixed among the native plants. It can look like violet leaves, wild ginger leaves, or a number of other plants. The second year, the plant sends up a flower stalk that drops thousands of seeds. Thousands and thousands of seeds are spread along a general area after a few years. Animal traffic expands the spread.

This biennial sounds pretty normal, but there is a point at which these plants reach a critical mass in numbers. They outcompete all the native plants by using a diabolical strategy: Their roots exude chemicals that kill beneficial mycorrhiza in the soil (underground fungi that are good for many native plants) and inhibit other plants from germinating. The result is whole areas being overrun with garlic mustard plants.

This is particularly bad for forests that contain native plants. Garlic mustard can take over the forest floor—good if you like to eat garlic mustard; bad if you like mushrooms and the great natural diversity of a native forest. So my priority when foraging for garlic mustard is to check my local native forests first. Upon finding the plants, I pull them up by the roots. The forest wins, and I win by gaining some great greens.

In Maryland, they have taken this harvesting to a new level. The Patapsco Valley State Park, which has a huge garlic mustard problem, sponsors an annual Garlic Mustard Challenge. This is a fair they put on with live music, nature displays, storytelling, plant hikes, a garlic mustard pull, and a garlic mustard cooking contest. The contest is for cooks of all ages: kids, amateurs, and professionals. This kind of event only works well if there is enough garlic mustard around for all the cooks to use. When the park has succeeded in eradicating its garlic mustard, the park will have to retire the event.

areas, particularly soft forest floors, roadsides shaded by trees and shrubs, floodplains, shading fences, and trail sides. It will even grow in open fields.

Edible Parts:
- Growing tips of leafy stems
- Leaves
- Buds
- Flowers
- Seeds

Garlic mustard invading a natural area. On the well-shaded edge of this area, these garlic mustard plants slowly spread into the woods. They are 12 to 36 inches tall, in flower, and not yet producing seed pods.

Young garlic mustard growing in a large open field. This is only one part of a 2,000-square-foot area of garlic mustard in this field with full sun.

Garlic mustard is good for you

Garlic mustard is one of the most nutritious leafy greens ever analyzed. In fact, of all the leafy greens in my two nutrient charts, garlic mustard finds itself at the top of the list for about a third of all the nutrients listed. There are no greens higher in fiber, beta-carotene, vitamin C, vitamin E, and zinc. Just to hammer in the point—garlic mustard beats spinach, broccoli leaves, collards, turnip greens, kale, and domesticated mustard for all these nutrients, and it is very high in omega-3 fatty acids, calcium, iron, and manganese.

And what about phytochemicals? Many plant chemicals that were originally considered toxins are now classified as good for you when found in the amounts in plants we eat. Phytates and selenium are good examples. Both were historically thought to be bad for you. Selenium was considered a toxin and phytates were considered anti-nutrients. Now selenium is considered a nutrient, and phytates are being investigated for potential health benefits. Too much selenium and you get poisoned. Too much phytates and you will start having mineral deficiencies. Eat just enough of both of these and you may benefit from them.

Many of the phytochemicals discovered recently have roles in protecting plants from their enemies. Some plants use these chemicals to protect themselves against viruses, bacteria, and fungi. Some use plant-inhibiting chemicals to keep other plants from growing too near. Some have bitter, acrid, or astringent flavors to protect themselves from being eaten by herbivores.

Garlic mustard is bitter and pungent, with chemicals in it that work as natural herbicides. It is known to have isothiocyanates and glucosinolates like other mustards. It is clear that garlic mustard is filled with phytochemicals yet to be discovered. So, while much needs to be done, it is not unreasonable to assume that garlic mustard is really good for you on a variety of levels.

Knowing Garlic Mustard

In the early spring, before the daffodils have flowered, you will find garlic mustard leafing out from overwintering roots. Small roots produce smaller and fewer leaves. Larger roots produce more and larger leaves. All of them, small and large, begin flowering in April to early May. Around the same time, before the flowering plants can set seed, a new crop of seedlings emerges.

New sprout of garlic mustard, life-size. The cotyledons are to the left and right of the true leaves.

Let's cover garlic mustard from seed and follow it throughout its life. First, let me say that different authorities have labeled this plant an annual, biennial, and even a perennial. I have seen all three forms, but mostly annuals and biennials.

I've seen some biennials transform into perennials if they have a taproot and their tops keep getting clipped before they can go to seed. Areas that are mowed regularly could theoretically produce perennials for garlic mustard. But I am speculating here.

As garlic mustard grows from a seedling, it puts down an underground stem-like root. Aboveground, leaves are

Spring garlic mustard. One way to identify garlic mustard is by a unique underground stem-like structure that is twice-curved and leads to the root. The first curve is just below the leaves, bending the stem to almost a right angle; the second curve is less dramatic, occurring further down where it looks like the true root begins.

growing, but no stem develops in this first year. The leaves are rounded to kidney-shaped with rounded teeth along the margins. The leaf stems (petioles) are long, relative to the size of the leaf blades, and have hairs. Plants sprouting in April or May tend not to grow a noticeable stem, at least through the warm summer months.

The upper root is intriguing. While it may or may not be made up of root cells, it acts and looks like a stem. Its apparent purpose seems to be to get the true root deep enough to have access to water, even under dry surface conditions. This underground stem sports two characteristic bends. The first bend is at the base of the leaves; the second is just above the true root. At the base of the leaves, this stem curves to the side at almost a right angle, then slopes gently downward. It bends again just above the root. This uniquely shaped underground stem helps to clearly identify garlic mustard. A true botanical morphologist is needed to tell us if this part is really a modified stem or just looks like one.

As their roots grow, these plants produce more and larger leaves. The first leaves are about an inch wide or smaller; later leaves can be three or four inches wide. Those early leaves can be rounded, kidney-shaped, or almost arrowhead-shaped. After a period of study, garlic mustard leaves should be easy for you to identify. Until that time, you can always check for that garlic odor (crush the leaves and smell), or investigate the unique stem-like root.

As winter arrives, garlic mustard adjusts to cold and freezing conditions. Like other cold-tolerant plants, it loses some moisture and produces sugars and alcohols to survive freezing temperatures. In extreme cold, it loses all its leaves. In moderate climates like the Pacific Northwest, the leaves remain either static or slow-growing. I have harvested good healthy garlic mustard leaves in the middle of winter here in Oregon. I cannot imagine doing that in Michigan, where the winters are much more severe.

As winter ends and spring begins, overwintering garlic mustard comes back to life, producing new sets of leaves. Different patches of garlic mustard may have different-size leaves, suggesting that different microclimates promote germination at different times of the year. So some plants get a head start over others.

Almost as soon as garlic mustard leaves appear in the spring, the plant begins growing a stalk (stem). That stalk goes mostly unnoticed at first. Most people trying to gather garlic mustard before the stalk appears don't realize that the stalk is already there, mixed among the leaves and not obviously overtopping them.

As spring progresses and the days get longer, the high temperatures warm into the 50s and the stalk elongates suddenly. The larger the root, the faster the aboveground stem growth, the more a multitude of stems will arise from that root. Smaller roots will produce fewer stems, often only one. I've seen spring roots anywhere from an eighth inch to a full inch in diameter.

WINTER CHEMISTRY

The development of winter chemistry in garlic mustard is probably very complex—more complex than just reducing internal moisture and producing sugars and alcohols. The leaves won't taste sweet, and the alcohols won't give you a high. Instead, healthy thriving winter leaves will taste similar to the spring leaves but will not be as bitter or garlicky, and they will be slightly tougher.

A young second-year plant sporting a hairy stem. The stem is about 2 inches in length. Some stems (like this one) are hairy, some are not.

Vigorous early growth of overwintered garlic mustard. This more-developed plant was found at the same time as the last two photographs. Note the curves in the underground root stem and the branching root system. A couple of upper stems have begun to grow.

Several garlic mustard plants that have bolted. At about 18 inches tall, these plants have not quite reached their flowering stage. You can see the newly formed buds at the tips of each plant and the triangular leaves in their upper growth.

Garlic mustard producing different-shaped leaves. The leaves vary in shape, from rounded at the base to triangular at the top of the plant.

(right) Clusters of flower buds and white flowers at the tip of a stem.

Once the stem gets tall enough for buds and flowers to form at its tip, differences in leaf shape become apparent. Basal leaves (leaves growing from the stem at or near ground level) have a rounded heart or kidney shape. As you travel up the stem, the shape changes progressively to triangular at the top.

Flowers are in clusters at the tip of stems. Each flower has four white petals. And, like other mustards, they have the characteristically odd six-stamen configuration: four long and two short. Stamens are the male reproductive organs containing the pollen.

As the flowers are fertilized and the plant ages, the stem eventually stretches upward. Long pods develop on elongated stems where the flowers used to be. The pods go from green to brown as they age. The pod snaps open when the seeds are mature and the pods dry, ejecting the seeds around the base of the plant. Seeds must go through a freezing process before they will germinate, so all germinating seeds have lived through at least one winter.

(left) Opened garlic mustard pods and seeds in hand. Mature garlic mustard seedpods split open and release their seeds, which drop close to the base of the plant.

(right) Flower stems elongate, transforming into seedpod stems.

Harvesting Garlic Mustard

There are two considerations when gathering garlic mustard: first, the size of the leaves, and second, the quantity of the leaves available to you. Larger roots produce more and larger leaves.

Size variations of spring garlic mustard. While the climate in some areas of North America may produce a consistent size of leaves in the spring, mild winter climates like those found in the Pacific Northwest and the Southeast may allow more than one germination season. The plants on the left were young, as defined by small roots and small leaves. The plants on the right had clearly overwintered, had larger roots, and had produced more and larger leaves. Both containers contain intact plants, roots and all. They were spray-misted to keep them moist and carefully positioned to keep the dirt from hitting the leaves.

When I have a choice, I prefer to focus on more vigorously growing, larger-rooted, second-year plants because they produce more food for less work. See how much bigger the leaves are for the larger-rooted plants in the photo above.

The leaves really begin multiplying when the temperatures range from the mid-50s during the day to the mid-30s at night, just around the time that daffodils start blooming in your area. Perhaps this, or just before this, is the time to go harvesting.

If you are harvesting in a natural area that you are trying to save, take a digging stick or pick-shovel to help you and uproot every plant that you can. Take their roots and all, even if you only want the leaves. Try to be careful to keep the roots and their dirt separate from the leaves. This can be done with some success by stacking the plants in a container with the roots facing downward (see photo above). Gathering them when the ground is somewhat dry will make this job less messy because much of the dirt will fall away and not stick to the leaves.

If you only have a few healthy plants in an old field where you want to continue producing leaves, then do not uproot them. Instead, use scissors to harvest the leaves. Pull all the leaves upward and, with one snip, cut the cluster of leaf stems. Place the leaves in a plastic bag, spray-mist, and take the harvest home. The lower-leaf stem stubs and the root system remain undisturbed in the ground. The larger the root system, the more likely the plants will survive to produce more leaves. Return regularly to harvest the returning leaves. If this is a safe place to let them grow, as in your garden, let them go to seed. If it is a sensitive area that you want to protect, uproot them after several harvests before they can go to seed. Never, never let them go to seed where you do not want them spreading!

WARNING: Throwing the discard roots into the compost might be a mistake. The roots can often regrow into new plants and spread uncontrollably. Unless you are a great composter who knows how to cook the compost, dispose of the roots in some other way. You can shred them in a food processor or briefly cook them (the microwave is good for this) before composting them. Some noxious weed organizations bag them and take them to the landfill—but I hate that idea. Of course, if you want them to grow in your garden, just throw the old roots out there, rake them under, and water.

Harvesting leaves without uprooting the plant. A cut like this allows the plant to send up more leaves for future harvesting. Repeated harvests are possible as long as the root produces new leaves. Do not allow the plant to go to seed unless the plant is in a controlled area. Uproot any plants that are growing in or near natural areas with native plants.

The upper few inches of the rapidly growing plant stems are edible. The thicker the stem, the better. As the plant gets taller and goes to flower, the length of the upper stem that remains tender will shrink to zero. Pre-bud plants will have longer usable stems than plants in bud. These upper plant stems (rapidly growing tips) are less bitter than the leaves and are tender in texture.

As the plants grow tall, the new triangular upper leaves that develop are increasingly bitter in raw form. They are still edible and great to eat, but you need to manage the bitterness. The raw leafy stems, flower buds, and flowers are also edible, just bitter. So collect whatever you want to work with. If you love garlic mustard's kind of bitter, you'll love this plant as is. If you hate bitter, stick with me—the foods you can make are delicious.

By the time the plant is in bud and flower, an interesting thing happens: the lower round leaves begin losing some of their bitterness. So consider gathering them over the triangular upper leaves.

Some people gather the seeds for various uses, but I have not yet tried to do anything with them. The seeds are pretty hard.

Garlic mustard should be well hydrated (spray-misted and/or soaked in water until crisp) and used right away or placed into your fridge. Because garlic mustard is cold-tolerant, refrigeration will preserve it well for up to ten days.

Processing Garlic Mustard

LEAVES: Besides cleaning, the only processing that garlic mustard requires is the removal of the leaf stems (petioles). This is a Zen kind of activity that takes some time, depending on how much of the greens you need. Larger leaves make this less work. Relax, sit down, and pluck the leaf blades from the leaf stems.

The leaf stems of garlic mustard are stringy even on the young leaves, so discard them. Usually with other plants, you can keep about a half inch of a petiole and get away with it; that is, you will not notice the fibrousness. But garlic mustard petioles are just too stringy, unless you inhale your food rather than chew it. I suppose the stringiness can also be managed by chopping the petioles into thousands of tiny pieces, which mix into the other mass of food you are eating and go unnoticed. I tend not to use them.

If you plan on eating the bigger leaves fresh (bigger meaning greater than 1½ inches wide), you might want to chop them up. Most of the time, garlic mustard will be bitter to the extent that you do not want to get a whole huge leaf in a fork full of mixed salad at one time. The bitterness would be too much. This, of course, makes more of a difference in some dishes than others.

UPPER MAIN STEMS: These will be tender as long as the plant is still growing rapidly. Doing the snap test like you would use with asparagus does not seem to work with this plant. The fibrous segment just below the good stuff still snaps cleanly, so try the following: find where the stem snaps cleanly, then cut off an additional inch; what remains should be tender. Since the leaf stems of the regular leaves will be tough and stringy, remove all leaf stems attached to the plant stem except for the baby leaves at the very top.

ROOTS: Those large enough to make it worth your while will have a central fibrous core throughout much of their length and tributaries. I have not spent enough time figuring them out to give you any good advice. The core can be either woody or crunchy. For the most part, the outer rind

Upper 4 inches of main stem topped with flower buds and the uppermost baby leaves. This is an edible upper stem, though bitter when raw. In preparation for cooking, all leaves with petioles (leaf stems) over ³⁄₈ inches long were pulled off due to fibrousness, exposing a tender naked stem.

is sweet and mildly pungent. The core, when I find it chewable, is crunchy and very peppery. Its pepperiness stays on the tongue for a while after eating. If it is typical of other biennials, the first-year roots will be tender. The second-year roots will become more and more woody, particularly after the flower stalks begin developing.

SEEDS: I have not worked much with the seeds. They may have potential for making condiments or being used as spices.

Serving Garlic Mustard

Eating garlic mustard fresh out of your hand is not for the faint of taste. Garlic mustard is pretty bitter most of the time. And while its winter greens, its very early spring greens, and its lower leaves at the flowering stage are less bitter than other parts, they are all still bitter. If its brand of bitterness goes to the pleasure centers of your brain, then you are all set to eat garlic mustard any way you want. If its bitterness is not your cup of tea, then we have great ways of managing it.

Garlic mustard has three flavors in this order of strength: bitter, garlic, and pepper. Being peppery is consistent with the mustard family, of which garlic mustard is a member, but this pepperiness is usually mild. When you manage the bitterness in different dishes, you are also managing the other two flavors at the same time. Temper the bitterness and you temper the garlicky-ness.

If you search the Internet for garlic mustard recipes, notice that most of them add copious amounts of garlic. That is the curse of the garlic mustard name. Even though this green has its own fine flavor when the bitterness (and concurrent garlicky-ness) are muted, people still expect it to taste garlicky, so they add garlic. And while you are encouraged to prepare garlic mustard any way you want, none of the examples I give include garlic. Please note that I am not a chef. These recipes are simple and designed to show you how to work with garlic mustard. They will not win any recipe contests.

On a personal note—I do not smell or taste much garlic in garlic mustard. Others I know experience it as a strong odor and flavor. So your experience with the taste of garlic mustard may be different from mine.

Most people today are not very tolerant of bitter foods, so the raw and cooked recipes included here are designed to temper that bitterness. Here, I will tell you *how* I prepared the foods. To know more about the hows *and* whys, read the introductory section of the Bitter Greens on pages 261–68.

Garlic mustard is a great addition to any salad; for most of us, it should be the only bitter green included. To use garlic mustard fresh in a salad, I recommend making it about a fourth of the total amount of greens; a 100 percent garlic mustard salad would be very hard to eat. You can always adjust the amount to suit your individual tastes. Chop the garlic mustard into shreds so you can spread them evenly throughout the salad. Experiment— add foundational and sour greens to this mix. Adding other strong-tasting greens that are pungent, peppery, or bitter will make the salad a little overpowering for some.

The bud heads and particularly the flower heads and their surrounding leaves can be used just like the leaves, although they are the most bitter part of this plant. Consider that bitterness when using them in any of these recipes.

The bitterness of garlic mustard is muted by the macronutrients: protein, fat, and carbohydrates. The greens can be added fresh or cooked in dishes containing these things. Add chopped fresh garlic mustard to pasta, bean, cheese, or egg dishes.

RAW: A turkey sandwich benefits from garlic mustard when used in place of lettuce. Amid the meat, bread, and tomato, bitterness is a welcome nuance in the mix of flavors. Garlic mustard would also work well with other meat sandwiches.

Recipe shown garnished with a garlic mustard flower head and leaf as well as a dandelion flower head.

Beans with Garlic Mustard

This is a simple cold plate recipe. *Makes 4 servings.*

INGREDIENTS:

2 cups of drained and rinsed canned red kidney beans
½ cup chopped garlic mustard
⅓ cup raisins
2 tablespoons extra virgin olive oil
2 tablespoons balsamic vinegar
Salt and pepper to taste

DIRECTIONS:

Mix all ingredients. No cooking required. Add other herbs and spices to really make this sing.

BOILING: For a basic cooked green, preheat a pot of rapidly boiling water with the top on to conserve fuel. Use enough water so the leaves can move around freely during boiling. Once the water is boiling, remove the top and throw in the leaves, buds, or flower heads. After about six minutes, you have a fine cooked green with a small amount of its three initial flavors remaining. It can now be eaten like spinach. Just add a little oil, some lemon juice, a pinch of salt, and you are all set. If you want more of its initial flavors, boil it less. If you want to remove all vestiges of its bitterness, boil it longer. Boiling garlic mustard transforms it into a foundational green; that is, it can then be used in almost any recipe where a spinach-like green is required. It will have a nice cooked green flavor but no bitter, garlic, or pepper flavor. And the cooking broth remaining from boiling the leaves makes a fine soup stock.

STEAMED AND SAUTÉED: These techniques remove most of the garlic flavor and only a fraction of the bitterness. Even after 10 minutes of steaming, there is not much change in the bitterness. Sautéing is not much better. In either of these cooking methods, if bitterness is a problem for you, you might want to treat the steamed greens like you would the raw plant to mask the bitterness.

Young garlic mustard main stem tips, boiled for about 8 minutes. I like to cook the stems a little longer than the leaves because they contain the uppermost, most bitter leaves of the plant. Treat like asparagus.

GARLIC MUSTARD OMELETTE

Add ½ cup chopped garlic mustard leaves and ¼ cup diced sweet pepper (red in this case) to 2 beaten eggs and set aside. Put 1 tablespoon olive oil in a preheated skillet, sauté ½ medium-sized red sweet onion and 1 cup sliced mushrooms (wild or store-bought) until the onions have caramelized. Add 1 heaping teaspoon of finely chopped fresh rosemary to the pan, stir quickly, and add the egg mixture. Cook until desired doneness. Gently flip or fold the omelette. Salt and pepper to taste.

Cooking, in general, seems to remove most of garlic mustard's garlic flavor. Since I like to appreciate whatever flavors come with a plant, I tried an experiment. Rather than make my typical omelette, where I sauté or steam a bunch of vegetables before I add the eggs, I chopped the raw garlic mustard into about half-inch-size pieces and mixed them in with my beaten raw eggs. Then I made my omelette. It worked because the egg part of the omelette is not cooked very long, the egg somewhat insulates the garlic mustard from the heat, and the protein and fat in the egg seem to mute the bitterness but retain the gar-licky-ness, which is never very strong for me. But this technique works fairly well to maintain whatever garlicky flavor there is.

Garlic mustard is a nutritious and often plentiful green whose potential as a food is tremendous. Help out your local natural area by harvesting their garlic mustard. Invent some innovative recipes. And if you want, add garlic.

Chapter 15

FAMILY: Brassicaceae
SPECIES: *Capsella bursa-pastoris*

Shepherd's Purse

A small, unassuming, nutritious plant—few know its true virtues.

Young healthy shepherd's purse plants with short stems, just beginning to flower.

Estimated Range

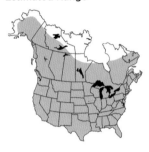

Official Species Name:
- *Capsella bursa-pastoris* (L.) Medik.

Synonyms (Historical Names):
- *Capsella rubella* Reut.
- *Bursa bursa-pastoris* (L.) Britt.
- *Bursa bursa-pastoris* var. *bifida* Crépin
- *Bursa gracilis* Gren.
- *Thlaspi bursa-pastoris* L.

Common Names:
- Shepherd's purse
- Shepherd's heart
- Shepherd's pounce
- Toywort
- Bolsa de Pastor
- Pickpocket

An herbaceous weed naturalized from the Mediterranean, shepherd's purse is widespread and abundant in North America,

continued

SHEPHERD'S PURSE

This plant is easily identified when mature. Unfortunately, prior to the appearance of the mature pods, the leaves can be mistaken for all those other basal-leaved dandelion-like plants. How can you identify this plant prior to seed production? We'll try to solve that problem in this chapter.

This is a prolific plant that can be the bane of farmers, who, as a result of crop losses, called this plant *pickpocket*. But for you, this plant should be called *great benefactor*, since it will give you free food as long as you can find it in good enough condition.

Shepherd's purse leaves are a nutritional powerhouse, very high in omega-3 fatty acids, calcium, iron, and zinc, with vitamin C and manganese levels as good as our most nutritious domesticated greens.

Knowing Shepherd's Purse

Shepherd's purse loves moisture, loose fertile soil, and cold weather. That being said, as long as the seeds have enough moisture to germinate and the plant can get established, it can grow just about anywhere, even in poor soil, hot weather, and dry conditions.

Shepherd's purse seeds may require two winters of conditioning before they will sprout. After that, they can germinate in any nonfrozen growing season. They prefer sprouting when temperatures fluctuate around 60 degrees F. But if the soil is disturbed and moisture is present, it has a wide latitude beyond that temperature. The major sprouting time is in the spring, with a secondary sprouting in the fall. It can sprout in the summer if the soil is turned and watered.

Earlier sprouts will have a longer vegetative growing season before producing a flower stem; that is, they will produce a lot more leaves, particularly if the weather is cool and there is plenty of moisture. Later sprouts, like those germinating in the summer, will have a shorter vegetative life, though with enough water, great leaves can still develop.

With summer heat and drying conditions, shepherd's purse will ignore leaf production to put all of its energy and focus on generating a seed-producing stem.

If shepherd's purse sprouts late enough in the year, perhaps in a late-autumn warm spell into the 60s, and then temperatures dip below freezing, growth will slow but continue until temperatures reach into the low 20s. At that point, the plant goes into hibernation for the winter.

Leaf shape varies somewhat. Some leaves are more

primarily where humans have invaded and where soil has been disturbed. It also grows in more stable soil, like lawns, vacant lots, old fields, and landscape beds.

Edible Parts:
• Growing tips of leafy stems
• Leaves
• Buds
• Flowers

VEGETATIVE GROWTH

This includes plant parts that are not reproductive; leaves and stems are vegetative.

Young shepherd's purse. To gauge size, the largest leaves in this photograph are just less than 3 inches long.

Leaf shapes commonly found in shepherd's purse basal rosettes. Some leaves are more deeply lobed then others. At the lower center is a flower stem.

Tough stringy cores are inside the leaves. If you stretch a leaf until it breaks, it will leave a tough core string. Cat's ear (*Hypochaeris radicata*) and plantain (*Plantago major*) have a similar attribute.

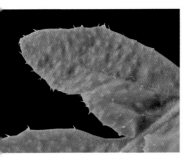

Tiny hair-like spines are found on the leaf margins. This shows an extreme close-up of the margin of one of the tiny lobes of a shepherd's purse leaf. This lobe is about ¼ inch long in actual size. It has been magnified so you can see the tiny hair-like spines at the tips of tiny leaf angles along its margin. There will also be a few to lots of scattered hairs found randomly around the leaf's edge that are not related to the angles.

pointed than others, some are more lobed. But there is an overall look that will become clear to you after awhile. First, shepherd's purse leaves are consistently smaller than dandelion, cat's ear, and sow thistle. Second, they are very regular in design. Look at the leaves of the plants in the lower photograph on page 251; note how consistent in shape the shepherd's purse leaves are to each other. There is a tapered leaf stem (petiole) leading to regular lobes on each side of the leaf. The top third of the leaf is larger than the middle or the lower third.

Another trait to look for are the tiny leaf spines. If you look closely at the margins of the leaves, you will see tiny hair-like spines arising from edge angles of the leaf blade. These spines are miniscule. To see them, hold the leaf up to the light. Look for the angles, then look for the spines at their tips. You might need a hand lens or a magnifier to see them. In contrast, dandelion will have smooth margins with obvious lobe tips or teeth tips. Its tips are typically brown, but you might have to use a magnifier to see them. Cat's ear will just have hairy margins—much larger conspicuous hairs and about five times the number of hairs you see in shepherd's purse.

If leaf shape and spines are not enough for you, there

Young shepherd's purse with about a 5-inch stem. Note that even though the stem is still forming, it already has flowers at its tip.

A mature but still-growing plant showing its characteristic elongated stem. Flowers are found at the top, and heart-shaped seed capsules form along the stem. Over time, this will continue to elongate, branch, grow more stems, and produce hundreds of seed pods (purses). Note the new branch arising from the base of a stem leaf. That branch will soon look just like the main stem.

is also the core string of each leaf. If you grab the leaf about at its center and then pull the leaf apart, a core string will remain. That string will either be attached to the base of the leaf stem (petiole), as in the adjacent photograph, or it will protrude from the upper leaf you just pulled off.

At some point—depending on the season, environmental factors, or the age of the plant—shepherd's purse sends up a flower stalk, typically one at first, then sometimes more. Like many of our plants, the more lush the growing conditions, the more leafage will be formed relative to flower and stem production. The harsher the conditions, the less leafage. So habitat has a lot to do with how much greenery there is on these plants.

The stem of this plant is how most people identify shepherd's purse. It has a characteristic look: tiny white flowers at the top, heart-shaped seedpods along its length, and small leaves below the pods. Stem leaves are typically small and get smaller as they travel up the plant.

Flowers are tightly clustered at the tops of all stems, tiny and closed most of the time. They open in the middle of the day when the conditions are right. Sometimes they have a reddish coloration, but mostly they are green parts with white petals. Like all other mustards, there are four

(above) Stem leaves are small and shaped differently from the basal leaves. The stem leaves are narrow, unlobed, get smaller as you travel up the plant, and have bases that clasp (wrap around) the main stem. New branches emerge from where the stem leaves meet the main stem.

(right) Shepherd's purse buds and flowers. In the middle of a sunny day, you might be lucky enough to see shepherd's purse flowers opening—they are typically closed most of the time. Deep within the flower, the pistil (female flower part) is in the form of a heart-shaped purse. This photograph has been magnified many times to show the tiny 3mm-wide flowers.

petals, four sepals, one pistil, and six stamens.

The pistil, once fertilized, transforms into a pod. When this happens, all the other flower parts fall away. The heart-shaped pod is green and is divided into two halves, each half containing a number of seeds. The distinctive shape of shepherd's purse pods helps distinguish this plant from close relatives like pennycress (*Thlaspi arvense*). The longer the stem gets, the more pods develop along its length.

Gathering Shepherd's Purse

LEAVES: These will be larger, more tender, and flavorful if you gather them from excellent habitats—moist rich areas with soft soil like gardens, landscaping, and farmland. You will find more of these conditions in the very early spring and late fall. Either uproot them for later leaf extraction or snip off the rapidly growing leaves.

Like most mustards, shepherd's purse dries out very quickly, so keep all parts moist and cool until ready to use. If they wilt, crisp them by immersing in very cold water for fifteen minutes. Once hydrated, they will last well in the refrigerator.

Shepherd's purse leaves are a little chewy, particularly those with long thin petioles (leaf stems). Before I use the

Six healthy young plants held as one bunch. These are young basal rosettes prior to any significant flower stalk development. Clustered like this, it looks like one plant. Note how lush the leaves are. This kind of growth is found in healthy well-watered soil in landscaping, adjacent to a garden, or on a farm. Shepherd's purse roots are typically thin and insubstantial.

Trimming shepherd's purse leaf stems. Large shepherd's purse leaves typically have long leaf stems (petioles). I usually cut off and discard the fibrous leaf stems. Leaf stems on smaller, younger leaves are not as fibrous and can be used whole.

PETALS
The showy flower parts; they are white on shepherd's purse.

SEPALS
The green flower parts that enclose the bud and then surround the base of the petals once the flower has opened.

PISTIL
The female part of the flower, found in the center; it contains the ovules that become the seeds. The pistil turns into the heart-shaped seed capsule that defines shepherd's purse.

STAMENS
The male part of the flower; each stamen has a stem and a pollen-packed tip. Stamens are *the* identifying characteristic for mustard family plants. Of six stamens, four of them are tall and two of them are short.

New shoots (flower stalks) that rise from the basal rosettes of shepherd's purse.

larger, longer leaves, I chop off their lower 40 percent, which is mostly petiole.

FLOWER STALKS: The short, very young, just-forming flower stalks are edible and delicious. At first, all you see are a cluster of leaves arising from the center of the basal rosette of leaves. Then the flower stem emerges. Eventually new stalks branch off the main flower stalk. On younger plants, the upper few inches are chewable. On older plants with long flower stalks, only a small part of the uppermost stem is chewable but not very tasty.

SEEDS AND SEEDPODS: These are just too fibrous for any use I can find. Even when they are green, there is not much to like about them. The seeds are the most-talked-about part of this plant in wild food literature, but they are tiny, tough, and generally disappointing. I do not see any practical use for them.

There have been repeated reports that Native Americans collected and used the seeds for a "nutritious flour." These reports stemmed from a single reference in a 1902 book by Victor Chestnut called *Plants Used by the Indians of Mendocino County, California.* Here is what Chestnut said under one of the old Latin names for shepherd's purse, *Bursa bursa-pastoris:* the seed "is used to a slight extent to make pinole." That is *all* Chestnut said. Pinole, if I understand it correctly, is a food made from seeds that are roasted and ground into a meal. Typically associated with corn, it can refer to any grain. Chestnut's information is really too vague to be useful. Was shepherd's purse seed, along with whatever other grains could be added, used to extend the corn? To flavor the corn? What does *slight* mean? Was it ever used on its own to make shepherd's purse flour?

It is difficult to imagine gathering enough shepherd's purse seed to make even a small amount of flour. I could not find any peoples in Europe or the Mediterranean (its native growing areas) who used the seeds at all. My guess is that the seeds have never been seriously used. I believe this not only because they are tiny and would take a lot of work, but because there are so many more useful and efficient grain alternatives. If you try doing something with shepherd's purse seeds that is worth doing, let me know what you discover.

It is not clear from the literature but it seems like both the pods and the seeds are recommended for use to spice up soups and stews. I do not remember reading about anyone who had actually tried this. I've tasted the green pods raw, and they do not have enough flavor to make them worth using as a spice.

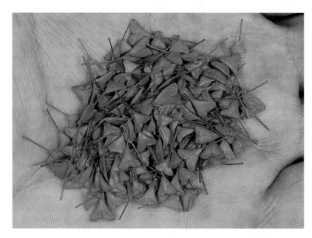

Seedpods collected while still green. When they fully mature, they turn light brown, break open, and release their seeds.

Cooking and Serving Shepherd's Purse

LEAVES AND STEM TIPS, FRESH: When lush and fast-growing, shepherd's purse leaves and emerging stem tips are delicious and can be very mild. In fact, it can be so mild that it could be used as a foundational green in some circumstances. Sometimes you get a little more of the pepperiness. It is excellent in salads, sandwiches, and anywhere you would use lettuce or spinach. Occasionally the leaves are just a little chewy—particularly leaves over four inches long. If so, remove the petioles and chop them into smaller pieces before putting them into whatever you are serving.

Wild Shepherd's Purse Salad. Included are mallow, nipplewort, sheep sorrel, English daisy flowers (*Bellis perennis*), and some domesticated carrot slivers. Shepherd's purse makes up about 1/4 of this salad's greens. Both leaves and shoots are included here.

Years ago, a major hotel restaurant in Seattle hired me to take a master chef, whom they were trying to recruit, on a wild food tour of Washington. It was November, so I could only show him the cold-tolerant plants. Even though there was frost covering everything, we found some shepherd's purse looking lush and still growing. They were at the stage where they were just sending up the first few inches of stem. After tasting both leaves and stem, this master chef (did I mention he was a master chef?) declared that it was one of the best-tasting greens he had ever eaten.

The flower heads at the tips of the tall mature stems are edible and can be added fresh anywhere you add the leaves. I have heard they are super peppery, but I've often experienced mild flavor in rapidly growing plants. I do not consider the flower heads to be choice, but they are edible; if you want to add diversity to your diet, they can easily become part of a larger dish, and you won't even realize you are getting the added diversity. For me, they are not pretty enough to be used as a garnish, but you might disagree.

LEAVES AND STEM TIPS, COOKED: Shepherd's purse leaves and rapidly growing stem tips are excellent greens whether steamed, boiled, stir-fried, or baked with some dish. Its mildness works wherever spinach is used.

But be forewarned: shepherd's purse leaves reduce down tremendously when boiled. It takes about ten servings worth of fresh greens to make one serving of boiled greens. While this amount of greens is not out of the ordinary for me, eating this much concentrated shepherd's purse gave me a five-hour low-level headache. Frankly, I do not know what the cause was. The headache could have been unrelated to the shepherd's purse. I could have been having a unique physiological reaction to something in the greens. Or perhaps there is some chemistry in shepherd's purse that is harmless until you consume a certain quantity. Who knows, it could be an overdose of beneficial phytochemicals. Dandelion flowers in large quantity have the same effect on me.

Shepherd's purse greens are powerful. This innocent-looking serving of shepherd's purse is actually about 10 hefty servings of fresh greens that boiled down to a fraction of its original size.

The ginger flavor claim for shepherd's purse root is an example of how misinformation gets inserted into the wild foods literature and then repeated author after author. Since I personally found no ginger flavor to the root, I thought I'd investigate. I checked through my library and found the original source (Harrington, 1967) of the "ginger flavor" statement. The author had not tried using the roots as a ginger substitute himself, but he was responsible enough to give the source of his information: Nelson Coon's book *Using Wayside Plants* (1960). So I read Coon's account of shepherd's purse. There was nothing about ginger flavor or candied root. Then I glanced at the page to the right that covered the next plant—wild ginger. Wild ginger root, Coon said, can be used as a substitute for store-bought ginger. So the original misinformation was nothing more than the offending author reading from the wrong page. The ginger flavor and candied root were all about eastern wild ginger (*Asarum canadense*), not shepherd's purse. Book after book and now certain Web sites dutifully repeat that misinformation.

I believe shepherd's purse greens to be nutritious and good for you. But due to my limited experience eating it boiled in this quantity, I caution anyone from eating that much in one sitting. So if you cook shepherd's purse, make sure that the finished greens are spread throughout a larger dish. And try not to eat the equivalent of more than five fresh servings in one sitting.

ROOT: It has been reported often that fresh or dried ground roots of shepherd's purse have been used as a substitute for ginger, and that they have been candied by boiling them in a rich sugar syrup. I've chewed on the roots of both young and old plants to search for that ginger-like flavor. None was to be found. And to top that, young and old roots are absolutely woody—not making them suitable for grinding. I have no use for the root.

Shepherd's purse is an excellent addition to the diet. It's nutritious and delicious, and is found all over North America. The key thing is finding lush plants with large, healthy, rapidly growing leaves. It is easy to find old struggling plants growing in hard dry ground, but wait for the good stuff. Go visit a local organic farm or possibly your own garden.

Bitter Greens

This introduction is designed to help you understand and manage bitter qualities in the plants that follow. It would be unfortunate if you skipped this section just because you might not be a fan of this class of flavors—I wasn't until recently. The benefits you will gain in flavor, dietary variety, and nutrition are worth it.

I'm defining the bitter greens here as ones that, in the *raw unadorned form* (having no added sauce or other ingredients), range from moderately to strongly bitter to most people. These are greens and vegetables that are suitable for occasions where you want to add some character to the dish you are making. Bitter greens are often paired with milder greens (foundational greens) or complex dishes to add interest and nuance. They are edible raw and cooked, but their best uses depend on your flavor goals for whatever you are preparing. They have the potential to greatly improve a dish by using just the right amount or to destroy it by adding so much that it overpowers everything else in the dish. Most people will prefer to use them as flavor enhancers for other foods or to cook them in ways to produce more moderate flavors.

Each of the greens in this section has its own characteristic flavors and textures. Served fresh, they are excellent when used in combination salads, added to sandwiches, employed as garnishes, and made into green-based sauces. Cooked as a side dish, their flavors vary tremendously—some remaining bitter while others transform into foundationally mild but rich flavors. Cooked in more complex dishes, their qualities shine. Add them to soups, stews, lasagna, pizza, pasta, and rice dishes.

The plants covered in this section include dandelion, cat's ear, sow thistle, and nipplewort—all in the aster or dandelion family. The aster family, the Asteraceae, have many representatives in our supermarkets—primarily lettuces. Plenty of other plant families have bitter greens, including ones mentioned in other sections of this book, so our grouping is a matter of convenience. Note that many members of the Asteraceae family, like some of the lettuces, are not bitter—including ox-eye daisy (*Leucanthemum vulgare*) and salsify (*Tragopogon* spp). The plants I cover are here because they are common and important from a wild food perspective. They are great foods that should be enjoyed, so read on.

Flavors offered by bitter greens are an excellent addition to the gourmet's arsenal of tastes. From a food perspective, the plants in this chapter are primarily cold-weather plants, providing their best eating in the early spring. Some are even good in the fall. If they are growing in your garden or yard, and if you nurture them, you can extend their availability into the summer.

Perceived Bitterness—Understanding Bitter

Historically, while many peoples ate bitter greens, they typically did not eat them raw and unadorned in their full bitter glory. In American culture prior to World War II, country folk and immigrants ate all sorts of wild greens, including the plants in this section. But they would eat them cooked and/or smothered in substances like hot bacon grease. In fact, this is the classic way to eat "wilted greens" in North America: Take a mess of wild greens and pour liberal amounts of hot bacon grease over them, then add the chopped-up bacon, diced hard-cooked egg, and whatever else strikes your fancy. People striving for healthier diets might ask, "Where are the greens under all that?"

Today, many people get hardening of the arteries just hearing the words "bacon grease"! These added foods and preparations transformed the greens into a whole different flavor experience than the lone bitterness of the raw greens.

Native Americans of the Pacific Northwest added eulachon grease (a fish oil) to greens and fruits with strong and/or unusual flavors. Mediterraneans added generous amounts of olive oil and lemon juice to their greens. And in both these groups, most of the bitter greens were cooked before these dressings were added.

Today, because we know so much about dietary-caused diseases and because our lives are so sedentary (we have to force ourselves to exercise), many more people are interested in eating fresh raw fruits and vegetables covered in less animal fats and calories. The benefits are better health; the downside is that bitter and other harsh flavors formerly concealed are exposed.

Taste is more complex than most people think. Most people I talk to classify foods as bitter or not, or they give a simple scale of intensity. In reality, there are thousands of bitter-flavored chemicals in plants, and our taste buds probably have hundreds of ways of sensing those chemicals. Since each of us has a unique array of taste buds, that explains why different people can disagree on whether a food is bitter or not. Some people can taste certain bitters in certain foods while others may taste something different in that same food.

If you were fed raw dandelions as a child, then you would be more likely to have developed a tolerance for their bitterness and some taste connections to your brain's pleasure centers. But people trying them for the first time as an adult do not have this advantage. If you are determined, as an adult, to eat raw unadorned dandelions for philosophical, health, or machismo reasons, you will probably tolerate more bitterness with time and practice. Your body adjusts somewhat. Mine has. But if you still want no bitterness in your foods, then that can be arranged.

Managing Bitterness in Fresh Greens

The only way I can enjoy bitterness is if it is managed into pleasantness. So how exactly do you manage bitterness? Here are the ways I've discovered:

1. GATHER THE GREENS AT THEIR PRIME

The biggest mistake novices make is just consuming whatever plant they find whenever they find it and expecting great results. If you gather greens at their prime, you will experience better flavor and texture, and you'll have an easier time managing what bitterness it does have. The plant chapters in this book will help you understand and find leaves and other edible parts at their prime.

2. TURN THE GREENS INTO A FLAVORING

Spearing a forkful of mixed greens in a salad is one thing. Spearing a forkful of nothing but bitter greens is a whole different experience. One way to take the intensity out of leaves is to chop them into shreds and distribute them throughout a mixed salad or some other food.

Your chopping is doing two things here: first, you are making small pieces, and second, you are diluting their intensity by mixing them with other foods. Instead of a slap-in-the-face hit of bitterness, this adds a mild bitter bite throughout a more complex medley of flavors.

When making a salad, bitter greens are typically mixed with milder greens to dilute the bitterness. The degree of bitterness of the greens I'm using will determine the degree of dilution I'll try to achieve. Real bitter greens may only make up a sixth of a mixed salad, where mildly bitter greens could be as much as a third of a salad. The goal is not to get rid of the flavor but to use it to its best advantage.

A very effective way to dilute bitter greens is to combine them with foods rich in protein, fat, and/or carbohydrates—the macronutrients. Greens cooked with meat, salad dressed with oil or fatty fruits like avocado, or greens cooked with pasta or potatoes are excellent ways to dilute bitterness. These macronutrients provide calories that mild greens alone do not. Those calories can absorb a lot of bitter flavor.

FATS

These can be found in the form of oils, butter, or animal-rendered fat.

Vegetable oils work well because they flow as a liquid, even at room temperature. This allows them to easily absorb lipid-soluble bitters that are found in greens. They are also better fats from a health perspective.

Animal fats tend to harden at room temperature. They work better as bitterness absorbers when they are heated into a liquid form. Animal fats also have a tendency to solidify your arteries, particularly in high-carbohydrate diets.

3. MASK THE BITTERNESS

Fat is the main ingredient for doing this. This is why many of the old-timers (like Euell Gibbons) poured hot bacon grease over their dandelions. Aside from the dilution factor that added fat provides, fat can mute and/or even change the flavor of different bitters. Fat flavored with bitters it has absorbed can provide a melded flavor that is often better than each one tasted separately. Fat may also coat the tongue, serving as a sort of shield or mask for taste bud receptors, reducing their exposure to the harshest forms of bitterness. My fat of choice is cold-pressed extra virgin olive oil.

4. ENGAGE ALL YOUR TASTE BUDS

Diluting bitter greens with mild greens helps to soften bitterness. But if you want to maximize the proportion of bitters to other foods in your dish, then engage more of your taste buds. If bitter taste buds are the only sensory organs firing signals to your brain, then that is all your brain will focus on. If you engage sweet, sour, salty, and umami taste buds, the brain hears a symphony rather then one note. Fruity vinaigrettes add sweet and sour to a salad. Smoked salmon shreds add smoked, salmon, umami, and salt flavors as well as protein to dilute the bitterness. Bitterness, while still there, would only be one of many sensations competing for your brain's attention.

Cooking Fresh Greens

The first four management practices above also apply to cooked greens.

1. HEATING

There are thousands (millions? billions?) of different bitter or just unpleasant substances in the plant kingdom. Each has different physical and chemical properties. They all react differently to processing techniques we throw at them. Some bitters are volatile and will evaporate with heat

UMAMI TASTE RECEPTORS

The existence of umami taste receptors is a fairly new concept based on the ability of glutamate, an amino acid, to enhance flavors in an analogous but different way than salt does. My understanding is that glutamate magnifies the savoriness, or meatiness, of foods. Glutamate is the same as glutamic acid. It is found naturally in meats, seaweeds, mushrooms, nuts, legumes, and dairy products. A fermented version of glutamate is sometimes added to processed foods and to restaurant dishes as MSG (monosodium glutamate).

in the escaping steam. Bitters in other plants will remain and break down into non-bitter substances. Others leach into the cooking water. Others are just persistent, unaffected by heat, and you have to live with them. Heating and boiling will not universally remove bitterness. You have to customize your behavior to what the plant demands.

Cooking will destroy a small proportion of nutrients—mostly the water-soluble ones; some will be lost in the cooking water. When I cook, my goal is to minimize loss and maximize flavor and texture. Cook things as little as necessary to make a delectable food. If the food is too bitter, you won't eat any of it, wasting ALL those nutrients. If you are worried that your body is going to go into fits of deprivation over a 5 percent loss of some nutrients that are cooked out, then eat 5 percent more greens.

2. LEACHING

Just as fat-soluble bitters are absorbed in fat that you might add to a dish, water-soluble substances are absorbed in water. In both these cases, the process of extraction is called leaching. Water-soluble bitters may leach out of a plant and into any surrounding water. Fat-soluble bitters may leach out of a plant and into any surrounding oil. Leaching can happen in cold water but is more effective under two conditions: first, if the greens are cut into small pieces, then there are more open areas for the bitterness to escape; second, the heat and agitation caused by boiling water speeds up the removal process. The greater the volume of liquid to the mass of greens, the more bitterness that escapes into the water. With some greens, leaching is not useful because they lose all their flavor. Your goal is to manage bitterness, not destroy all flavor. Many bitter wild greens, including dandelions, reveal a wonderfully rich flavor after being leached properly.

Nature Is NOT Here for Our Convenience

Bitterness varies in nature

Since you will gather at different times during the season from a variety of locations that experienced a variety of growing conditions, the degree and tenacity of bitterness may vary, even if you know what you are doing. So your job is to taste things before you commit them to recipes, particularly if you are planning to share your food with others. Following a recipe using a bad ingredient only gets you a bad result.

Bitter greens tend to be more powerful than other greens

In my experience, the greens in this section, particularly when eaten raw, can initially result in a more laxative effect than other greens. This makes sense because some of the bitters that may be beneficial in small amounts tend to be mildly toxic in large amounts. Sesquiterpenes and terpenes are two such classes of chemicals. Your intestines have to decide what to absorb and what not to absorb, your liver has to metabolize these substances, and your kidneys have to excrete them. So the first few times that you eat a bitter wild green, you may have softer stools then normal. Your body will adjust gradually as you eat these greens more and more. This is not something to worry about. Just be aware that softer stools are a normal thing when you are new to this.

Nutrition

Bitter greens can be nutritional powerhouses packed with nutrients and phytochemicals. Of our four plants, only dandelions and sow thistle have been studied to any extent. Both are high in calcium, iron, zinc, and copper. Dandelions are also a great source of riboflavin, folic acid, beta-carotene, and vitamin E. Sow thistles are a great source of omega-3 fatty acids and are the highest source for manganese I've found for any green plant.

Bitter greens tend to be great carriers of phytochemicals, of which sesquiterpenes and terpenes are members. There are many reports these days about phytonutrients—substances in plants that may have protective effects against cancer, heart disease, and some of the effects of aging. This is promising stuff. And while the bitter greens certainly have their share of phytochemicals, it is clear that the non-bitter greens and just about all other plants do too. If you want phytochemicals, go ahead and eat bitter greens, but also eat non-bitter greens, fruits, nuts, seeds, and legumes. One of the nutritional benefits of wild foods is that they increase the variety of the plant part of the diet and, hence, the variety of phytochemicals in the diet.

The bitter greens that follow add a wonderful contribution to the overall diet. You can make the best use of them by making them taste as delicious as you can in ways that suit you. Using the techniques above, you should be able to experiment and improvise with bitter wild greens you read about here and ones not covered in this book. Appreciate wild greens for whatever they bring to the table and use them to your advantage, bitter or not.

Chapter 16

FAMILY: Asteraceae
SPECIES: *Taraxacum officinale*

Dandelion

A nutritious, delicious vegetable: great if you know what you are doing—a disappointment if you don't.

Spring dandelions in a growth stage that is great for gathering leaves, buds, and flowers.

Estimated Range

Official Species Name:
- *Taraxacum officinale* G.H. Weber ex Wiggers

Synonyms (Historical Names):
- None

Common Misspelling:
- *Taraxacum officinalis*

Common Names:
- Dandelion
- Dent-de-lion
- Diente de león
- Blowball
- Pissenlit

An herbaceous perennial weed naturalized from Europe, dandelion is widespread and abundant in North America, primarily where humans have invaded and where soil has been disturbed.

continued

DANDELION

One summer when I was a kid, my grandmother walked to the vacant lot next to our house and gathered dandelion greens—greens our Greek ancestors have eaten for centuries. A second-generation, fully American suburban kid, I had never seen such a thing. My mom washed the greens, boiled them for about 10 minutes, poured off the water, and served them with a little olive oil and lemon juice. Everyone at the table began eating the greens, suffering at every bite. It was an excruciatingly bitter experience. But my mom did not want to hurt her mother-in-law's feeling and was dragging us along for the ride. After much torture, my mom took pity and allowed us to leave the rest. It is a good thing that I could ignore this common and unpleasant experience in my adult life, or I would never have learned to enjoy dandelions.

Popular and wild food literature is filled with inaccurate and misleading information about the use of dandelions for food—making it almost impossible for the novice to have a really enjoyable dining experience. Articles are commonly written by people who are intrigued with wild foods but have little practical experience. Even people with experience do not seem to have the ability to give practical advice. And worse, there are many wild food authors/proponents/cheerleaders who give the impression that every wild food is delicious no matter how it is prepared.

There is also a long history of dandelions being used by health-care practitioners to aid in digestion, to stimulate bile secretion, to clean the liver, to purify the blood, and to help manage insulin. Before you start eating raw dandelion, be forewarned that the leaves are considered mildly diuretic and laxative, the roots can be mildly laxative, and the milky juice is used to kill warts. Educational papers found in libraries and on the Internet describe all the potential health and medicinal benefits of dandelions. Because medicine is not my area, neither am I an herbalist, I will not try to summarize this information for you except to say that, in the end, dandelions are a great food in the context of a healthy diet. I can eat a great deal of it without any pharmaceutical effects that I know of—as do millions of other people. Dandelion leaves are packed with nutrients and are generally considered one of the more healthy vegetables. Try giving it a chance. In this chapter, I'll lead you through the natural history of dandelion and describe the points of greatest opportunity. With a little experience, you may learn to love dandelions as much as I do.

Knowing Dandelion

Dandelion sprouts from seed whenever the soil is moist. It will emerge in your garden when you turn the soil and then water the area, or it will show up in your yard if you continually water to keep your grass looking fresh. It is a cold-loving plant that seems to prefer moist springs and autumns. This plant will continue to grow more and longer leaves as time progresses, and it sends down a taproot that thickens with age.

First-year development

How much leafage and root that a first-year dandelion produces is totally dependent on growing conditions. Great growing conditions—lots of water, rich soil, and no cutting back—will produce lots of leafage. The more leafage, the larger the root and the deeper it digs. As far as I can tell, dandelion is capable of flowering before its first winter, but it takes energy to flower. Through photosynthesis, the plant must build up a storehouse of enough energy in the roots to support flower and seed growth.

Dandelion seedling, about 1½ times life-size.

Dandelion is a perennial, a plant that survives for two or more winters. Like other winter-tolerant plants, dandelion adapts to survive the cold in a variety of ways. Water content decreases while sugar and alcohol content increases.

Dandelion plant and root size. This display shows dandelions in early March that grew wild in my garden. The soft, rich, well-watered soil allowed them to flourish more than the dandelions growing in the lawn. The roots here are up to 2 feet in length. Unless the top of the plant is damaged, like the center plant here, leaf growth is generally proportional in size to the root size.

These are protective measures that reduce the damage from ice forming in the cells during a freeze.

I've seen dandelion leaves survive several days of 20-degree temperatures during several cold blasts in an otherwise moderate Pacific Northwest winter. They look all shriveled and dead during the freeze, only to recover when the temperature warms again a few days later. Surviving, however, is not thriving. In northern regions, dandelion leaves have been known to survive under the snow. But months of below-freezing temperatures tend to kill all the aboveground growth.

Second-year development

The second-year dandelion is the one that most people are familiar with. Once winter passes, the aboveground leafage grows rapidly, fed by overwintering roots and watered from rainy springs and snowmelt. The number and size of the leaves are roughly proportional to how big the root is. Overwintered dandelion plants tend to burst into flower around the same time, typically in April or May, depending on where you are in North America.

LEAVES: These are extremely variable in shape. This variability causes dandelion to be confused with other plants that have similar-shaped but variable leaves. Cat's ear, chicory, and shepherd's purse are plants with similar leaves. Dandelion apparently got its name from the teeth on the leaf blades. Many people say it comes from the French name *dents-de-lion,* referring to "teeth of the lion." This may be true, but before that, the Latin name was *dens leonis.*

Dandelion leaf stems are almost white where they attach to the base of the plant. That base is often called the root crown, where leaves are attached to a short compact stem above the root. There is often a reddish tinge somewhere on the leaf stem. The leaves are variably lobed, and those lobes are pointed, mostly downward; sometimes they point outward. Some of the lobes divide the leaf all the way to the central vein; other times the lobes are shallow, not cutting deeply into the leaf. Look at the leaves in all the

Several dandelion root crowns growing from a single large root. The root crown is that area created by the bulge of the leaf bases down to where the root begins. Younger plants will have a simpler structure—a single straight root leading to a single crown.

(right) Dandelion leaf (center two) compared to cat's ear (left) and chicory (right). These represent common shapes, but many variations exist for all three species. Much more detail will be given in the chapter on cat's ear. Chicory will be covered in another book. While you cannot see it here, chicory leaves often twist instead of lying flat. Check this chapter for more dandelion leaf variation.

(facing, above) Leaf surface comparison of cat's ear (left), dandelion (center), and chicory. Cat's ear has coarse hairs all over its upper surface; dandelion and chicory are mostly hairless. If they have any hairs at all, they are small, sparse, and inconspicuous. Note also that the main veins on cat's ear and chicory do not stick up from the blades' surface. Dandelion's main vein does stick up above the blade and is more likely to have some redness to it than the other two species.

(facing, below) Leaf underside comparison of cat's ear (left), dandelion (center), and chicory. Both cat's ear and chicory have coarse hairs all over the undersides of their leaves. Hairs are particularly evident on the main veins, which stick up/out from the underside of the leaf blade. Dandelion leaf undersides have no obvious hairs.

pictures in this chapter to get an idea of the variation you are likely to see. The leaves can range from just a few inches to over eighteen inches long. What few hairs they have are tiny and barely noticeable.

Dandelion leaves can look like a variety of other plant leaves. To help you distinguish between them, I've taken side-by-side comparison photographs. Those comparisons will focus on shape and hairiness differences. Dandelion is compared to cat's ear (*Hypochaeris radicata*) and wild chicory (*Cichorium intybus*); all three have edible leaves.

In summary, dandelion is virtually hairless on both sides, cat's ear is quite hairy on both sides, and chicory is hairy on its bottom side, often with little or no hair on its top.

FLOWERS AND SEEDS: Like all the other plants in this section of the book, dandelion has what is known as a composite flower. That means that what looks like one flower is in fact a cluster of flowers, also known as a *flower head*. Each petal you see is actually the tip of a separate individual flower. Each flower results in the development of a single seed on the seed head. So a head of flowers results in a composite or cluster of seeds on the seed head.

What most people call the flower bud on dandelion is actually a *flower cluster* bud surrounded by green bracts. An opened flower head is cradled/subtended by those bracts.

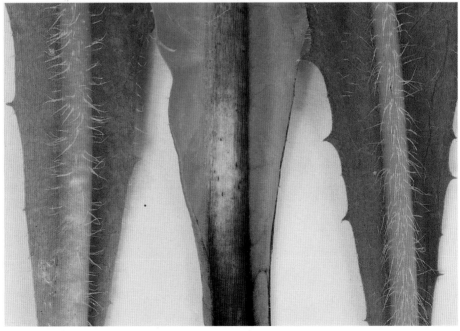

The flower head opens and closes once each day for about three days before transforming into a seed head. By the fourth day, the closed head appears white at the top before opening. The fully open seed head is sometimes called a puffball, blowball, or faceclock. The puffball has generated lots of folklore. I've heard of two ways to tell time over the years. The first view says that the number of puffs it takes to blow off *all* the seeds tells you what time it is. So, if it takes four puffs to blow off all the seeds, it's four o'clock. The second view is that after three puffs, a count of how many seeds remain on the head tells you what time it is. Einstein would love this method, as time would be relative to each puffball you picked up.

New leaves and flower stalks arise from the top of the root crown. Flower stalks can reach a length of up to two feet under excellent growing conditions.

Developmental progression from dandelion bud to seed dispersal. Progression goes from upper left to upper right, then lower left to lower right: (upper) bud, bud opening, fully opened flower head, flower closed, seed head closed; (lower) seed head opening, seed head fully open (puffball), seed head releasing seeds, flower/seed receptacle denuded.

After spring's massive flowering, dandelion will continue to flower sporadically and infrequently throughout the rest of the year. A small upsurge in flower blooming occurs again in the fall.

Edibility

Dandelion has six edible parts: leaves, flower buds, upper bud stem, flowers, heart, and roots. Flavor and texture are highly dependent on growing conditions, your ability to choose the best specimens at the appropriate stage of growth, and your management of the bitterness.

LEAVES: In much of popular wild food literature, you are often told to gather dandelion leaves before the flower stalks appear. This is limited advice since dandelion can be collected and enjoyed during all the nonfrozen seasons. But there is some reasoning behind the idea. Non-bitter or less-bitter dandelion is "possible" to find in the early spring because a variety of environmental factors create conditions that allow it to be that way. In my experience, dandelion bitterness is caused by the following three factors: excessive sun, slow growth, and possibly root storage of bitterness. Since I am not a plant physiologist, the following discussion is speculation based on observations I've made.

The first and most important source of bitterness is sunlight. Dandelion's bitter chemicals are made in proportion to the amount of sunlight the leaves receive. The more intense and longer the duration of sunlight baking a leaf, the more bitter it will be. Conversely, less bitter greens are produced during a period of rapid spring growth; the plant receives low amounts of sunlight since the sun is still low in the sky and the days are short. At this time, dandelion has less stimulation from the sun to produce bitters.

The second source of bitterness is slow growth, primarily caused by a lack of moisture; but it can also be caused by a lack of growth-promoting nutrients like nitrogen. Slow growth means that whatever bitters are produced will concentrate as the leaf sits there stagnantly, baking in the sun. Conversely, plentiful soil moisture left over by winter and prolonged by spring rains, nonfreezing temperatures, and energy stored by the roots result in explosive spring growth. Rapid growth means that whatever bitter chemicals the sun stimulates in the leaf gets spread out (diluted) as the leaf expands.

The third source of bitterness may be root storage. During the longest days in the year, the sun is at its strongest. This results in bitterness buildup in the whole plant, including the roots. So my theory is that bitter roots feed and produce more bitter new-leaf growth. Conversely, the winter root that feeds spring growth may not be packed with stored bitters as a summer root might be. When spring rolls around, the root has little bitterness to pump back into the rapidly growing spring leaves. In addition, the root's chemistry has otherwise changed to adapt to survive winter's harshness. Like the leaves, there has probably been an increase in sugars, alcohols, and other chemicals to survive freezing temperatures. So spring roots feeding spring leaves should have less bitterness than they will have at any other time of the year.

Early spring, therefore, creates the best possible conditions for the leaves to have little or no bitterness. But don't be misled; bitter-*free* dandelion leaves are still difficult to find, even in the spring. But that is the time you are most likely to find them.

Of course, warm hot summers are when most people are enjoying the out-of-doors without the chill of spring, and that is when most novices try dandelions for the first time. The result is bitterness so tenacious that you cannot easily cook it out; hence, all the recipes asking you to boil dandelion leaves into oblivion (two or more changes of water).

Most people do not think of eating dandelion leaves in seasons other than spring. But, under the right conditions, dandelion is manageably great during the non-winter months—what I call the *growing seasons*. They can

(facing) Dandelion gone wild. Here is a robust dandelion plant in late May with almost full sun. Very rapid growth in rich well-watered soil tempers the bitterness enough to be perfectly useful. Too bitter for me raw, unadorned, and eaten by itself, but it's fine if managed well. It would be just a little less bitter and have fewer leaves if growing in the shade. Direct sunlight produces rapid growth and a greater number of leaves when adequate water is present.

be found at various degrees of bitterness—some tolerably bitter (manageable), others excruciatingly bitter (too bitter to manage). So the question becomes, How do you identify the manageably bitter dandelion leaves?

As I've said, you are looking for rapid growth. The more rapid, the less bitter the greens, even in the summer. Rapid growth becomes even more important in the summer because you have longer days; and the sun is higher in the sky, causing more intense rays; and the roots are no longer sweet. Rich soil, abundant moisture, lack of competition, and shade are the most important factors for the leaf growth to keep pace with the production of bitters. Non-spring dandelion will always be bitter. Rapidly growing dandelion leaves will, however, be manageably bitter.

After spring, the sun is a double-edged sword. On the one hand, it becomes a potent source of the plant's growth energy; on the other, it is a potent dryer of the available soil moisture. This drying out stresses the leaves during the day and is the source of the plant's bitterness. So the indirect sun that a plant gets in the shade allows for the best summer dandelions, assuming other rapid growth factors are working to give you a thriving plant.

Soil and leaves dry out less when dandelion is growing in the shade. Whatever moisture is there can stay on the plant and in the soil instead of evaporating into the dry air. This protected moisture allows the leaves to grow more rapidly using only ambient light. Look for dandelions shaded by tall surrounding plants, rock features, topography, and other natural features.

Man-made settings for shade include buildings, fences, and other structures. Fences are sometimes the best unnatural locations because where there are fences, there are often landscape plants that are being watered or maintained. Dandelions getting this additional moisture can continue to thrive throughout all the growing seasons.

So how do you identify leaves undergoing rapid growth? Look for luxuriant growth where the leaves look so good they could be sold in the produce section of a super-market. No marks, no insect damage—just beautiful-looking leaves. These leaves can be big, anywhere from three to eighteen inches long. Also check the habitat for signs that the area you are picking from is regularly moist.

Center leaves are younger and grow more rapidly then the outer leaves. Younger rapidly growing leaves are a bright green. Slower growing leaves or *end size* leaves tend to be a darker green.

You'll find authors suggesting that you cover actively growing dandelion plants in your yard with large bowls to shield them from sunlight. Come back weeks later and you'll have blanched (white) dandelion leaves growing beneath that are not bitter. You can also transplant large dandelion roots into the dirt in your cellar. Water these and they will produce white non-bitter leaves until the roots become depleted. If this is correct (I have not tried either technique), this proves that sunlight drives some sort of chemical pathway in the plant that produces bitterness. The lack of photosynthesis will also mean the lack of production of many nutrients and potentially beneficial phytochemicals.

If you have a yard, you can enjoy "manage-able" bitterness throughout all the non-winter months if you can find or encourage dandelion in areas and conditions that promote rapid growth.

DANDELION HEART: The dandelion heart is a new concept I use to describe an edible part of the dandelion. It overlaps with and therefore replaces what people have called the *root crown.* According to Euell Gibbons in *Stalking the Wild Asparagus,* the root crown is "on the top of the root," and reaching up to "where the leaves start getting green."

I have always had misgivings about including

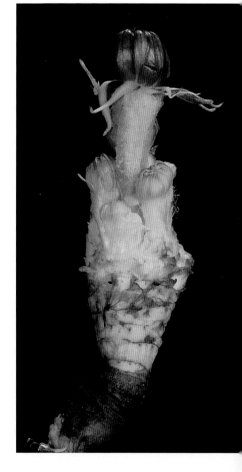

Dandelion heart. One or more dandelion hearts can emerge from a single dandelion root. This includes all emerging flower buds and the naked stem all the way down to the top of the root. The root starts at the very bottom of this photograph and is brown in color and fattened. All the leaves and long flower stalks (ones over an inch) have been peeled off.

DANDELION HEART

The dandelion heart is made up of the dandelion stem and young bud stems up to an inch long. It does not include the root, leaf stems, or flower bud stems over an inch long.

DANDELION STEM

The dandelion stem is defined as the area above the root that supports the leaf bases. It is distinguished from the root by the existence of leaf scars. A previous year's stem may appear to be part of the root, as it shrinks in size and darkens with age. While one thinks of a typical plant stem as long and easily observable, the dandelion stem is short, stubby, and hidden below the leaves.

The Euell Gibbons version of a root crown. What I used to call the root crown (right center) was a smaller piece for cooking than Gibbons' version. His root crown would have included much more of the leaf stems and more of the stem leading to the root. My smaller version allowed me to have a somewhat-uniform size when working with several crowns for cooking and presentation.

leaf bases in the crown. In my experience, they have always been chewy, tough, and bitter. I find myself removing them, revealing the tender underlying stem. I call this the *dandelion heart*, sort of like an artichoke heart—where you have to peel off fibrous parts to reach the tender core.

In the past, you often saw recipes of the root crown battered and fried. Frying probably helped to tenderize the fibrous leaf bases. If you remove the leaf bases, the remaining stem with buds is tender, manageably bitter, and quite delicious if prepared properly.

Bud stems of four inches or less are typically tender enough to eat. Those longer tend to be fibrous anywhere below that upper four inches of stem. For easier handling, bud stems over an inch are too long to be considered part of the heart, so I remove them.

BUDS, FLOWERS, AND STEMS: The buds are found on straw-like stalks that arise from the top of the dandelion stem. Collect the buds with the first three to four inches of their stalks. They are more tender and less bitter if you get them before the stalks have elongated. If you search down into the leaves of a dandelion plant, you can often find the emerging buds. In rapidly growing plants, there is very little bitter in the bud and its adjacent stem when that stem is still short. Below that first three to four inches, the stem is too fibrous to be worth your while.

The more mature the buds—that is, buds ready to open into flowers—the more bitter and powerful they become. By powerful I mean that overeating them can cause a headache; at least, they cause me to have a headache (perhaps I am unusual and you are different). So keep the number of mature buds down to ten at a time unless you are boiling them and pouring off the cooking water. This headache thing is true for me, even if I am eating them mixed with other foods. The bitterness is caused by the green bracts that surround the unopened flower. The flower petals tightly packed inside the bud do not contribute any bitterness.

Open dandelion flower heads are one of the great foods from this plant. They are decorative and flavorful. Arising from long stems, they open and close three times over three days. They are best if you can get them on the first day of opening but are still great on days two and three. The flowers—actually the flower petals—have the same headache issue for me as the buds if I eat more than twenty in one setting. Twenty is a lot of flower heads. Try not to eat more than ten at a time.

The straw-like stalks leading to the flowers are too fibrous to eat once its flower opens.

If you have some dandelion near your house (and who doesn't?), you can increase the plant's production of flowers,

BUD & BUD STEM TENDERNESS

If the first three or four inches of a bud stem are tender, it is assumed that you are gathering from a healthy, vigorously growing plant. A plant struggling to survive will produce short fibrous bud stems that flower quickly. The tender edible part of those stems will be proportionately shorter than those growing in optimal conditions.

Dandelion flower bud with edible upper 4 inches of stalk. Before the bud stem elongates fully, this whole thing is edible.

extend the flowering season, and prevent seed production. Just keep plucking the flowers and using them before each flower stem can go to seed. This stimulates the plant to keep producing flowers because it wants to reproduce and spread its seed. I tend to pluck the flower stem as close to the base of the plant as I can, in the hope that that will stimulate even more growth.

SEED HEADS: One seed head is produced for every flower head. The seeds are found at the center of the puff-ball. The filamentous structure attached to the seeds and creating the fluff is called a *pappus.* The pappus is light and works like a parachute to catch air and help the seed fly to a distant location.

Dandelion seed head. Blow it away to wish for new plants to feed you. One seed head is produced for every flower head.

I have not heard of any food uses for the seed. But should a use turn up, I have come up with a way to gather it or any other similar seed and fluff. The problem with these seed heads is that by the time the seed is mature enough to be released, it floats away—making it difficult to gather. The solution? I took my trusty shop vac, strapped it to my back, hooked it to a long extension cord, and went hunting. The secret to this technique is to put a mesh filter at the end of the suction tube. The mesh traps the seed and pappus on the way in so it does not end up in the large cavity of the shop vac. The other secret is to have a *long* extension cord or portable power supply.

This collection technique can be used to collect the seed for some use or just to prevent more dande-

lion seed from spreading without killing the plants you are enjoying. Once collected, you would still have to separate the seed from the pappus.

ROOTS: I have had little experience with the roots. I've eaten them and know others that have eaten them sporadically throughout the years, but I have not figured them out yet. The problem is that since dandelions are a perennial, you may be digging roots that are one year old or roots that are several years old.

Then there is the issue of rapidly growing conditions vs. slow-growing and highly competitive conditions. I've eaten roots that were potatoey in texture, and the bitterness was manageable. I've eaten others that were woody, and

Dandelion seed head collector. A shop vac is strapped to my back and powered by a long extension cord. A red mesh material I taped to the end of the vacuum tube folds inwards about six inches to create a cavity for the seed to collect.

there was no way to remove the bitterness. I can only guess that the same principles involving bitterness in the leaves and other parts also apply to the roots. New roots are probably tender and old roots are not.

Harvesting and Serving Dandelion Leaves

Harvesting involves finding leaves that look great (like you would find them in the produce section) and selecting the center-most elevated leaves (those not touching the

Harvest from the center of a rosette of dandelion leaves. Those leaves will be the most tender, the fastest growing, and the youngest of all the leaves.

ground around the perimeter of the plant). These lower outer leaves are older, more bitter, tougher, and they have more dirt to clean off. The less dirt you bring with you, the less you have to clean.

Harvesting the leaves requires attention to two things: keeping the leaves fresh in transit and managing the milky juice that will bleed from the cuts. To keep the leaves fresh, gently pull together the ones you want and use a pair of scissors to cut them within a couple of inches of the base. Take this bunch and carefully aim them, cut stems first, into your collecting bag. This keeps all that milky juice in one corner of the bag so it does not stain the leaves. Spray-mist these leaves and move to the next plant. Keep the bag in the shade if at all possible. Repeat this technique from plant to plant until you have all the leaves you want. As long as the root is left in the ground, harvested plants will grow all new leaves for a later culling.

Once you get the leaves into your kitchen, wash and crisp them. This involves soaking them in cold water for about five or ten minutes and then draining them. The leaves are now ready to use fresh, to cook with some dish, or to store in the fridge. For storing, put them in a clear plastic bag. They will keep in the fridge for a week, but try to use them while they are still fresh.

Before you decide on any particular recipe, taste them first so you don't go through the work of making some elaborate dish, only to find out that the leaves are too bitter for normal humans to eat. If the dandelion you have is truly not bitter, you can use it in any dish from any cookbook that requires lettuce, spinach, endive, or broccoli. Just estimate an equivalent mass of dandelion to whatever you are replacing. Or better yet, experiment using dandelion in dishes you typically make for yourself—omelets, salads, lasagna, etc. If they are normally bitter, you'll have to manage that bitterness.

One issue that is annoying to some is the fibrousness or chewiness of the lower leaf stem on larger leaves.

DANDELION RECIPES

If you want dandelion-specific recipes, get the book titled *The Great Dandelion Cookbook*, by Strauss and Gail. It contains over 125 dandelion recipes from the first five National Dandelion Cookoffs held every May in Ohio.

UMAMI

A flavor likened to savoriness. It is different from sour, sweet, and bitter flavors that add specific sensations. Like salt, umami enhances other flavors. Salt tends to magnify existing flavors. Umami works differently from salt in that it adds savoriness, enriching existing flavors. Originally discovered in kombu (a seaweed kelp), the ingredient causing the flavor is known as glutamate.

Just before you are ready to use dandelion leaves, lay a stack of them together and chop off the lower third of the leaves. Either put that third in the compost or chop them into tiny pieces and include that in the dish you're making. If you compost this part, you are not losing much of the leaf—this third of its length includes very little of the leaf blade. Smaller and younger leaves are not as much of a problem.

Managing bitterness

MANAGING BITTERNESS INTO ENJOYABLE FLAVORS

Read pages 261–68 to understand bitterness and to learn how to manage it into flavors that suit your particular likes and sensibilities.

Many people today want to eat fresh raw foods. In order for that to work with dandelion, you either have to love their bitterness, or you must work it into other foods that can dilute the bitterness. The ideal mix is when the dandelion you include adds character to the dish rather than overpowers it with bitterness. If you have selected your leaves well, here are some general recommendations:

A lettuce-style salad with somewhere between a third to a tenth part of dandelion greens is a good mix. Try a fifth first; you can always add more dandelion. Don't just add the whole leaves, chiffonade them into narrow ribbons so that any one forkful will not have a large bitter leaf to contend with. Unless you really love bitterness, you want to spread these greens throughout the mix. As explained in detail in the introduction to this section, oil and additional flavors that add sour, sweet, salt, and umami will help temper the bitterness.

CHIFFONADE

A cutting technique. Leafy greens are rolled up for easy handling, then cut into narrow pieces or ribbons.

Fresh narrow dandelion leaf ribbons can be added to fruit, fish, bean, or ethnic salads as well as vegetable medleys, sprouted grain medleys, cold soups—you are only limited by your imagination.

Cooking the leaves

There are three basic cooking methods that I will talk about here: boiling, steaming, and sautéing. These were selected because experience with them will give you a basis to move on to other options.

For all three of these techniques, I like to chop the leaves into one- to two-inch-long pieces. This allows them to move easily in and out of pans and to move freely in water. Do not chop them until just before cooking. Chopping them too early will result in the milky juice that bleeds from them, drying and staining the cut ends.

BOILED: This is the best method for removing most of the bitterness. If the greens you've gathered are good, it takes anywhere from four to eight minutes for them to go from strongly bitter to not being bitter at all. But do not depend on that time! Taste the greens at four minutes, six minutes, eight minutes, ten minutes. If they are good for you before eight minutes, take them out. They may take longer than eight minutes. Bitterness is somewhat unpredictable.

Dandelion Greens. Boiled for 8 minutes, drizzled with extra virgin olive oil and a spritz of lemon, sprinkled with a touch of salt and dandelion flower petals, and garnished with a dandelion flower.

The bonus of boiling is that dandelions have a fantastic underlying flavor that is masked by the bitterness. By lowering the bitterness, you reveal more flavors. The greens are now ready to be eaten just as greens or added to any dish requiring greens. Unless you've done a poor job of selecting the plants you gathered, you do not have to boil the greens in two or three changes of water, as some of the wild food literature suggests.

When I say *boiling* for eight minutes, the proper timing technique is to start the water boiling before adding the greens. This gives you a full eight minutes of boiling without a variable/unpredictable warming-up time. It is also important to use a large pot with plenty of water. For boiling to work properly, the greens need to move freely around in the water. If there is only a small amount of water, the bitterness has nowhere to go. To save energy, put a lid on the pot while warming the water. Once the greens are added, remove the lid so any volatile bitters can evaporate away.

The cooking water makes a fine broth for soups and stews.

SAUTÉED: By itself, sautéing provides only a small degree of relief from bitterness before the greens get overcooked. But if you mix them with other foods during the cooking process, there is a much better result. Folding them into a still-cooking stir-fry works surprisingly well. Sautéing them with caramelized onions and mushrooms before adding egg makes a marvelous omelet. Stir-frying them with non-leafy vegetables works great. Add enough dandelion to suit your own tastes.

STEAMED: The process of steaming dandelion has never really worked for me because it seems to trap most of the bitterness. I encourage those of you who are fans of steaming to experiment. Perhaps you will have more success then I did.

Harvesting and Preparing Dandelion Heart

Harvesting the dandelion heart will put a temporary damper on the production of leaves for a dandelion root. It will take time for the plant to recover and form a new stem, the benefit being that you can have a lawn clear of dandelions for a few weeks! Before harvesting the dandelion heart, consider collecting the upper leaves first, using the techniques discussed earlier. Harvesting the upper leaves from all the plants before going after the dandelion heart will help keep those leaves clean.

To harvest dandelion heart, grab all the remaining aboveground leaves that you can, pulling them upward as if to stretch the plant, and cut the root just below the ground. Lift out the heart. Cut off the still-attached leaves and long flower stems, leaving their bases still attached to the heart. As soon as possible, soak the heart in water, which washes away the milky juice and helps soften any attached dirt. Don't let it soak more than fifteen minutes before refrigerating it or moving on to the next cleaning phase.

To clean, work on only one stem at a time. Pull off any remaining leaf bases and flowering stems over an inch long. Use a soft brush to remove any dirt. Once clean, place it in a bowl of clean cold water and start on the next

Vegetable Stir-fry. Any stir-fry can include chopped dandelions. This one is garnished with a dandelion flower.

Mushrooms Stuffed with Dandelion Hearts. Baked, drizzled in rosemary-marinated extra virgin olive oil, and sprinkled with salt and pepper to taste. Boiling the hearts and mushrooms separately for 5 minutes prior to baking will reduce bitterness and moisten the mushrooms. Once assembled, oiled, and spiced, stuffed mushrooms can be steamed instead of baked for a different result.

one. Continue until you are done. Doing these one by one allows the stem to hit the water soon after the leaf bases have been torn off and before browning can occur. Once cleaned, dandelion hearts are ready for eating raw, boiled, sautéed, or baked.

RAW: Serving dandelion heart this way is not very pleasant if this is all you are snacking on. The milky juice and bitterness will result in a bitter sticky feeling in the mouth. Raw dandelion is fine if you mix it in with other foods. To do so, slice it into thin pieces directly into cold water to slow browning. After about five minutes, those slices can be sprinkled onto any food.

BOILED: This is a good solution. Once boiled, they can be used in any dish as a vegetable. Use the same technique here as for the leaves.

SAUTÉED: This process works better with the heart than with the leaves. If the stems are thick, slice them lengthwise just before cooking so they will cook evenly. Always sample for bitterness as cooking progresses.

BAKED: You can also bake the stems, which will not remove much of the bitterness. Make sure you cook them with other foods that will neutralize some of that bitterness. Always sample before and during the cooking process to determine when the stems are tasty and cooked to perfection.

Harvesting and Preparing Buds, Flowers, and Stems

Flowers can be plucked directly from the plant to garnish dishes or to add to sandwiches. If you want to eat them fresh, I suggest separating the petals from green bracts supporting them. Independent of the bracts, the petals are dry but sweet to the taste. The bracts are bitter.

If it will be a while before you use the buds or flowers gathered, take your scissors and cut the stem down to about ten inches. Or if stems are shorter than ten inches, cut them as long as you can. Immediately put these in cold water, just as you would put flowers in a vase. Spray-mist liberally and keep them in the shade. You might have to

Separating the sweet petals from the bitter green bracts. Squeeze the bract area with force while twisting. After a little practice, the petals should release and fall into your hand.

Tuna Fish Sandwich. Served with whole dandelion flowers, garnished with a pickle on the side for tartness and with wild carrot leaves (*Daucus carota*) and field mustard flowers. Eat as an open-faced sandwich or topped with another slice of toast.

change the water they are sitting in if it gets too cloudy from all the milky juice. Try to use them within three hours; they will last longer then that, but their quality will deteriorate with time.

When ready to use, clip the buds and flowers from their stems and add them to your dishes. Remember that you can leave three to four inches of stem on the younger buds if that suits your needs.

The buds are delicate and can fall apart if processed too much. They can be pickled like capers, mixed in raw with other foods, or cooked like the leaves. You do not want to eat more than ten or so at a single sitting unless they are really young—by young I mean early in their development, not growing on stalks more than six inches long.

Raw dandelion buds, soaking in extra virgin olive oil marinated with rosemary and salt. Buds prepared in this way can be used as appetizers. Young buds are not bitter. Older buds add a predictable bite to the taste.

The mature flower stalks also make great straws for cool summer drinks. (Portrait of Kris Freitag, 2001.)

The flower petals are very flavorful. Once boiled, their flavor transforms from a sweet dry flower to a wonderful green leafy flavor. To make dandelion flower petal soup, use five to eight heads worth of petals for every cup of soup, boil for a couple of minutes, add salt to taste, and enjoy.

Pond Lily Soup. Made with dandelion flower petals as its flavor base. Use 5 to 10 heads' worth of petals for each cup of soup—depending on how thick you like the broth. English daisy flowers (*Bellis perennis*) and miner's lettuce (*Claytonia perfoliata*) leaves simulate pond lilies as they float atop the soup. The asparagus was the thin kind found in the supermarket. The broth temperature has to be at or below 120 degrees F for this to work. So make the soup, then let it cool down before adding the floating flowers and leaves. If it is too hot, the floaters will wilt, making this swamp soup—just as tasty but not as attractive.

Other things can be made from dandelion flowers, including wine, syrup, and dandy burgers. (Gail, 1994; Strauss, 1997.) You are only limited by your imagination.

Dandelions are one of the most common and versatile greens you will find. Different parts of them are available most of the year under the right conditions. Their bitterness, once managed, allows them to be enjoyed in a wide variety of dishes.

Chapter 17

FAMILY: Asteraceae
SPECIES: *Hypochaeris radicata*

Cat's Ear

*Often mistaken for dandelion, this Old World green
works well in many dishes.*

Cat's Ear in full glory. It is more prevalent then dandelion in some parts of the country, grows
in the same habitats, is much more annoying to lawn keepers, and is as good in flavor.

CAT'S EAR

Estimated Range

Official Species Name:
• *Hypochaeris radicata* L.

Alternatively Spelled:
• *Hypochoeris radicata*

Synonyms:
• None

Common Names:
• Cat's ear
• False dandelion
• Gosmore
• Flatweed
• Frogbit
• Hairy cat's ear
• Spotted cat's ear

An herbaceous perennial weed naturalized from Eurasia, cat's ear is widespread and abundant in North America, primarily where humans have invaded and mostly where soil is stable, particularly lawns, vacant lots, waysides, pastures, and old fields.

continued

Cat's ear is an odd name for a plant. It is not as soft as a cat's ear, but it is shaped like one if you just consider the tip of the leaf, which is hairy on both sides.

There are good reasons that cat's ear is confused with dandelion. In fact, it is better known as "false dandelion." Its leaves and flowers are similar, it grows in the same kinds of habitats, it is a lawn nuisance, it bleeds a milky juice, and it has similar food properties.

In many parts of Europe, cat's ear and dandelion have names that, when translated into English, both signify "dandelion." This raises the question: How many traditional dandelion recipes actually originated from the consumption of cat's ear and vice versa?

The confusion also makes it more difficult to know what the research has found when plant identification is not verified. A nutrition or cardiac researcher studying the dietary habits of villagers in rural parts of Greece might ask participants what wild foods they eat. If the local name of cat's ear translates into dandelion, whatever nutrition or health data they generate may mistakenly be attributed to dandelion.

You might have seen cat's ear many times but just did not know it. Most people mistakenly think it is dandelion taking over their yard. Cat's ear is also more destructive to lawns than dandelion.

The range map I've shown you skips a part of the central U.S. and Canada. Cat's ear can likely grow anywhere within the map. I think the problem is a matter of poor and outdated records. I've seen it almost everywhere I've traveled. In some areas of the northeastern U.S. and in the Pacific Northwest west of the Cascade mountain range, the plant is prolific and in a huge variety of habitats.

I have seen secondary reports that cat's ear is high in calcium, phosphorus, and copper, but I will not commit that to the nutrient chart until I can verify those claims. Regarding phytochemicals, the flowers appear to have significant amounts of lutein and total carotinoids (Valadon,

Edible Parts:
- Leaves
- Buds and bud stems
- Flowers

1967). Extracts from the leaves have shown high antioxidant activity and antiradical power (Zeghichi, 2003).

Knowing Cat's Ear

Under normal circumstances, cat's ear germinates in the spring and fall. It requires enough moisture to establish a root that will sustain it. Cat's ear prefers solid soil to germinate, unlike many of the other plants in this book. My lawn is filled with cat's ear, but my garden next to it nurtures only one or two plants a season. There are seeds in my garden—they just prefer to grow in the lawn.

Cat's ear takes over many lawns. You might first notice this plant during its flowering season, as seen below. There are some dandelions in this yard, but it's about a month past their flowering season. In contrast, cat's ear flowers most during the longest days of the year.

The seeds can sprout soon after being dropped from the seed head of a mature plant. All they need is moist soil. I've heard that the viability of dried seeds saved indoors decreases dramatically for every year of storage. I have not tested these claims.

LEAVES: The seedling's cotyledons are round to slightly oblong. The first true leaves have the look of a baby dandelion leaf, sort of. As more and larger leaves develop, they remain relatively flat or their sawtoothed margins curve upward.

Cat's ear seedling. From left to right, this sprout is only ³/₄ of an inch long. The cotyledons are roundish. The first two leaves are barely toothed. The third leaf in this image is just starting to unfurl. At the upper right are wood sorrel seedlings.

A young cat's ear plant. This one is about 5 inches in diameter, still just a baby.

Once cat's ear develops a full healthy basal rosette of leaves, it can take two general forms: flat and upright. Those forms are situation-dependent. The fact that cat's ear can morph into the flat form is a wonderful example of co-evolution. From many years of lawn mowing, this plant has apparently learned to grow low to the ground—below where blades can cut. The plants actually depress down somewhat into the earth so their leaves and young stalks are below the grass-cutting level. I call this *lawn-adapted* cat's ear.

Lawn-adapted cat's ear. This plant is obviously avoiding lawn-mower blades. This growth form gives you a clue as to why this plant is also known as flatweed.

Cool as that is, even the eventual flower stalks adapt. At first, the stalks are hard to cut and can survive by bending as a push mower passes over. After a day, many of those stalks have recovered, uprighted themselves, and continue to reproduce. If they are cut and recut from frequent mowings, new rapidly growing flower stalks get shorter and shorter, maturing faster and faster.

Not only does this flat version sink into the earth, it depresses the growth of plants it is competing with. Even its own offspring will not sprout within leaf distance. This is one aggressive plant! These flattening, growth-depressing characteristics make cat's ear worse than dandelions from the perspective of weeding or harvesting. If a dandelion is pulled up by its roots, the scar left over is minimal, and the surrounding grass covers the hole. If cat's ear is pulled up by its roots, there is a big bare spot of soil exposed. Like pulling the toupee off a partially bald head, a big bare spot is revealed that's hard to ignore. If you pull up thirty to ninety cat's ear rosettes, your yard looks like a detonated minefield. Each bare spot can be three to five inches in diameter.

The upright form (as seen on page 297) is my favorite of the two forms because it produces lots of easily accessible leaves. It occurs anywhere the plant is allowed to grow freely without the fear of mowing. In fact, a lawn-adapted form can convert to an upright form if you stop mowing the area.

The upright form will roughly resemble the flattened form if it is starved for nutrients and water throughout its life; it will be a small plant with a minimal number of leaves. In contrast, if it gets a good supply of water over long periods in the spring and summer, it will grow many healthy leaves.

The growth spurt of cat's ear follows dandelions by about a month. In mid-May to mid-June, cat's ear leaves begin to grow rapidly, lengthening, and the flower stalks emerge. Up until the growth spurt, cat's ear leaves stay small—4 to 6 inches—and limited in number.

Cat's ear flourishes when the ground is moist and rich, and when it gets full sunlight. It can be shaded out by other plants—shrubs, trees, and thick tall weeds.

As I've shown in the last chapter, cat's ear leaves are similar in shape to dandelion and chicory leaves. Distinguishing them is more difficult prior to stalk development because all you see is the leaves. There are ways to tell them apart. Close observation helps, as well as experience that you will get over time. Since nature is not here for our convenience, you might see some variation from my list of differences, but it is a pretty good list.

First, cat's ear leaves are conspicuously hairy on both sides, like the ears of a cat. Dandelion leaves have no hair to speak of—a few tiny random ones here and there, but nothing easily observable. Chicory is hairy on the bottom side, particularly along the main vein.

Second, neither dandelion nor chicory have a lawn-adapted flat form that presses into the ground.

Third, the lobes along the leaf margins of the upright form of cat's ear are typically long, fat, and often twisted. Even when they are short and toothed, like in the photograph here, cat's ear teeth are slightly fatter than chicory teeth.

Fourth, whole chicory leaves often gently twist or coil. Dandelion and cat's ear may cup or bend downward, but they do not twist. Cat's ear lobes may twist, but the leaves do not.

ROOT SYSTEM: Cat's ear roots typically have somewhat of a bulge at the top, just below where the leaves emerge. This is called a caudex. It gets larger as the plant matures. It may be a storage organ for water or some kind of protective

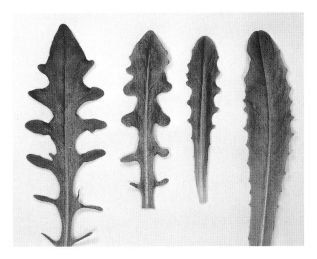

Cat's ear leaf variation. These are all cat's ear leaves showing some of the possible variations.. Compare these to the photographs on pages 274 and 275, which contrast cat's ear, dandelion, and chicory.

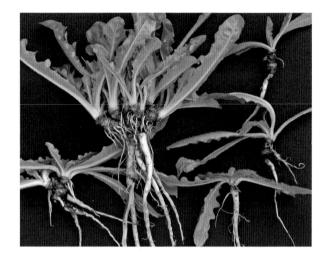

Cat's ear caudex and roots. The caudex is the enlarged portion of the stem just below the leaves. The two plants on the left are more than a year old, producing a more complex combination caudex. The three on the right are this year's plants with a simple caudex.

A healthy cat's ear plant producing its first flowering stalk. This first thick young stalk is great for eating. Flower buds are just forming at the tip.

or supportive structure. Older ones seem to get woody.

The caudex and rind, combined with a deep root system, help cat's ear survive harsh dry conditions. It's sort of like the camel of the plant world.

FLOWER STALKS, FLOWERS: At some point after the first month of spring growth, overwintered plants send up one or more flower stalks. If growing conditions are good, the stalks are thick and plentiful. Very early on, you can see immature flower buds and early branching at the tip of the stalk. The stalk is nearly leafless.

The flower stalks are a solid green in color and branch, eventually forming a flower head at the tip of each branch. In contrast, dandelions have a single, unbranched, greenish-white stalk per flower head.

Under harsh sun and lack of water, cat's ear will favor producing flower stalks and flowers over leaves. If you run across a lawn exposed to these conditions, the grass will be dead and brown. The cat's ear plants will be green with small leaves and lots of branching, flowering stems.

Major simultaneous blooming of cat's ear occurs in June or July. That is about a month after the dandelion burst. Cat's ear flowers can appear sporadically from May

Cat's ear flowers at different stages of maturation. This process takes about 3 days from first opening to the full flower you see at right. A dandelion flower head "looks like" the fully open cat's ear flower head on the right, except the dandelion is larger and looks that way from the start.

Water-stressed cat's ear produces small and few basal leaves. Even under stress, this plant produces many thin branching flower stalks.

through early November, depending on the individual plant and its environmental influences.

When mature, cat's ear flower heads can look remarkably like dandelions from the top. And like dandelions, cat's ear flowers open in the morning light and close as the sun lowers in the sky. The flowers are different in a couple of ways. Dandelion flowers open on the first day with all their petals fully developed. In contrast, cat's ear flowers bloom on the first day with only the outer petals open, with the remaining petals unfolding gradually over several days. Newly opened flowers are smaller, growing in size as they mature. Given the same conditions, mature cat's ear flower heads are, on the average, only 40 to 75 percent the size of dandelion flowers.

Cat's ear seed head. Similar to dandelion, except for seemingly stray fibers that jut out unevenly from the puff ball. It is like a smaller dandelion puffball that has had a bad hair day.

BRACTS, PUFFBALLS, SEEDS: The green bracts subtending the flower heads are different. Dandelion has two sets of bracts—one that curves upward and a second set that curves downward. Cat's ear bracts all curve upwards and have an overlapping pattern like shingles on a roof.

Cat's ear is fast-growing, proceeding from germination to seed production in about sixty days. These are perennials that produce flowers their first year and every year thereafter.

The puffball that develops is similar to dandelion, except that it seems to have a pattern of stray fibers jutting out here and there. The seeds attached to these fibers are dispersed by wind once they have matured enough to be released. On the average, these heads are smaller than dandelion puffballs.

Harvesting Cat's Ear

LEAVES: Cat's ear leaves are edible. Like dandelions, healthy rapidly growing leaves are preferable to slow-growing leaves. So find them in places where they get plenty of moisture. Season does not matter; as long as the plant is healthy, thriving, and producing new leaves, the leaves are good. Great conditions are more likely to exist in the spring while the soil is moist on its own, in well-watered grass, or on the edge of watered gardens and landscape.

If I have a choice, I prefer to harvest from cat's ear that is growing upright, but lawn-adapted leaves are acceptable. Always gather the inner upper leaves, particularly with lawn-adapted plants. The lower outer leaves will be older and will be clinging to dirt. Choose beautiful-looking young leaves. End-size leaves have very chewy mid veins.

Like dandelions, cat's ear bleeds a milky white sap—about half to a third as much sap as dandelions. This juice stains everything brown it touches—gathered greens, your clothes, and you. The staining is much greater than that of dandelion sap. Natural fabric dye might be made from this stuff. So if you care about such things, gather the greens with care.

Use a pair of scissors to clip the leaves. This makes a clean cut in a location of the leaf that you can control. As you gather, keep the cut ends in one place. When you bag them, point the cut ends into a bottom corner of the bag. If you follow these steps, you are less likely to drip the sap on something.

No matter how you collect them, keep them hydrated like all the other plants you gather. The sooner you get them soaking in water, the easier it is to wash away the sap.

After a short period, the sap dries, discoloring the leaf ends you've collected. If you want to use the fresh greens and you want them to look good, put a bowl of cold water next to your cutting board. Cut off and discard the already-discolored ends. Then chop the greens into the size suitable for your use and put them immediately in the cold water. The water will wash away the sap and refresh the leaves. Swish them around to make sure the sap gets dispersed. Then spin the water out of the leaves and use to your liking.

BUD STALKS: Cat's ear bud stalks are an excellent food. They are very easy to gather and almost always free of dirt and other debris. In a healthy, rapidly growing plant, the upper four inches are typically tender enough to eat. Their tenderness is revealed when you snap them free from the lower stalk. On stressed plants, the stems age more quickly and fibrousness develops sooner. So if you collect from stressed plants, you may have to be satisfied with a shorter

Cat's ear flower bud stalks. These are easily gathered in quantity for use in your kitchen.

piece of the upper bud stem. If the stem is just emerging from the basal rosette, you can take the whole thing. With a little practice, you'll soon figure out how to make use of the buds and their stems.

The same sap management technique used for the leaves can be used with the bud stalks. Scissors, however, are less necessary because the stalks snap cleanly. You can easily keep all the sap-dripping ends together. Point all the cut ends into one corner of your collecting bag. As with the leaves, you'll want to trim off the brown cut ends and put them in water prior to food preparation to keep them aesthetically pleasing.

Cooking and Serving Cat's Ear

RAW: Cat's ear leaves and bud stems are, to me, only 50 to 80 percent as bitter as dandelion leaves, so use them accordingly. They work well in mixed dishes where a little bitterness adds character and interest. I enjoy a fresh salad that is about a third cat's ear, a third foundational green, and a third sour green. Whole salads of cat's ear are way too bitter for me. The raw leaves and bud stems have a sticky texture if eaten alone. This is not an inherently bad feel, just different. It is likely caused by the milky sap.

When whole, the leaves are somewhat chewy. The lower part of the leaf stem is particularly tough. I typically chop off the lower fourth of the leaf blades I want to consume. That lower part is mostly stem anyway, with very little leaf blade. The remaining upper three-quarters of the leaf then needs to be chopped into bite-size pieces. These work better in salads and as cooked greens. I prefer chopping the leaves to no smaller than half-inch squares unless they are unusually chewy. (If so, I chiffonade them.) The bud stems are tender and do not need to be chopped.

Cat's ear flowers have much in common with dandelion flowers. They are both edible and can be used in many of the same ways. Put them in salads and sandwiches or

MANAGING BITTERNESS INTO ENJOYABLE FLAVORS
Read pages 261–68 to understand bitterness and to learn how to manage it into flavors that suit your particular likes and sensibilities.

throw them in soups, stews, and omelets. The differences are practical. Cat's ear flowers are slightly smaller than dandelion flowers and only about 30 percent the mass. That smaller mass means that they will have less presence and less impact when used to replace dandelions in recipes. This difference becomes apparent if you boil the flower heads. The cat's ear head shrinks into a tiny mass.

Cat's ear flowers can close up quickly once picked. To keep them open for better presentation, don't pick them until the last minute; gather them with enough stem to put them in a vase of cold, preferably iced water as they are cut; assuming they are in water, keep them in the brightest light of the day (sunlight keeps them open); pluck them from their stems as you are serving your meal.

Unlike dandelions, the petals themselves have some minor bitterness to them. You only notice this if you are plucking the petals to eat out of hand. You do not notice the bitterness if you are sprinkling the petals on a salad for color or making flower petal soup. Like dandelion flowers, try not to overdo it—eating more than ten or fifteen full heads at a time might induce a mild headache.

BOILED: The bitterness is easily removed from cat's ear by cooking, and boiling is the fastest method. Throw your chopped cat's ear leaves or bud stems into boiling water, and they should be free of bitterness in two to five minutes. Taste as you boil and remove the greens as soon as you are happy with the flavor. Remember, you do not have to remove all the bitterness. Leave some in. Drain the cooking water, drizzle with a little extra virgin olive oil, add a spritz of lemon and a little salt, and try it. The slight remaining bitterness will add depth without harshness. Boil them eight minutes or more to completely tenderize the leaves.

STEAMED: This method removes about 80 percent of the bitterness in about eight minutes. Leaf tenderness

improves gradually as the greens are boiled or steamed. After about ten minutes, they are cooked enough to be considered tender.

The broth left over from the steaming process is quite good for use as a soup stock. I prefer it over the cooking water used for boiling.

SAUTÉED: The whole bud stems and the chopped leaves work great in sautéed dishes and stir-fries. I really enjoy adding them to sautéed or steamed vegetables that go into my breakfast omelet.

Cat's Ear Stems. Steamed and served like asparagus. You have to place them carefully to look like this because the stems relax quite a bit once cooked. Directions: Steam the stems for 5 minutes or boil for 3 minutes. Add your favorite sauce. Season with salt and pepper to taste.

Cat's Ear with Peppers and Onions. Cat's ear works great in any stir-fry.

Cat's Ear with Peppers and Onions

Add garlic at the same time you are adding the greens. You'll love the results. *Serves 2–5 as a side dish.*

INGREDIENTS:

2 tablespoons extra virgin olive oil

1 small onion, sliced

⅓ red bell pepper, sliced

⅓ yellow bell pepper, sliced

1 clove garlic, minced

5 cups chopped cat's ear greens

Salt and pepper, to taste

DIRECTIONS:

In a skillet, heat the olive oil on medium high until shimmering. Add onion slices and sauté until softened and somewhat translucent. Add the peppers and garlic, stirring until slightly cooked. Add the cat's ear leaves and cook until wilted. Season with salt and pepper.

The stems relax so much upon cooking, you could use them like green noodles. Just cook, add your favorite spaghetti sauce, and serve with a little Parmesan cheese.

Chapter 18

FAMILY: Asteraceae
SPECIES: *Sonchus oleraceus*

Sow Thistle

A delightful food that is one of the most widely used wild edibles in the Mediterranean

Vigorously growing sow thistle. Young stems are developing and buds are just beginning to form at the growth tips.

Estimated Range

Official Species Name:
- *Sonchus oleraceus* L.

Synonyms:
- None

Common Names:
- Sow thistle
- Annual Sow Thistle
- Smooth Sow Thistle
- Hare's Lettuce
- Quelite de leche
- Zochos or Tsochos (Greece)
- Zuccho or Sivone (Italy)
- Cerrajas or Forrajas (Spain)
- Yellow Pualele (Hawaii)

An herbaceous weed naturalized from southern Europe and Asia, sow thistle is widespread and abundant in North America, primarily where humans have invaded and where soil has been disturbed.

continued

SOW THISTLE

I do not know where or when I first learned about sow thistle. As a mild bitter, I initially avoided it, as I did most of the other bitter greens before I understood them better. But over the last couple of years, I have become more and more impressed with this plant's capabilities. I now look forward to eating it every year.

For those of us who did not grow up on a farm, *sow* is a strange word. A sow is a female pig. So why "sow thistle"? Why not "pig thistle"? Female pigs are mammals that breastfeed their offspring. Sow thistle is notorious for bleeding a milky sap, and lots of it. It may have seemed logical for farmers to hope that sows eating this plant would produce more milk for their offspring. Of course, the sap is only milk-like in appearance. The chemistry of plant sap and breast milk are unrelated. It is unknown if sow thistle has any effect on milk production in mammals, other than being another nutritious food.

There are several plants in the *Sonchus* genus known as sow thistle. The one I'm focusing on in this chapter is annual or smooth sow thistle (*Sonchus oleraceus*) as opposed to spiny sow thistle (*Sonchus asper*) or perennial sow thistle (*Sonchus arvensis*). All three have similar edibilities.

Apparently sow thistle is not a true thistle. As far as I can tell, that distinction has been bequeathed to three genera: *Cirsium*, *Carduus*, and *Onopordum*. I do not know what the criterion for a true thistle is or if the distinction is scientific or folklore. All I know is that *Sonchus* is not one of those three.

Like many vegetables, some edible parts are fleeting, meaning that you have a short window of opportunity to harvest some of the good parts before you lose them to adult onset fibrousness or bitterness. So you adapt by eating seasonally—which is one of today's popular trends. The cool thing about sow thistle is that it can produce multiple crops during the growing season if the soil is repeatedly disturbed.

Nutritionally, sow thistle is higher in omega-3 fatty

acids, zinc, and manganese than any of our domesticated greens. In fact, it has the highest source of manganese of any of the foods in our two charts. It has good amounts of copper and iron, and average amounts of beta-carotene, vitamin C, calcium, and fiber.

From a phytochemical standpoint, the edible parts of sow thistle have shown a high antioxidant activity in laboratory tests (Pieroni, 2002). The greens contain polyphenols and flavonoids, including aspigenin, kaempferol, luteolin, myricetin, and quercetin. *Sonchus oleraceus* has four times more myricetin than red wine and twelve times more than black tea. It has about half as much quercetin as onions. (Trichopoulou, 2000b.)

Knowing Sow Thistle

SEEDS: Sow thistle is an annual that only grows from seed. If it gets a late start, it can overwinter to complete its life in the spring. Overwintering can happen in moderate climates, but I am not sure that sow thistle can survive harsh winters. Its seeds can germinate anytime during the growing seasons when conditions are right. So if there is moisture and seed near the surface, sprouting can happen.

SEEDLINGS: Sow thistle seedlings are somewhat difficult to distinguish from nipplewort and a few other plants. The cotyledons resemble Ping-Pong paddles. The first true leaves are shaped like tennis rackets with spines around their margins. Some of the spines point up, some out, some down towards the base of the plant.

The third set of leaves has a choice: the leaves can be elongated versions of the tennis racket shape, or they can be miniature versions of the shape that the mature basal leaves will become. The mature shape is somewhat dandelion-like but with its own character.

Two sow thistle seedlings so close to each other that they are overlapping. The cotyledons look like Ping-Pong paddles. The first true leaves look like tennis rackets. All but the cotyledons will continue to grow in size. You can see the sharply pointed adult form leaves emerging from the growth point of each seedling. These seedlings are about ⅝ inch in diameter.

Young sow thistle, about 3 inches in diameter. The two tiny cotyledons are partially obscured by the growing true leaves. Notice the tennis-racket-shaped leaves as intermediaries between the cotyledons and the more raspy mature form of the leaves. The tennis racket leaves are now about ten times the size of the cotyledons. Note the chickweed sprouts and small clover plant.

Why all this detail on seedlings? Because it helps you to know which ones to let grow when you are weeding your garden—taking out all those inedible weeds.

If you still need help identifying a plant as sow thistle, spray-mist it. If the water beads up and drips off the leaves, you have one more piece of evidence that it is sow thistle. If the leaf just gets wet, it is an indication that you have nipplewort or some other plant. Sow thistle is hairless—further distinguishing it from nipplewort. And finally, the color of the leaves tends towards cyan but can be green. Nipplewort is mostly just green.

LEAVES: At some point, the leaves start to multiply, forming a basal rosette. The more the plant is under stress (lack of water and nutrients), the fewer and smaller leaves are produced. If it is growing in lush conditions, a large amount of leaves will form.

Adult leaves also vary in shape, depending on where the plant is in its growth cycle. Younger plants, particularly

Basal rosette of fully formed leaves. This plant shows both rounded and more triangular tipped leaves. The basal leaves can get much bigger than this.

Young sow thistle sending up its new stem. This plant is about 8 inches tall and shows leaf tips in the fat triangular form.

within the basal rosette, tend to have round-tipped leaves. As the plant gets older, there is a tendency to produce leaves whose tips are more triangular. The leaf tip outline transitions from fat triangular to thin triangular as the leaves are followed up the plant stem.

A full basal rosette lasts for a couple of weeks before a stem is formed. How quickly it produces that stem and goes to seed is determined by the season and its growth needs. Sow thistle germinating early in the spring will live longer and produce more leaves and larger stems before it buds and flowers than if it germinates in the summer or fall.

Spring-germinated plants are in no hurry to reproduce; they've got lots of time to grow vegetable matter prior to seed production. That extra vegetable matter has the capacity to do more photosynthesis, which provides more food for the plant to feed its eventual seed production. This not only produces more food for us in its vegetative forms, it produces more seed later, which is its true mission in life.

Sow thistles germinating in the summer or fall do not

(above, left and right)
A comparison of sow thistle's basic two forms: sharply triangular and rounded triangular:

(left) The upper 14 inches of a 32-inch-tall plant This plant's upper leaf tips are clearly in the sharp triangular form and are bright green in color.

(right) A 40-inch-tall sow thistle plant. The leaves are larger, fatter, and softer than the more triangular form. Note the color variation in the stem. While the predominant color is bluish green, this plant sometimes produces some purplish coloration to leaves and/or stems.

live as long as spring plants. Nature somehow tells them to have a shorter life, to go to seed sooner, before they die from the heat of summer or the cold of winter. Both these scenarios make the plant want to produce seed quickly before the end arrives. These plants are shorter in height, produce less vegetative growth, and pass their prime (from a food perspective) very quickly.

Each leaf is directly attached to the stem in an alternating pattern. Down past their tips, individual leaves have a series of lobes extending from each side of the main vein. The lobes follow the example of the tips and get thinner and more pointed as you examine leaves up the plant stem.

Sow thistle leaves tend to *look* spiny due to the shape of their margins. The margins are toothed, often ending with sharply pointed tips. The margins are often wavy, and the teeth can be irregularly shaped. Some individual leaves have lots of large and obvious points; others are more subtle. The softer the leaves, the softer the pointed teeth along the margins. Older leaves stiffen up, making the points stiffer so that they begin to feel spiny. Sow thistle has no real spines or thorns.

Sow thistle leaf variation. These mature leaves found near the base of the sow thistle plants are about 8 inches long. The lower leaf stems are cut out of the picture. The lobes of these leaves vary in shape, size, and number (some have more lobes than others).

All sow thistle leaf bases wrap around the main stalk. But as you observe upwards, you see that leaf stems transform from long and narrow to short and wide until they disappear. These upper teardrop-shaped leaves wrap all the way around that stem; its leaf blade itself wraps around the stem. The wrapping lobes often overlap each other.

As you can see in these photographs, sow thistle plants demonstrate a lot of leaf variation. But after a short learning period, you will be able to spot a sow thistle plant from at least thirty feet.

Every location where a leaf attaches to the stem is a potential spot for a new shoot to grow; new shoots form new branches.

Upper leaves are teardrop-shaped and clasp, or wrap around, the stem where it is attached. It wraps all the way around to the point of overlapping itself. A new shoot is emerging where the leaf meets the stem.

STEM: Sow thistle's stem is quite stout, oddly shaped, and roughly five-sided. The stem twists gently as it travels upwards. On close observation, you'll see that these sides are related to how the leaves are attached to the stem. There is actually a sixth side, but it is much reduced. Now that I've told you about this five-angled stem, I have to add that sometimes that stem is more rounded. Don't ask me why—I do not have a clue. I chalk it up to natural variation. Always remember that nature is not here for our convenience.

Spiny Sow Thistle
Sonchus asper

Edible brother of sow thistle with similar uses

Spiny sow thistle is like the wild misbehaving brother of smooth sow thistle. Some people think smooth sow thistle is spiny—but wait till you see spiny sow thistle. Like smooth sow thistle, spiny sow thistle has no true spines or thorns. But the teeth on its leaf margins are wild, pointing this way and that. The margin itself is undulating—curving those wild teeth into even more wildness. The shape of the margins gives the impression of being on fire.

Another thing making it *feel* spinier is that the leaves, in general, are tougher, stronger, and more solid than smooth sow thistle, making the teeth and their tips tougher/sharper to the touch. These differences impact its use as a food. To make its spininess more palatable, it requires longer cooking times to soften it up and/or chopping into smaller pieces to lessen the chewing discomfort.

Basal rosettes of spiny
sow thistle (left) and
smooth sow thistle.

In almost all other ways, smooth and spiny sow thistle are similar: both form a basal rosette of leaves prior to developing a stalk, both form a five-sided stalk, leaf stems (petioles) get shorter as they travel up the main stalk, and they both have similar buds, flowers, and seed heads.

Upper leaf on a spiny sow thistle stem. Like smooth sow thistle, this leaf is teardrop-shaped, and its basal lobes clasp the stem. The leaf margins here are distinct, due to their wild spinyness.

A maturing spiny sow thistle plant with buds and almost-open flower. This is an adult plant even though it is stunted to only about 14 inches tall. It germinated in the summer, so got a late start in the growing season for this species. Because of that, it grew a short stalk and went into flower within a few weeks. Had it germinated earlier in the spring (allowing it a much longer season), it would have been a much taller plant.

A 4-foot-tall mature sow thistle showing buds and flowers on upper branches. This plant germinated in the spring under normal circumstances and enjoys normal growth to maturity.

Sow thistle buds, flowers, and seed heads. The buds are tiny and cylindrical in shape. The closed flowers are fat at their bases and narrow at their tips. The white seed head is smaller than an inch in diameter.

BUDS: Sow thistle buds form early in stalk development. But if the plant is growing in good conditions, the stem can get quite tall before those buds bloom into flowers. The buds are distinct in shape. They resemble human nipples—cylindrical in shape and about the right size (see page 325). So you'd think that this plant would be called nipple thistle. But no. The next plant in the book (nipplewort) got that name even though its buds are tiny—about the size I would imagine guinea pig nipples to be: tiny, thin, and narrow.

FLOWERS: The flowers are yellow and dandelion-like, growing in clusters at the tips of branched stems. They are smaller than dandelion flowers, about three-quarters of an inch across or less.

Bloom time is determined by local climatic conditions. For instance, in southern British Columbia, sow thistle blooms around June. In Phoenix, Arizona, it blooms around early March. That is a three-month difference.

Once the flowers mature, they produce rounded seed heads reminiscent of small dandelion puffballs. Once the seeds mature, the puffballs break apart, allowing the seeds to be carried away by the wind.

TAPROOT: Sow thistle and spiny sow thistle each grow from a taproot.

Harvesting Sow Thistle

Like other plants in the aster family, sow thistle bleeds a milky sap. As I advised with cat's ear, you want to consider managing the sap that bleeds out. You'll have better control if you cut parts off with a pair of scissors. Then keep all those parts together while you are handling and bagging them. Sow thistle bleeds more milky sap than most plants, so be prepared.

Like with all other harvested plants, keep sow thistle greens fresh by spray-misting them, storing them in plastic bags, keeping them cool and out of the sun, and using them as soon as possible. Any part that you cut will bleed the milky sap. Anything the sap touches will stain brown. For appearances, you should trim off any cut stained parts just before using. The brown dye here is not as strong as the stain from cat's ear.

Sow thistle leaves can be almost as tough as collard greens. So for almost all uses, I chop them into small pieces. This goes a long way in tenderizing them for fresh or cooked applications. Chopping is even more important when using the tougher, spiny, sow thistle leaves. Do not chop sow thistle leaves until you are ready to use them. And when you do, soak them immediately in cold water. The water will wash away the sap from the cut ends—preventing staining and keeping the leaves looking fresh and green.

Leaf stems are particularly tough, almost as tough as collard greens stems. So I typically discard the leaf stem below the leaf blade; that removes about one-third the length of the leaf. When gathering the upper five or six inches of the rapidly growing

Hollow stems, mostly five-sided. Nodes separate the hollow stem into separate air chambers. A sort of sixth side is at the top of this view. Sow thistle is a prolific producer of milky sap that bleeds whenever the plant is injured.

main stem, make sure your knife or scissors slices through easily. If you feel toughness while you are cutting the stem, it indicates that that part of the stem is too tough to eat. So cut higher until the slice is easy. If any attached leaves are longer than three inches, remove them. You can leave on all the buds and smaller leaves if you want. The more leafage you remove, the more the stem will look asparagus-like. Any leaves removed can be used elsewhere.

The first harvest off a particular plant will always be the best. Whenever you cut the stem, you stimulate new growth in the remaining plant. This means new leaves and stems can be harvested later. But be aware that once the stem is cut, the plant goes into survival mode and wants to go to seed as soon as possible. So while more vegetative growth forms, it will be smaller with the plant rapidly progressing toward seed development.

Prior to cooking the upper stem (or *sowsparagus*, as I call it), take a barbecue skewer and force it up the hollow stem. This will pierce all the chambers trapping air within the stem. Doing this prevents the stem from exploding when you heat the greens. The explosions are minor but fun to hear—giving off a "POP" sound as each air-trapped chamber bursts. You do not see food flying across the room, but allowing the bursts deteriorates the appearance of the cooked sowsparagus.

Sowsparagus. The upper 6 or so inches of a rapidly growing healthy plant is tender and collectable. At the cut point, they can be anywhere from ³/₈ to 1 inch in diameter. Note the buds located near the base of the top leaf. Everything you see here is tender and edible.

As the stem gets older and more fibrous, you can always gather the still-tender tips containing the buds and one or two leaves. But once the flowers have opened, you've passed the time when the stem will still be usably tender.

No matter how old the stem is, if you can see unopened bud clusters, you can still collect buds. They will be tender and delicious when prepared properly. Be aware that aphids

Flower bud clusters. The buds and their short supporting stems are edible and ready for use. Once the buds start opening into flowers, the stems quickly become fibrous. Closed flowers are vase-shaped and too fibrous to eat.

love sow thistle upper stems and buds. Sometimes when I am hoping to collect some, there are so many aphids that I can barely see the buds. Be brave—cook and eat the whole thing. I'll bet aphids are highly nutritious.

If you are collecting the buds, make sure you remove all the open and closed flowers as well as the seed heads. All parts except the buds and uppermost bud stems are fibrous. In fact, the flower heads are so fibrous, you could use them as a masticator (a non-sweet chewing gum). But it's not like gum; it is like chewing on soft vegetable matter that won't break down easily. I don't find it bitter like most of the rest of the plant. Try it for the fun of it.

Serving Sow Thistle

LEAVES: The younger the leaves, no matter how old the plant, the more tender they will be. The most tender leaves

MANAGING BITTERNESS INTO ENJOYABLE FLAVORS

Read pages 261–68 to understand bitterness and to learn how to manage it into flavors that suit your particular likes and sensibilities.

are found on healthy, rapidly growing basal rosettes. The faster the plant grows, the less bitter the rapidly growing leaves. Sow thistle leaves are only a fraction of the bitterness of dandelion leaves.

When managed appropriately, sow thistle is a delicious green, and its mild bitterness works well in complex green, fruit, and meat salads. It can work almost anywhere that collard greens can.

Cooking sow thistle reduces both the bitterness and the crunchiness found in some of the older leaves. Boiling young rapidly growing leaves for three to five minutes can remove the bitterness completely. Boiling them for ten minutes makes them much more tender. If you boil them, how long you boil them is determined by how you want to use them. If they are destined for a mixed dish, they need less boiling. If you are making a pure batch of sow thistle greens, only boil them until they reach your desired flavor and texture. Remember to keep sampling the cooking greens for the flavor and texture you are looking for. The cooking water from the boiling process makes a great broth or soup stock.

Steaming sow thistle leaves has about the same effect on chewiness as boiling. But it does not remove the bitterness as well. Steaming for longer periods can help some, but so can adding lemon juice, olive oil, salt, or some kind of sauce to the cooked greens. Salad dressings work wonders to help temper the bitterness.

SOWSPARAGUS: This is my favorite part of sow thistle. If you are lucky enough to find a bunch of lavishly growing plants producing thick upper stems, call me. It is the tenderest part of the plant and is delicious. Raw, the upper stem and buds are only mildly bitter—good in many mixed dishes or chopped into salads. Boiled two to five minutes, they have a flavor reminiscent of asparagus crossed with artichoke hearts. Mmmmm—my mouth is watering.

FLOWERS: These become less chewy after fifteen or more minutes of boiling. They are at their best when used in soups and stews that require long boiling times.

TAPROOT: The taproot of the basal rosette works fine as a cooked vegetable. Rip off all fibrous roots attached to the taproots you've gathered and boil them for five to ten minutes. They are good anywhere you would use potatoes. Use them as an accent in mixed dishes. Once the stalk is forming, the taproot gets fibrous and bitter. Even boiling for twenty minutes in two changes of water will not improve the flavor or texture of the older roots.

Sowsparagus. Boiled and served with extra virgin olive oil, lemon juice, and a touch of salt.

Pasta with Sow
Thistle Greens.

Pasta with Sow Thistle Greens

Many kinds of sauces and creams would work in this recipe in place of olive oil. Try spaghetti sauce or pesto. *Serves 4.*

INGREDIENTS:

1 pound of pasta, any kind
⅓ cup extra virgin olive oil
4 cups finely chopped young sow thistle leaves
3 cloves garlic, finely minced
Salt and pepper, to taste
Parmesan cheese (optional)

DIRECTIONS:

Cook pasta, remove from heat, and drain. Over medium heat in a separate skillet, heat 3 tablespoons olive oil until shimmering. Add greens and sauté for about 7 minutes, or until the greens become tender. Stir in garlic and continue sautéing for about 3 minutes. Pour cooked greens and remaining olive oil into your pasta pot. Return to heat and stir the greens and pasta mixture until hot. Remove from heat. Season with salt and pepper, and add Parmesan if you'd like. Serve immediately.

Chapter 19

Family: Asteraceae
Species: *Lapsana communis*

Nipplewort

A delicious green with character and an odd name

Nipplewort rosettes, just prior to bolting—a prime time to collect the leaves.

Estimated Range

Official Species Name:
• *Lapsana communis* L.

Synonyms:
• None

Common Names:
• Nipplewort
• Dockcress
• Swine's cress

An herbaceous weed naturalized from Eurasia, nipplewort is widespread and abundant in North America, primarily where humans have invaded.

Edible Parts:
• Growing tops of leafy stems
• Rapidly growing leaves.
• Buds and flowers

NIPPLEWORT

Nipplewort originated in and grows all over eastern and western Europe, western Russia, the Mediterranean, parts of Asia, and it has naturalized in most of the populated areas of northern North America.

Most of the popular literature attributes the name "nipplewort" to the shape of the flower buds. But, as I joked about in the last chapter, that never made sense to me. Nipplewort buds were too small and not the right shape. With a little more digging, I found an explanation that seems to make more sense. According to ethnobotanical research done by David Allen and Gabrielle Hatfield and reported in their book *Medicinal Plants in Folk Tradition* (2004), they found the following: Historically, in the British Isles and other parts of Europe, nursing mothers would apply nipplewort leaves— possibly directly (it's not specified) as a poultice, or in some other application—to their nipples to relieve soreness from breast feeding. In Gaelic, the original names for the plant evidently translated to "good leaf" and "breast leaf."

"Nipplewort" makes sense from a medicinal standpoint. The word *wort,* which typically means "plant," is from German and English origins and was generally applied to plants that had some medicinal value. *Wort* has nothing to do with "warts," a virus-caused growth of abnormal cells.

I could find no nutrient or phytochemical data on nipplewort. It is safe to assume that nipplewort adds to the diversity of the diet with whatever nutrients it contains. Just like all the foods in this book, the value is in the diversity and the quantity of greens you eat, not in specific nutrients.

Knowing Nipplewort

SEEDS: Nipplewort is an annual that grows from seed. It can germinate in any of the growing seasons when the soil is moist enough. I find it germinating much more in the cooler seasons of spring and fall than it does in the heat of summer.

Seeds need moisture and light to germinate. When

buried where light cannot penetrate, nipplewort seeds will not germinate. Germination is more successful if the seeds are less than a year old and have gone through one drying period. As the seedling emerges, the cotyledons are tiny, hairless, and spoon-shaped.

LEAVES: The first two true leaves are tennis-racket-shaped with three to five subtle points defining the margin. Those first two leaves remain different in shape and size from all other true leaves that follow. Close inspection shows tiny hairs on all true leaves.

POULTICE

Plant material, typically a soft moist mass, that is held against the body to relieve localized inflammation, soreness, or to draw things out of the body. It works sort of like today's bandage—only instead of gauze, you have plant material. Instead of just protecting the infliction, you are treating it medicinally.

Nipplewort seedling, about an inch in size from left to right. The cotyledons are tiny and spoon-shaped. The first true leaves are on the left and right of this view. One is a rounded pentagon shape (left), and the other is a rounded three-pointed shape. From the third true leaf onward, the leaf blades get longer, the margins have more points, and lobes develop on the leaf stem, as seen on the leaf stem at upper right.

Nipplewort—still young but past the seedling stage. The tiny cotyledons are partially hidden by the overtopping true leaves. The first two true leaves pointing left and right will remain smaller and different in shape than all the other true leaves that come after them.

All true leaves from the third one onward gradually start taking on the adult leaf shape—a longer more pointed leaf blade, wavy leaf margins, more points on the margins, and lobes forming along the leaf stem.

Nipplewort, when growing as an individual, shows a clear basal rosette of leaves. Often, due to massive amounts of seeds on the soil, the plants grow so close together that they form a loose, salad-like ground cover (see pages 329 and 334). Under these crowded conditions, it is impossible to see basal rosettes or where one plant stops and another begins without pulling the plants apart.

Upper leaf surfaces are covered with short tiny hairs that give a velvety feel. Individual hairs are more obvious on the leaf undersides—particularly along the veins. The main central vein has the largest hairs; secondary veins have hairs that are almost as large.

As the basal rosette of leaves develops, the leaves evolve in shape. Like sow thistle, the large blade at the tip of each leaf, while rounded, becomes more triangular with each

Undersides of young nipplewort leaves (left) and sow thistle compared. Nipplewort has obvious hairs on its veins with others scattered in between. Sow thistle is hairless on both its upper and lower sides.

new leaf that grows in. Just below that tip are a pair of lobes—each about one-tenth the size of the tip. Farther down the stem are even smaller lobes about a fifth or a tenth the size of the first set of lobes.

Nipplewort basal rosette of leaves. Plants like this can be anywhere from 8 to 24 inches in diameter.

The leaf stem is triangular in cross section. The very base of the leaf stem, where it attaches to the plant stem, is curved and cupped like celery.

Nipplewort leaves are green, thin, delicate, and velvety to the touch. In contrast, sow thistle leaves are bluish-green, sometimes with reddish accents, sturdy and smooth to the touch. On more mature plants, sow thistle lobes are more numerous and larger in size.

TAPROOT: Like every plant in this section, nipplewort has a taproot.

STEM: At some point in the plant's life, a flower stem emerges from the center of the basal rosette of leaves. This initiates because the plant reaches its own form of puberty and because of weather and other environmental stimuli. Seeds germinating in the spring all seem to bolt (grow a stem) at the same time. In contrast, seeds germinating in the summer or fall, tend to bolt much earlier in their lives in an effort to go to seed before inclement (bone-dry hot or freezing) weather kills them. Or if it is really late in the season, they do not bolt until they have overwintered.

Stems are primarily round and hollow. If you examine the stem, you will find it covered with hairs. Upon closer examination, you will see some minor ridges running up and down the stalk. Under ideal conditions, the stem will be thick, supporting plenty of fully-formed leaves. As it branches and extends upward, the stems thin out, supporting fewer full-sized leaves.

In great conditions, adult plants can reach six feet in height. The branching flowering stems narrow, increase

Nipplewort plants growing in high density and starting to bolt (grow a stem). The leaf tips are more triangular (less rounded) in shape as the plant continues to grow upward. The stems here, though difficult to see, are about 4 to 5 inches tall.

in toughness, and increase in bitterness as the plant matures. The leaves change shape as they travel up the plant. Small narrow leaves grow on the upper branching flower stalks. The top half of the plant is almost bare of foliage relative to the bottom half.

If nipplewort stems are broken or harvested, the plant will be stimulated to produce more growth and to go quickly to seed. Cut stems often stimulate the growth of multiple replacement stems.

(above) A 4-foot-tall, healthy, maturing nipplewort plant. The tall, lean reproductive stems are clearly reaching above the more leafy lower part of the plant. This plant is just forming its first buds and flowers.

The upper 8 inches of a healthy, spring-germinated, 14-inch-tall nipplewort plant. No buds or flowers have appeared yet. The stem is thick and straight. I call it nipsparagus.

Leaf shapes found on the upper half of a fully mature nipplewort plant. The higher they are on the plant, the smaller and narrower the leaf. The bottom three leaves shown here had their stems trimmed somewhat to fit the photograph. Lower leaves nearer the base of the plant can be seen in my hand on page 338.

BUDS, BRACTS, FLOWERS: Nipplewort buds are small and green at the tips of branching stems. They are less than an eighth inch in diameter. There are eight bracts surrounding each bud. Yellow flowers emerge from the tops of the bracts. Like other members of the aster family, these are composite flowers—really a flower head of a bunch of smaller individual flowers clustered together to simulate one flower. Each petal is from a different flower and has five teeth at its tip. When fully open, nipplewort flower heads are about a half inch in diameter. The anthers carrying the pollen are somewhat brown in color.

Once pollinated, all showy flower parts fall away from the bracts, leaving the seeds to mature in their now stiff, brown bract encasement. Fully mature seeds detach from their bases and rattle around within these vase-shaped containers until they get knocked out and fall to the ground.

Harvesting and Managing Nipplewort

LEAVES: Nipplewort is a prolific plant. Its seeds sprout predictably, and it produces most of its edible offerings in the spring, right around the time that asparagus shoots

are being harvested. As with the other plants in this book, the goal is to gather young, rapidly growing leaves from whatever part of the plant you find them. Leaves from the basal rosette prior to stalk formation are the most tender. A leaf of any size can be good as long as it looks healthy and vibrant.

If you can find enough of this plant growing in dense clusters prior to bolting, use your scissors to clip many leaves at once. Otherwise, just using your hand to snap leaves free works fine. Just grab them at the leaf stem so you don't injure the leaf blade. Like the other plants in this bitter plants section, nipplewort bleeds a milky sap, but it is not enough quantity to have to manage carefully.

It is helpful, however, to keep the leaves lined up as

(left) Buds and flowers of nipplewort. The flowers are mostly open here. Fully open, the petals reach out more to the sides.

(right) Brown dry bract encasements holding nipplewort seeds. The seeds, once mature, rattle around inside the open-topped casings until they are knocked out. The casings resemble the green buds in size and shape, but the plant has died by the time the seeds are ripe.

Fully mature nipplewort leaves from the lower parts of the stem. These leaves have just reached their full size—still great for use as food. Lining them up like this makes them easier to trim in the kitchen. I cut off the fibrous leaf stem where my thumb is holding the leaves.

you gather them for other reasons besides sap. Nipplewort leaf stems are fibrous. As with sow thistle, you'll want to chop off most of the leaf stem. While it may seem more efficient at the time, do not pluck the blade tips free from their stems as you gather unless you plan to use them right away. Leaving the stems on helps to keep the leaves fresh until ready for use.

As with all other plants, keep them cool and well hydrated until ready to use. Try to use them as close to the time you pick them as possible to preserve freshness. They will last for about a week in the refrigerator.

There are parts of North America where winters are generally mild and wet enough to support slow growth of basal rosettes. Check them out; nipplewort leaves found under those conditions can be delicious raw without more than a hint of bitterness.

STEMS: Gather the upper four to eight inches of the rapidly growing stems for nipsparagus. This can be the first four to eight inches of stem from ground level all the way up to the top part of a two-foot-tall stem. The best stems are thick, tender, and straight like the one shown earlier (see page 335). The length to take is determined by tenderness, which is determined by how healthy, well-watered, and rapidly growing the stem is. The thicker and straighter they are, the earlier in maturation they are. Maturing stems that are getting ready to produce buds begin to zigzag slightly from leaf to leaf. Zigzagging stems will be thinner, tougher, and more bitter. Younger, thicker, straighter is better.

Finding the tender part of the stem takes some practice. I have found that if you cut just below the point that feels tender, all that stem will be tender once boiled. Whether using a knife or scissors, there is a certain feel you will understand over time that helps you gauge tenderness in a stem. To get the maximum amount of tender stem length, cut about two inches below the point you think is tender—taking more stem then needed. Later in the kitchen, just before using, cut off a half inch more at a time, working your way up the stem, until you find an acceptable tender feel from the cut-through. Then you'll know the stem will be good from that point upward. Snapping the stem like you would asparagus to determine the tender point can work, but it is a little difficult.

Once gathered, pull all but the very topmost baby leaves from the stem just before using. Remember that the more developed leaves will have fibrous leaf stems, so you do not want to include them when serving nipsparagus. Use the removed leaves separately. The other benefit of removing the leaves, is that the nipsparagus looks more asparagus-like, which will please anyone you serve it to.

Serving Nipplewort

**MANAGING
BITTERNESS INTO
ENJOYABLE FLAVORS**
Read pages 261–68 to
understand bitterness
and to learn how to
manage it into flavors
that suit your particular
likes and sensibilities.

Greek Salad with Nipplewort
Leaves. Also included are wild
spinach leaves, cucumber
slices, sliced olives, fresh
tomato, and feta cheese, all
drizzled with extra virgin
olive oil and lemon juice,
sprinkled with oregano,
and salted to taste. One
of my favorite salads.

Nipplewort leaves and nipsparagus can be mildly to strongly bitter depending on a variety of factors. One of the things I appreciate about nipplewort is that the bitterness there does not linger on the tongue like raw dandelion or wintercress.

The younger and more rapidly growing that nipplewort is, the less bitter; the earlier in the season, the less bitter. Sometimes young basal rosette leaves growing under mature stems can be less bitter. This is where your judgement comes into play. Taste as you gather to decide how you want to use the greens you harvest. Remember, bitterness is a feature, not a limitation. Learn to manage bitterness in meal preparation. If they are less bitter, use more in mixed dishes. If they are more bitter, use less.

RAW: I enjoy mixing them raw in vegetable, fruit, and meat salads. You want them in just enough quantity so that they add a nice bite but don't overpower. The greens

are great in sandwiches, pestos, and salsas. They are often slightly too bitter for me to eat raw or unadorned.

As you prepare dishes, keep in mind the hair factor. The short velvety hairs that cover the leaves are unnoticeable in mixed or properly cooked dishes, but they are dominant if you make a salad of nipplewort alone. Also, I find the buds, flowers, and still-tender upper elongated flower stems quite bitter. Cooking does not reduce their bitterness to any degree. To use them, chop tiny amounts into mixed dishes so they won't overpower you. Experiment so the amount you use suits you.

BOILED: This is the best way to reduce bitterness and reveal the great underlying flavor of nipplewort greens. Boiling for two minutes leaves a very mild bitterness; around four minutes removes it all. Of course, your experience might vary. Always sample as you boil to get the taste you want. When I boil nipplewort, I enjoy eating it as a

Poached Egg on Nipplewort Greens. Sauté red onions until translucent. Add the nipplewort greens and continue sautéing until the greens are fully wilted. Place the cooked greens and onions on toast and top with a poached egg. Salt and pepper to taste. Very satisfying.

cooked green all by itself. I just add a little olive oil, balsamic vineger, and salt to taste.

STEAMED: This process has almost the same bitter-reducing effect as boiling, but the hairs remain more prominent. So adjust accordingly. Steamed nipplewort greens are a great addition to an omelette.

SAUTÉED: As long as the greens aren't too bitter, sautéing works well. The extra virgin olive oil enhances the flavor quite a bit, transforming the bitterness without totally removing it. Sautéing nipplewort greens and then adding them to whipped egg for an omelette is wonderful.

Nipsparagus. Steam or boil nipplewort stems and serve with your favorite sauce. I decorated this dish with columbine (*Aquilegia chrysantha*) and chive flowers. For comparison, a fresh uncooked stem is displayed on the table. Lining up stems like this take some patience because they are limp once cooked.

PART III
THE POTENTIAL
OF WILD FOODS

In this section, I take on the human side of the equation. How do wild foods fit into our modern world? Why pursue them, study them, eat them? How nutritious are they? How would you increase your access to wild foods in order to eat them daily, and what considerations come into play for people wanting to bring wild foods to market? Oxalates and nitrates are mentioned as hazardous substances in almost every wild food book—what should you think about them? There is also a chapter proposing a name for the field of wild foods.

Amid all the fun, I take the field of wild foods very seriously, as have more and more scientific researchers. The research on wild foods takes place in a variety of disciplines with no apparent unifying agent. In this section, I collect, organize, and present some of the information produced by researchers, and suggest some beginnings of a framework for thinking about wild foods.

And while the potential of wild foods can be clearly seen throughout this book, this section helps provide the information, perspective, and motivation to foster a more active use of these plants.

Chapter 20

Why Eat Wild Foods?

There are many reasons to learn about, find, gather, and eat wild foods. The primary reasons I put forth are that it's fun, it satisfies a variety of human needs, and this food is good for you spiritually, intellectually, and physically.

Getting involved with wild foods taps into your adventurous spirit, satisfies the drive to be more self reliant, and fulfills the desire to connect more intimately with the earth and its bounty. It sets you on a path to be a student of the plant world, an investigator, an observer, a history detective. You find yourself spending more "dirt time"— learning the secret life of plants.

There is a lot of joy in finding that original recipe for sarsaparilla, making that first acorn muffin, or serving your friends an omelet made with wild greens.

Wild foods provide a fun, knowledge-based recreational activity that meaningfully engages the heart and mind. The gathering of substantial sustenance directly from the earth, as opposed to finding a sanitized plastic-wrapped product in the produce section of a supermarket, has a great impact on the soul. It brings us closer to the earth and to our distant ancestors, and it engenders feelings of confidence and self-reliance. Knowing enough to forage, harvest, and eat your own wild food is a very primal experience. The study and use of wild foods can realistically become a lifelong outdoor recreational, educational, and culinary activity—new fun, new food, and new fascination for a lifetime.

Here are some practical additional reasons why people will benefit from learning about and eating wild foods.

"DIRT TIME"

Time spent learning about nature and its inhabitants while actually in nature, as opposed to learning from books, on computers, or in a classroom. Dirt time involves observational and experiential learning in the real world.

Wild Foods Are Good for Your Family

All of the benefits gained by you as an individual are amplified in a family setting. If you are a parent who enjoys wild foods, it has the added benefit of being really fun for kids at any age. Spending quality time together as a family, exploring nature close-up while investigating, gathering, and cooking the plants will be times you and your kids will never forget. Involving kids in the whole process, from identifying and collecting to preparing and eating, will engage their curiosity and begin a lifelong family activity.

Kids today are isolated from food systems. In a meaningful way, wild foods will teach them where food comes from. And there's the added benefit of exercise. Let's face it, childhood and adult obesity rates are epidemic in North America. In today's video game-, television-, and computer-focused sedentary existence, this outdoor activity can help to provide the kinds of physical exercise and dietary contributions that both parents and children need to foster a healthier lifestyle.

Treating Nature Deficit Disorder

Children today are isolated from food systems—ignorant of exactly what food is, where food comes from, and how it gets into the forms we see in the supermarket. Adding to the problem is their isolation from nature itself, no longer spending much time in it because of a constant barrage from "awfulizers" hyping fear of everything to the general population.

"Awfulizers"—sensationalized media, manipulative and pandering politicians, and laws that scare parents into monitoring and micromanaging their kids every second of the day—add up to kids who no longer play freely with their peers in neighborhoods and local woods. The hobby of wild foods is one way that parents and their children can play together in nature. Even in an atmosphere of fear, kids can get more exposure to nature.

Wild Foods Provide Motivation for Students

Most kids who love the outdoors and spending time in nature are fascinated by creatures like frogs, lizards, turtles, and snakes. Plants get slighted in our school systems because they don't move, hop, slither, or bite. Kids today do not know why they should care about plants. But if they see plants in a new light, one that goes beyond just learning taxonomy and morphology, then they will be motivated learners. Here are some of the concepts that may help motivate students:

—Plants form part of the lowest level of the food chain, a chain that we are a part of. Foods at lower levels accumulate/concentrate less environmental toxins.
—Plants are crucial to the students' own survival.
—The earth provides food, even if not grown on a farm.
—Native Americans and all preagriculture communities made their living by gathering and eating all of these foods.
—Many cultures around the world still eat wild foods today.

These concepts make plants more interesting, more rewarding. Plants become something to discover, to play with, to cook with, to eat and enjoy. And once they try wild foods, students may feel that primal connection that only comes from getting sustenance directly from something foraged from nature.

Euell Gibbons—outdoorsman and wild foods expert.

This motivational logic goes beyond grade school to college. Many students have to take botany as part of their curriculum. If these students have additional motivation other than "it is a requirement" to learn about plants, they will do so happily. And, in the end, they will learn more.

Wild Foods Are a Great Social Activity

Back in the late 1960s and early '70s, many people got excited about wild foods because of Euell Gibbons, a wild foods expert. The excitement generated in his fans and readers resulted in the creation of many clubs, festivals, and social events centered around wild foods. Some

of them are listed at wildfoodadventures.com.

The hobby of wild foods is a great social venue for people who love the outdoors, food, cooking, plants, and recreational survival. These group events are a great way for enthusiasts to share information and experiences, and to enjoy the company of like-minded people. Social networks also exist in cyberspace. A Yahoo e-mail group titled ForageAhead caters to the wild food community. Potlucks, wild food parties, dating centered on wild foods—so much is possible on a social level.

FORAGEAHEAD

To join this e-mail list, go to http://groups.yahoo.com and type in "forageahead." Yahoo requires you to register with them in order to join the group. This is by no means the only group, so search the Internet for one that suits you.

Wild Foods Are Good for the Earth

From a "love your mother" perspective, wild foods are a fantastic venue for motivating people to become better caretakers of the earth. First, the study and active use of wild foods brings you closer to nature in an extremely intimate way since you are gaining sustenance directly from the earth. You see all land—not just farmland and your garden—as a potential source of food. So any kind of pollution becomes all that much more apparent. Second, edible weeds are the ultimate in locally grown sustainable foods. They can be a component of simple living, voluntary simplicity, permaculture, and reduced-consumption lifestyles.

Wild Foods Are Good Nutritionally

Many people believe that wild foods are worth pursuing because of their tremendous nutritional content. And there is no question that wild foods represent a wonderful source of nutrients. Indeed, many raw food proponents believe that wild foods are the ultimate foods.

I firmly believe that it can do nothing but good for North Americans to be eating more fresh leafy greens and vegetables. That isn't to say you cannot select a healthy diet from the fresh greens and vegetables currently available in the supermarket—indeed, you can. What the edible plants in this book provide are new options, lots of nutrients and new phytochemicals, diversity in the diet, free food, and a focus on including more fresh and diverse vegetables. Nutrients in Wild Foods (page 351) delves more directly into nutrition and health issues.

People of all dietary sensibilities will benefit from the greater culinary and nutritional variety offered by wild foods. Omnivores will benefit by including more fresh plant life. Vegetarians, vegans, and raw foodists will benefit from more food choices that don't cost them an arm and a leg.

Wild Foods Are Good for Your Wallet

If you are living on a limited or fixed income, fresh supermarket vegetables can take a serious chunk out of your paycheck. The use of easily accessible edible weeds can spare your money for other things and expand the variety of your diet. Wild foods can be a hedge against inflation and fluctuating food prices, an alternative or addition to some store-bought foods, and an improvement in the quality of everyday life. If you think civilization will crumble some day, and you and Mel Gibson will be fighting it out for that last can of beans, the study of wild foods will help you become more self reliant. And in the process of saving money, you'll be having lots of fun—at least until the coprolites hit the fan.

Wild Foods Are Good for Farmers and the Economy

What!?? Weeds good for farmers? Well . . . yes. Farmers, particularly small farmers, are barely scraping by these days. Many are losing their farms because they cannot compete with the megacorporate farms growing conventional crops. Small farmers could start specializing in more niche crops like some of the wild foods in this book. They could also benefit by using gleaners who harvest wild foods. Feeding Yourself and Society (page 395) covers this idea in more depth.

MEL GIBSON
This actor played anti-hero Mad Max in a series of movies where global fuel and food shortages caused civilization to degenerate into chaos. The remaining inhabitants experienced lawlessness and fought over the few resources left.

COPROLITES
Fossilized dinosaur droppings. Unfortunately for my allusion to chaos, rather than splatting all over the place, coprolites would most likely break any fan.

Chapter 21

The Nutrition of Wild Foods

The nutrient values in this chapter are here because there needs to be some collected source of this information to refer to when it is deemed necessary. But please do not start memorizing nutrient charts! People consuming wild foods should not be bookkeepers and accountants of nutrient composition. Not only does that take the fun out of eating, it takes you on the misadventure of eating nutrients, not foods. The only reasons you might refer to these charts are if you are making initial decisions on what nutrient-dense foods you want to add to your diet, you have very specific nutrient goals, or you have a medical condition that requires monitoring such things. Otherwise, stop counting milligrams! Get a life. For most of us, just eating real food (less processed foods, less empty calories) with lots of diversity and gobs of fruits and vegetables is great advice. It is almost that simple.

NUTRIENT DENSITY

A nutrient-dense food is one that has a high proportion of nutrients to calories. And while the formula for figuring nutrient density varies depending on the institution doing the calculations, greens are typically at the top of the list.

Nutrients in Wild Foods

The conventional categories of nutrients we all know are proteins, fats, carbohydrates, vitamins, and minerals. Within those categories are specific nutrients, including some amino acids, fatty acids, vitamin C, etc., that we need for our bodies to function. These are some of the nutrients and fiber listed in our nutrient data tables.

New substances found in plants called phytochemicals are intriguing many scientists. They are trying to identify, measure, and determine their role in human nutrition. This is a complex field in its infancy. So the most I can do is list a few selected classes of phytochemicals and tell you wild foods that are known to contain them. You'll find them later in the chapter.

You can greatly improve the quality of your diet just by eating plenty of store-bought, dark-green leafy greens like kale, collards, turnip leaves, and spinach. And you can do yourself even more good by adding wild spinach, field mustard, dandelions, purslane, and other wild foods to that. They are all good for you. The major advantages of the domesticated greens are that they can be purchased and require no identification and harvesting knowledge. The advantage of the wild greens are that they are fun, free, and add tremendous diversity to the diet in terms of flavors, nutrients, and phytochemicals. Health benefits build through this diversity.

Are wild foods more nutritious than domesticated foods?

As a wild food educator, I am typically asked, "Are wild foods more nutritious than conventional foods?" and "What are the most nutritious wild foods?" I have been uncomfortable answering these questions because I am diet- and lifestyle-focused, not individual food–focused. I try to eat a great overall diet as a lifestyle. I do not like microanalyzing the nutrients in my food. If you are not eating wild foods for the flavors, for the joy of it, or to reach some overall dietary/lifestyle goal, you will not be doing it for long. If you do not have the time or enthusiasm to learn about and prepare these plants, their nutritional value is a moot point. According to the nutrient data I found, most of the wild foods listed in this book are nutrient powerhouses. In fact, garlic mustard (*Alliaria petiolata*), shepherd's purse (*Capsella bursa-pastoris*), wild spinach (*Chenopodium album*), spiny sow thistle (*Sonchus asper*), and dandelion (*Taraxacum officinale*) may be the most nutrient-dense leafy greens ever analyzed. The benefit of wild foods is that they add diversity, the kind of diversity that increases your intake of potential cancer-fighting, heart-disease fighting, and longevity-promoting phytochemicals. Each vegetable has its own array of nutrients. The most nutritious diet is a diverse diet of healthy foods. A greater diversity is possible with the incorporation of wild foods.

Domesticated greens produced on a massive scale may have less to offer then their historical counterparts. Many have been genetically selected for flavor and/or transportability characteristics rather than nutrition. Selecting for flavor would make lettuces and broccoli sweeter and less bitter. Selecting for flavor has a tendency to knock out many of the bitter phytochemicals. (Drenowski, 2000.)

In addition to the selection process, poor farming practices can deplete the soil of minerals over time. Significant decreases have been found in calcium, magnesium, copper, and iron on farm-raised crops since the 1930s. (Davis, 2004; Mayer, 1997.) Nutrient values provided by the USDA (reflected in my nutrient table for domesticated greens) may be outdated over time because of this soil depletion. This means that wild harvested foods may have an even greater advantage than the nutrition tables depict. However, wild foods placed in cultivation could suffer the same fate as domesticated foods if they are grown with poor management practices on mineral-depleted soils.

But, even with the minor reductions in mineral content that some domesticated greens may have experienced, it is better to eat them and eat more of them than not to eat them at all.

What nutrients do wild foods have to offer?

Because this book deals mostly with leafy greens, all the nutrients I discuss will only refer to and compare these greens. This idea of comparing greens to other greens creates its own range of what defines a high versus a low level of a nutrient. After all, each part of the well-balanced diet makes its own contribution, so why not let the leafy green contribution be as nutrient-dense as possible?

My nutrient chart gives you a general idea of where nutrients are and where they are not. If you want to eat foods that are nutrient-dense, you might want to start with ones that have a greater number of values shown in the color red. These will be good for you because not only will you get lots of great nutrients, but other possible nutritional factors will come along for the ride that are not listed here, including hundreds, perhaps thousands of phytochemicals.

The Mediterranean Wild Food Diet

I have been impressed by the traditional diet of the people on the Greek island of Crete. The Mediterranean Diet, as it became known, was an extremely diverse diet due to all the wild foods consumed, both plant and animal. The omnivorous diet and vigorous lifestyle of the Cretans resulted in long healthy lives with virtually no heart disease and little cancer and other degenerative diseases typically associated with modern living. Most of the wild foods covered in this book were eaten as a normal course of everyday life during the time they were studied. Those same wild foods are found right here in our own North American backyards.

Almost all the recent nutrient and phytochemical data regarding wild foods has emerged as a direct result of researchers studying the health benefits of the original Mediterranean diet. Researchers are trying to figure out the role that wild greens and their constituents (phytochemicals) play as metabolites, antioxidants, anti-inflammatories, etc., in human longevity and general health. I am not covering the whole diet here. I am just mentioning the way the Cretan people ate wild greens as part of everyday life. That life helped define the diet.

Leafy greens and other vegetables

In some form or another, greens were virtually part of every meal, almost every dish, for the Cretans. As Diane Kochilas wrote in her book *The Glorious Foods of Greece* (2001), "Greens and olive oil were consumed in mind boggling quantities." Antonia Trichopoulou, an active researcher of the diet, wrote that Greeks have been characterized as having one of the highest consumptions of vegetables in the western world. She went on to say that "there are at least three hundred edible greens on Crete, but most people who are knowledgeable recognize about a hundred" (Trichopoulou, 2003).

These wild foods, an integral part of everyday life, were gathered fresh everyday in season. Depending on their individual characteristics, greens were used as vegetables, flavoring herbs, spices, and teas. They were eaten fresh, often boiled, or baked with olive oil. Lemon juice and olive oil were regularly added to fresh and cooked greens.

There are two concepts that I'd like you to remember from this: 1) greens were consumed in incredible amounts, and 2) there was a huge diversity of species, particularly wild species, that were used.

Wild foods in this book

Considering the amount of wild greens that were eaten within the context of an overall diverse and healthy Mediterranean-style diet, it is not unreasonable to imagine that those greens were at least partially responsible for some of the health benefits enjoyed by the Greeks. And that perception is driving much of the research cited in our wild nutrient chart and additional research on phytochemicals. Almost all the plants discussed in this book grow here as well as there. And as you will see in the nutrient charts, those plants are highly nutritious. Considering the few varieties of greens you find in the supermarket, learning the greens in this book will add variety—one of the probable virtues of the Mediterranean diet. And while you can purchase large quantities of greens from the supermarket, finding the diversity of different kinds of greens that the Cretans enjoyed is only obtainable with the inclusion of wild species. There certainly is more to the Mediterranean diet than discussed here. As far as I know, no one has come up with a better dietary lifestyle. If you eventually want to live that diet (a healthy lifestyle diet, not a weight-loss diet), you will already have the wild food component started by using this book.

Additional information

The original epidemiological work discovering the Mediterranean diet was done by Ancel Keys in the 1950s and '60s (Keys, 1970: Keys 1980). His research has stimulated hundreds, if not thousands, of research projects and papers on the diet and its impacts.

Dietary guidelines and a pyramid-style food guide reflecting the Mediterranean diet were published by the Greek Ministry of Health and Welfare in 1999 for the Greek People (Supreme Scientific Health Council, 1999). That same guide could function well here in North America. Wild greens are mentioned in their guide. Unfortunately, wild animals they ate (snails, rabbits, frogs, and all sorts of sea creatures other than fish) were not.

It is clear that many of the health benefits enjoyed by the Cretans were also due to a vigorous lifestyle that could burn off all those olive oil calories and keep them physically fit.

The Nutrient Charts

The nutrients I report here are limited to those that North Americans have a difficult time obtaining in typical diets without fortification (nutrients added to processed foods) or supplementation (nutrients put into pills). Don't put too much stock in these exact values. What you see on my charts are often averages of widely different values.

Factors that might cause variation in these values are the richness or lack of minerals in the soil, the age of leaves at time of harvest, whether the analyses include only leaves or tender leafy stems, and whether the study plants were foraged or grown in greenhouses. Rarely are these details reported in the scientific literature. Sometimes, as you might note in my chart, researchers don't even specify the actual species used, only the genus. Much more research needs to be done regarding the nutrient content of wild foods.

Many of the values given for cultivated plants may no longer be the same variants as you eat today or even contain the same amounts of minerals as displayed in the chart or discussed here. Another problem with this listing is that many wild foods have never been analyzed, so no values exist at all. Green amaranth (*Amaranthus retroflexus*) and a few domesticated plants not covered in this book are included in my charts for comparison purposes. The numbers given are USDA values or are averages of values I found in the scientific literature.

Nutrient Data

Following are brief summaries of what each nutrient can do for you. Under each one, I list some plants that contain good amounts of those nutrients. Wild plants such as fennel (*Foeniculum vulgare*) and wild carrot (*Daucus carota*) are not covered in this book but are included in some of the lists below.

Dietary fiber

Fiber, while not really thought of as a nutrient, is an important part of a healthy digestive process and disease prevention. Dietary fiber represents a set of indigestible plant components. These include starches, inulin (not insulin), waxes, pectins, and other materials. Most do a combination of things such as absorbing water to keep the food mass soft so it can easily travel through the gastrointestinal tract. Other fibers can help stabilize glucose levels, increase good intestinal bacteria, and inhibit digestive tract inflammation. This, in turn, helps prevent type 2 diabetes, cardiovascular disease, and gastrointestinal disorders. The plant with the most fiber is garlic mustard at 5.38 grams per 100 grams of plant material. That is followed by wild spinach, collard greens, spiny sow thistle, and dandelion. Four of the top five leafy sources of fiber are wild in origin.

Omega-3 fatty acids

Fat in the diet is made up of a variety of fatty acids. Each one has a different impact on the body. Omega-3s are considered essential fatty acids due to their roles in growth and maintenance regarding skin, eyes, and the nervous system. There are two classes of essential fatty acids: omega-6s and omega-3s. The body uses them in balance. We generally need a higher proportion of linolenic acid (one of the omega 3s) than we are getting in typical Western diets. Omega-3 fatty acids are believed to be anti-inflammatory, to promote the body's good cholesterol

continued on page 365

OTHER OMEGA-3s

Omega-3 fatty acids found in fish and other sea creatures are eicosapentaenoic acid (EPA) and docosahexaenoic acid (DHA). Most of the research on omega-3s has been done using these two compounds.

Nutrient Values in 100 grams of Wild Greens

Values are red if larger than the largest value from the Common Domesticated Greens chart.

Values are green if larger than or equal to the top three Common Domesticated Greens.

Species	Common Name	Parts/Methods	Fiber gm	Om3 mg	RAE mcg	B-car mcg	Eα mg
Alliaria petiolata	Garlic Mustard	Leaves Raw	5.38	150	1,029	12,350	
Amaranthus retroflexus	Green Amaranth	Leaves Raw	1.30		305	5,540	
Amaranthus spp.	Amaranth	Leaves Raw		2	146	1,752	
Amaranthus spp.	Amaranth	Leaves Boiled		1	139	1,668	
Barbarea vulgaris	Wintercress	Leaves Raw			253	3,040	
Barbarea vulgaris	Wintercress	Buds Raw			101	1,209	
Capsella bursa-pastoris	Shepherd's Purse	Leaves Raw	2.52	233	433	5,200	
Capsella bursa-pastoris	Shepherd's Purse	Leaves Boiled					
Chenopodium album	Wild Spinach	Leaves Raw	5.15	36	520	6,233	
Chenopodium album	Wild Spinach	Leaves Boiled	2.10	32	485	5,820	1.85
Chenopodium album	Wild Spinach	Leaves Steamed	5.20		194	2,329	
Chenopodium album	Wild Spinach	Leaves Raw	5.15	36	520	6,233	
Hypochoeris radicata	Cat's Ear	Leaves Raw			133	1,600	.19
Hypochoeris radicata	Cat's Ear	Flowers Raw			161	1,768	
Oxalis corniculata	Wood Sorrel	Leaves Raw					
Oxalis stricta	Wood Sorrel	Leaves Raw					
Portulaca oleracea	Purslane	Leaves Raw	.90	383	222	2,657	13.10
Portulaca oleracea	Purslane	Leaves Boiled			93	1,116	
Rumex acetosella	Sheep Sorrel	Leaves Raw					
Rumex crispus	Curly Dock	Leaves Raw	.80		645	7,740	
Rumex obtucifolius	Broad-Leaf Dock	Leaves Raw	2.70	34	120	1,439	.85
Rumex spp.	Dock	Leaves Raw	2.90		200	2,400	.51
Rumex spp.	Dock	Leaves Boiled	2.60		174	2,088	
Sonchus asper	Spiny Sow Thistle	Leaves Raw	3.56	279			
Sonchus oleraceus	Sow Thistle	Leaves Raw	2.93	207	210	2,526	.63
Stellaria media	Chickweed	Leaves Raw			50	600	
Stellaria media	Chickweed	Leaves Boiled					
Taraxacum officinale	Dandelion	Leaves Raw	3.50	44	508	6,096	3.44
Taraxacum officinale	Dandelion	Leaves Boiled	2.90	38	342	4.102	2.44
Taraxacum officinale	Dandelion	Buds Raw			40	480	

Key to Abbreviations:

Fiber = Dietary fiber
Om3 = Omega-3 Fatty Acids (milligrams) Alpha Linolenic Acid
RAE = Retinol Activity Equivalents (micrograms). Vitamin A
B-Car = B-Carotene (micrograms)
Eα = Alpha tocopherol (milligrams). Vitamin E
C = Vitamin C (milligrams)
Ribo = Riboflavin (milligrams)
Fol = Folic Acid (micrograms)

Ca = Calcium (milligrams)
Fe = Iron (milligrams)
Zn = Zinc (milligrams)
Cu = Copper (milligrams)
Mn = Manganese (milligrams)
Se = Selenium (micrograms)
spp = Indicates that the exact species analyzed was not specified; only the Genus is known.

Compiled by John Kallas, Ph.D. © 2008
Institute for the Study of Edible Wild Plants & Other Foragables
wildfoodadventures.com

C mg	Ribo mg	Fol mcg	Ca mg	Fe mg	Zn mg	Cu mg	Mn mg	Se mcg	References (pp. 362–64)
261			200	3.20	.910	.130	.990		7, 22
141			404	3.90					1, 2, 3
43	.158	85	215	2.32	.900	.162	.885	.9	17
41	.134	57	209	2.26	.880	.158	.861	.9	17
141									2, 22
163									2
104			247	3.55	.550	.090	.890		4, 8, 9, 10, 22
77									10
112	.370	39	371	1.18	.580	.210	1.140	1.0	1, 3, 17, 17 (Lambsquarters)
37	.260	14	258	.70	.300	.197	.525	.9	17 (Lambsquarters)
	.270		349	1.15	.610	.100	.1.56		17 (Lambsquarters)
112	.370	39	371	1.18	.580	.210	1.140	1.0	1, 3, 17, 17 (Lambsquarters)
									15, 21
									18
78			150	8.00					11
105			102	1.80					4, 9, 22
27	.112	12	96	2.50	.170	.113	.303	.9	1, 2, 3, 5, 9, 12, 13, 14, 15, 17, 22
11	.090	9	78	.77	.170	.114	.307	.9	17
			56	1.40					9
110			43	2.10	.430	.130	.450		2, 4, 6, 9, 10
32			60	1.10	.400				2, 4, 6, 9, 10
48	.100	13	44	2.40	.200	.131	.349	.9	17, 21
26	.086	8	38	2.08	.170	.114	.303	.9	17
63			137	2.98	.880	.310	.310		3, 7
54			104	2.19	.635	.290	1.200		3, 4, 7, 15, 16, 19, 20, 21
37			73	3.00	.590	.120	.290		3, 4, 5, 6, 9, 10, 22
26									10
35	.260	27	187	3.10	.410	.171	.342	.5	17
18	.175	13	140	1.80	.280	.115	.230	.3	17
30									2

Details, details, details . . .
- Values are reported as 100 grams of the edible portion of the plant material (wet weight, not dry weight).
- Blank spaces mean that no analyses, hence, no data were found for that nutrient. A zero would mean that an analysis was done but none of the nutrient was found.
- Nutrients selected for inclusion in this table were ones thought to be the most difficult to get in the typical American diet.
- Vitamin B-12, an important nutrient, is not listed because it is assumed to be 0 for all plants.
- Nutrient values above originate from the references listed at the right of the table.
- Nutrient values above are derived from one of the following:
  1. Shown exactly as reported in the original research paper.
  2. Converted mathematically into the units represented here for comparability.
  3. Averages of several values from two or more sources.
- Values shown above will change in future publications as more information becomes available.
- Charts listing other wild foods will be included in future publications.
- If you are a researcher, please do the research to fill in the blanks above or redo this all systematically with the latest laboratory techniques. Then let me know about it.
- The *Brassica rapa* listed in the USDA database (citation 35) is spinach mustard, a cultivar, not field mustard, so there are no values here for *Brassica rapa*.

Nutrient Values in 100 grams of Common Domesticated Greens

Highest values in each category are in red.

Species	Name	Parts/Methods	**Fiber** gm	**Om3** mg	**RAE** mcg
Brassica juncea	Mustard	Leaves Raw	3.30	18	525
Brassica oleracea var. *acephala* C	Collards	Leaves Raw	3.60	108	333
Brassica oleracea var. *acephala* K	Kale	Leaves Raw	2.00	180	769
Brassica oleracea var. *italica*	Broccoli	Leaves Raw		129	800
Brassica rapa var. *rapifera*	Turnip	Leaves Raw	3.20	84	579
Lactuca sativa var. *crispa*	Leaf Lettuce	Leaves Raw	1.30	58	370
Spinacia oleracea	Spinach	Leaves Raw	2.20	138	469

Key to Abbreviations:
Fiber = Dietary fiber
Om3 = Omega 3 Fatty Acids (milligrams)
    Alpha Linolenic Acid
RAE = Retinol Activity Equivalents
    (micrograms). Vitamin A
B Car = B Carotene (micrograms)
EQ = Alpha tocopherol
    (milligrams). Vitamin E
C = Vitamin C (milligrams)
Ribo = Riboflavin (milligrams)
Fol = Folic Acid (micrograms)
Ca = Calcium (milligrams)
Fe = Iron (milligrams)
Zn = Zinc (milligrams)
Cu = Copper (milligrams)
Mn = Manganese (milligrams)
Se = Selenium (micrograms)

Source: USDA National Nutrient Database for Standard Reference
http://riley.nal.usda.gov/N DL/index.html
Greens only, Raw Edible Portion, Fresh Weight

car mcg	Eα mg	C mg	Ribo mg	Fol mcg	Ca mg	Fe mg	Zn mg	Cu mg	Mn mg	Se mcg
6,300	2.01	70	.110	187	103	1.46	.200	.147	.480	.9
3,842	2.26	35	.130	166	145	.19	.130	.039	.276	1.3
9,226		120	.130	29	135	1.70	.440	.290	.774	.9
9,600		93	.119	71	48	.88	.400	.045	.229	3.0
6,952	2.86	60	.100	194	190	1.10	.190	.350	.466	1.2
4,443	.29	18	.080	38	36	.86	.180	.029	.250	.6
5,626	2.03	28	.189	194	99	2.71	.530	.130	.897	1.0

SUGGESTIONS FOR THE NUTRIENT RESEARCHER

Here are my research design recommendations for analyzing and reporting nutrient analyses of edible wild plants and their parts to consumers.

1. All data should be reported as the amount per 100 grams of fresh weight. If the food is consumed in dry form or as a flavoring, attempts should be made to report the amount in average serving sizes in the form used.

2. All plants should be grown from seed in a greenhouse with standardized soil adjusted for the pH and other special needs of the plant. Plants growing in the wild should only be analyzed for comparison to this standard. Wild conditions (soil pH, rainfall, state of maturity, estimated time of germination relative to the natural beginning time of germination, etc.) should be documented. The more that is documented, the more reliable and meaningful the data will be. The difficulty analyzing plants growing in the wild is that they experience an infinite number of soil, moisture, and germination

continued

NUTRIENT CHART REFERENCES

1. Aliotta, Giovanni, and A. Pollio. "Vitamin A and C Contents in Some Edible Wild Plants in Italy." *Rivista Italiana* EPPOS 63 (1981): 47–48.

2. Gibbons, *Stalking the Healthful Herbs*. New York: David McKay Co. Inc., 1966, 271, 276–77. In Gibbons' acknowledgments (p. vii), he thanks Dr. George Baron, head of Foods and Nutrition in the Department of Home Economics at Pennsylvania State University, for the new wild food values in his charts.

3. Bianco, V. V., et al. "Nutritional Value and Nitrate Content in Edible Wild Species Used in Southern Italy." *Acta Horticulturae* (ISHS) 467 (1998): 71–87.

4. Burrell, R. C., and H. A. Miller. "The Vitamin C Content of Spring Greens." *Science* 90 (2329) (1939): 162–65.

5. Cowan, J. W., et al. "Composition of Edible Wild Plants of Lebanon." *Journal of the Science of Food and Agriculture* 14, no. 7 (July 1963): 484–88.

6. Guil-Guerrero, Jose Luis, et al. "Mineral Nutrient Composition of Edible Wild Plants" (Spain). *Journal of Food Composition and Analysis* 11, no. 4 (December 1998): 322–28.

7. Guil-Guerrero, José Luis, et al. "Nutritional Composition of *Sonchus* species (S. Asper L., S. oleraceus L., and Stenerissimus L.)." *Journal of the Science of Food and Agriculture* 76, no. 4 (1998): 628–32.

8. Guil-Guerrero, José Luis, et al. "Nutritional Composition of Wild Edible Crucifer Species." *Journal of Food Biochemistry* 23, no.3 (1999): 283–94.

9. Leichsenring, Jane M., et al. "Many Wild Greens Have Food Value." *Minnesota Farm and Home Science* 4, no. 3 (1947): 4–5. (Note: Leichsenring's ascorbic acid values were excluded from my chart because they showed a pattern of being systematically far below all other data points. Methodological problems were assumed. Calcium and iron values were consistent with other

studies, so they were included.)

10. Murray, Hazel C., and Robert Stratton. "Vitamin C Content of Wild Greens." *Journal of Nutrition* 28, no. 6 (1944): 427–30.

11. Sengupta, S. R., and B. Pal. "Composition of Edible Wild Greens." *Journal of the Science of Food and Agriculture* 21, no. 4 (1970): 215.

12. Simopoulos, Artemis P., et al. "Common Purslane: A Source of Omega-3 Fatty Acids and Antioxidants." *Journal of the American College of Nutrition* 11, no. 4 (1992): 374–82.

13. Simopoulos, Artemis P., and N. Salem. "Purslane: A Terrestrial Source of Omega-3 Fatty Acids" (letter). *New England Journal of Medicine* 315, no. 13 (1986): 883.

14. Simopoulos, Artemis P., et al. "Purslane in Human Nutrition and Its Potential for World Agriculture." In *Plants in Human Health and Nutrition Policy* 77. Series by *World Review of Nutrition and Dietetics*. Edited by A. P. Simopoulos. Basel, CH: Karger, 1995, 47–74.

15. Su, Q., et al. "Identification and Quantitation of Major Carotenoids in Selected Components of the Mediterranean Diet: Green Leafy Vegetables, Figs, and Olive Oil." *European Journal of Clinical Nutrition* 56, no. 11 (2002): 1149–54.

16. Trichopoulou, Antonia, et al. "Nutritional Composition and Flavonoid Content of Edible Wild Greens and Green Pies: A Potential Rich Source of Antioxidant Nutrients in the Mediterranean Diet." *Food Chemistry* 70, no. 3 (2000): 319–23.

17. U.S. Dept of Agriculture, Agricultural Research Service, USDA National Nutrient Database for Standard Reference Release 18: http://www.nal.usda.gov/fnic/foodcomp.

18. Valadon, L. R. G., and R. S. Mummery. "Carotenoids of Certain Compositae Flowers." *Phytochemistry* 6, no. 7 (1967): 983–88.

time variations. If the impacts of these variations are not understood, the nutrient values will have less meaning.

3. Plant parts analyzed should be clearly specified as to what is included and excluded. Here are just some of the parts that one may consider when defining the "edible portion" used: leaf blade, petiole, main leaf vein, whole tender leafy stem. For example, the edible portion used for a particular plant may be the whole leaf (leaf· blade + petiole), or it may be restricted to the leaf blade alone. If analyzing the leafy stem, how much stem? two inches? six inches? Wherever the edible/tender portion of the stem snaps cleanly from the main stem is a good standard for leafy stems. This specificity applies for other parts of plants as well—fruits, seeds, flowers, buds, stems, etc.

4. Vegetative plant parts analyzed should be gathered during their rapid growing phase, when they are at their most tender—when appropriate for human consumption. Reproductive parts (fruits and seeds) should be analyzed when at their peak of ripeness. The exception would be for anthropological or

continued

ethnobotanical research where the subject population has its own specified gathering criteria.

5. Overwintering spring roots may have a different chemistry than summer or fall roots. The first rapidly growing leaves of spring will perhaps have different values than the rapidly growing leaves of summer or autumn. Nuances like these are valuable for scientists to know and account for in their research.

19. Vardavasa, C. I., et al. "Lipid Concentrations of Wild Edible Greens in Crete." *Food Chemistry* 99, no. 4 (2006): 822–34.

20. Vardavasa, C. I., et al. "The Antioxidant and Phylloquinone Content of Wildly Grown Greens in Crete." *Food Chemistry* 99, no. 4 (2006): 813–21.

21. Zeghichi, Sabrina, et al. "Nutritional Composition of Selected Wild Plants in the Diet of Crete." In *Plants in Human Health and Nutrition Policy* 91. Series by *World Review of Nutrition and Dietetics)* 91. Edited by A. P. Simopoulos and C. Gopalan, C. Basel, CH: Karger, 2003, pp. 22–40.

22. Zennie, Thomas M., and Dwayne Ogzewalla. "Ascorbic Acid and Vitamin A Content of Edible Wild Plants of Ohio and Kentucky." *Economic Botany* 31, no. 1 (January 1977): 76–79.

(continued from page 357)
(HDL), and to decrease triglycerides. Purslane has more omega-3 fatty acids than any green ever analyzed, just under 400 milligrams per 100 grams of fresh greens. All the following plants are great sources of omega-3s for leafy greens: spiny sow thistle, shepherd's purse, sow thistle, and kale. Four of the top five leafy sources of omega-3s (lino-lenic acid) are wild in origin.

Vitamin A (RAE)

Vitamin A is important for vision; for maintaining the skin, all mucous membranes, the lining of the digestive tract; and for proper bone growth. In terms of RAE (Retinol Activity Equivalency, an international measure of Vitamin A), garlic mustard has the most at 1,029 micrograms per 100 grams of fresh greens. That is followed by broccoli leaves, kale, curly dock, and turnip leaves. Many of the greens in these charts have high amounts of RAE. Two out of the top five leafy sources of RAE are wild in origin.

Beta-carotene

Beta-carotene has beneficial properties of its own. It is considered to be a strong antioxidant, may provide protection against several types of cancer, and may enhance immune function. Beta-carotene is a precursor of vitamin A and is the only source of vitamin A that plants produce. So beta-carotene is found in direct proportion to RAE in my charts. As with RAE, beta-carotene is found in greatest quantity in garlic mustard, then broccoli leaves, kale, curly dock, and turnip leaves.

Vitamin E

Vitamin E in the form of alpha-tocopherol is considered a powerful antioxidant. In this role, it helps to stabilize cell membranes; to protect the lungs against environmental damage; to inhibit tumor growth; to protect the eyes, skin, liver, breasts, and other organs from damage; and to aid in maintaining the biological integrity of vitamin A. This is where wild foods shine. Purslane, at 13 milligrams per 100 grams of leaves, has almost four times the amount found in dandelions, the next highest leafy source. This is closely followed by turnip greens, collard greens, and spinach. Two out of the top five leafy sources of vitamin E are wild.

Vitamin C

Vitamin C is an important antioxidant. It helps support vitamin E, folacin, and iron; plays a major role in collagen formation in skin, tendons, scar tissue, bones, and teeth; is important in amino acid metabolism and hormone synthesis; and helps to manage cholesterol. Here, the top four plants are wild foods, starting with garlic mustard at 261 milligrams per 100 grams of leafy material. This is closely followed by wintercress buds, green amaranth, and wintercress leaves. These are all very high values, since the daily recommendation is only 75–90mg for adults.

Riboflavin

Riboflavin, also known as vitamin B2, is important for energy production, fatty acid synthesis, amino acid synthesis, and growth in general. Wild spinach is the highest source of riboflavin at .37 milligrams per 100 grams of leafy material. This is followed by dandelion, cultivated spinach, amaranth spp, kale, and collards. Three of the top six leafy sources of riboflavin are wild.

Folacin

Folacin, also known as folic acid, is vital for amino acid metabolism, for DNA formation, and for the manufacture of neurotransmitters. It was one of the most common nutrient deficiencies in humans until they started fortifying grains. The top four leafy sources of folacin are from cultivated plants. Starting with turnip greens and spinach at 194 micrograms per 100 grams of leafy material, the next in line are cultivated mustard and collard greens.

Calcium (Ca)

Calcium is most important for bone development and maintenance, nerve transmission, muscle contraction, and blood clotting. The top five leafy sources of calcium are wild. Wild carrot leaves are the highest source by far at 450mg per 100 grams of fresh material. They are not on this chart but are worth listing because they are so high in calcium. That is followed by green amaranth, wild spinach, shepherd's purse, and garlic mustard. Wild carrot (*Daucus carota*) is in the same family as poison hemlock (*Conium maculatum*), so keep away from carrot unless you really know what you are doing. The availability of minerals to humans is complicated by the presence of oxalates. Oxalates can bind with calcium in the digestive tract, making that bound calcium unavailable for absorption. Plants with high oxalates include spinach, wild spinach, rhubarb, French sorrel, sheep sorrel, dock, purslane, and wood sorrel, among others. The more oxalates present, the less minerals available while consuming that food.

Iron (Fe)

Iron is primarily used in hemoglobin and is involved in enzymatic activity. Iron is the key for oxygen being supplied to the cells. The top seven leafy sources of iron are wild greens. The highest source by far is wood sorrel (*Oxalis corniculata*) at 8 milligrams per 100 grams of fresh greens. The next six are green amaranth, shepherd's purse, garlic mustard, dandelion, chickweed, and spiny sow thistle. Iron from plants is poorly absorbed.

Zinc (Zn)

Zinc is a cofactor for over twenty enzymatic reactions, which include alcohol detoxification, bone metabolism, dietary protein digestion, and energy production. Zinc also works as an antioxidant. The top seven leafy sources of zinc are wild foods. Garlic mustard has the most at .91 milligrams per 100 grams of leafy material. That is followed by amaranth spp, spiny sow thistle, sow thistle, wild spinach, chickweed, and shepherd's purse.

Copper (Cu)

Copper acts as a cofactor for enzymes, serves as a catalyst in the synthesis of hemoglobin, influences iron absorption and movement, is considered an antioxidant, is involved in energy production, and aids the synthesis of protective coverings around nerve fibers. Turnip greens have the highest amount at .35 milligrams per 100 grams of leafy material. This is followed by spiny sow thistle, sow thistle, kale, and wild spinach. Three out of the top five leafy sources of copper are wild.

Manganese (Mn)

Manganese is involved in protein digestion and synthesis, collagen formation, carbohydrate metabolism, bone development, and a variety of other things. Manganese is also thought to be an antioxidant. Sow thistle is a great source at 1,200 milligrams per 100 grams of leafy material. This is closely followed by wild spinach, garlic mustard, spinach, and shepherd's purse. Four of the top five leafy sources of manganese are wild.

Selenium (Se)

Selenium is a strong antioxidant and a component of amino acid metabolism, helps detoxify heavy metals, and aids fetal development. While selenium content in plants is strongly a function of the selenium content of the soil, the highest source is apparently broccoli leaves at three micrograms per 100 grams of leafy material. This is two or three times that found in collards, turnip greens, spinach, and most of the wild foods listed.

What should you take from this?

First, wild foods have some significant nutrients to offer, particularly ones difficult to get in the typical Western diet. Wild leafy greens with the highest nutrient densities include garlic mustard, wild spinach, dandelion, spiny and regular sow thistle. Wintercress, sheep sorrel, wood sorrel, and cat's ear leaves have so little data representing them that evaluating their nutrient density is impossible at this point.

And a final note for emphasis: Nutrient data on wild foods is rare. What exists is often incomplete, which makes it all the more remarkable that our most nutrient-dense domesticated greens have been bested (for lack of a better term) in many respects by only a small sample of the thousands of North American wild foods available. Again, the point is not to say that wild greens are better, only that they offer additional nutritious variety that could help the modern diet in substantial ways.

Phytochemicals

Phytochemicals are organic compounds found in plants. Plants are filled with phytochemicals. Determining which of them have roles in human health is a big area of investigation today. Plants clearly have been shown to contain nutrient, medicinal, and poisonous phytochemicals. So there is no doubt that phytochemicals can have an impact on health. The big question of the new crop of phytochemicals is which will be shown to have clear benefits to human health and which will clearly deserve the term phytonutrient?

Researchers today genuinely believe that phytochemicals are one of the reasonable answers to why fruits and vegetables are so good for you, why certain diets and lifestyles have less heart disease, cancer, stroke, diabetes, neurodegenerative diseases, etc. The study of phytochemicals, however, is in its infancy. There are so many chemicals and the human body is so complex, it is not surprising that we do not know very much yet.

Phytochemicals might serve as antioxidants, anti-inflammatories, and general metabolites that facilitate health and long life (longevity). Like conventional nutrients, phytochemicals tend to be more prevalent in plants with deep colors of green, yellow, red, and orange.

Some of the most discussed phytochemicals today are resveratrol, found in the skins of grapes and in Japanese knotweed (*Polygonum cuspidatum*); carotenoids, found mostly in vegetables; and flavonoids, found mostly in fruits and nuts. But don't get caught up focusing on individual phytochemicals. If you want improved quality of life and perhaps a longer life, you might want to shift your diet by eating more and diverse fruits, vegetables, nuts, and seeds. They can only be good for you. Below is a listing of general classes of phytochemicals that have been identified in plants. Phytochemicals are often referred to as phytonutrients in both the scientific and lay literature. What follows each listing are some of the theorized metabolic functions and edible wild plants that are known to contain them:

—*Carotenoids* are antioxidants that may protect vitamins from oxidation and help protect the skin from sun damage. Beta-carotene, lutein, and lycopene are examples of carotinoids. Plants with ample carotenoids include garlic mustard, wild spinach, eastern blue violets (*Viola sororia*), dandelions, curly dock, shepherd's purse, ox-eye daisy (*Leucanthemum vulgare*), purslane, amaranth, sheep sorrel, cat's ear, and sow thistle. (Aliotta, 1981; Cowan 1963; Gibbons, 1966; Guil-Guerrero, 1998, 1999b, 1999a; Hu, 2004; Mercadante, 1990; Raju, 2007; Su, 2002; Trichopoulou, 2000b; Valadon, 1967; Zennie, 1977.)

—*Phenols* may help reduce inflammation at the cellular level and help prevent blood platelets from clumping. Both may be good for the cardiovascular system. Plants with phenols include docks, chicory, cat's ear, dandelion, and sow thistle. (Schütz, 2005; Trichopoulou, 2000b; Wiese, 1995; Yıldırım, 2001; Zeghichi, 2003.)

—*Polyphenols* may serve as antioxidant, anti-cancer, and antimutagenic agents. Polyphenols, like anthocyanidins, may have a role in the strength of collagen protein. Tannins are polyphenols and are found in curly dock, broad-leaf dock (Vardavasa, 2006), and acorn meat (*Quercus* spp.).

—*Flavonoids* are phenols that are antioxidants and may protect against allergies, inflammation, blood platelet clumping, ulcers, tumors, bacteria, and viruses. Plants high in flavonoids are wild carrot leaves (*Daucus carota*), dock, fennel, sow thistle, cat's ear, and dandelion. (Schütz, 2005; Trichopoulou, 2000b; Wiese, 1995; Yıldırım, 2001.)

In addition to the above, the following phytochemicals are commonly found in members of the mustard family. Mustard family plants covered in this book are field mustard, wintercress, garlic mustard, and shepherd's purse.

—*Glucosinolates* may block enzymes that promote tumor growth, help regulate white blood cells, and activate liver enzymes responsible for detoxification of undesirable metabolites.

—*Indoles* may work in the intestines to activate enzymes that detoxify substances and bind chemical carcinogens before they are absorbed.

—*Thiols* may help to prevent cancer and cellular mutations; they may also support the cardiovascular and immune systems. Glutathione is a thiol. Purslane (not a mustard) also has glutathione. (Simopoulos, 1992.)

So if this is more than you wanted to hear, just know that fruits, vegetables, and leafy greens are good for you because of the nutrients, phytochemicals, and fiber they contribute to the diet.

In Summary

Here are the things you should take away from this chapter:

- Greens are great; eat a considerable amount of a variety of greens.
- Wild foods are great; they increase the diversity of foods available to you.
- Greens and wild foods may improve your long-term health status, longevity, and quality of life.
- Many of the same good-for-you arguments can be made for wild and domesticated fruits, but that is a subject for another book.

Eating lots of diverse greens and vegetables can help provide you with a wide array of nutrients and phytochemicals. Wild greens are a fine addition to any North American diet.

Chapter 22

Oxalates & Nitrates

Almost every book written on wild foods mentions the substances oxalates and nitrates. Often in the context of giving you a word of caution: "Don't eat too much because this plant contains oxalates," or nitrates. These warnings are not generally understood by wild food authors and therefore are never explained. Some of the plants covered in this book contain either one or both of these substances. So it is only fair that I explain to you in detail why you should NOT generally be worried about them being in your diet. People ordinarily do not talk about these substances when eating conventional foods, even though they are present. They are mentioned with wild foods mostly because authors feel responsible to mention things they've heard about that *might be* a problem, but they cannot explain why.

Most substances like oxalates and nitrates only become a concern in certain unusual circumstances and not in the context of a normal healthy and diverse diet in normal healthy people. In fact, in certain amounts, these substances may have some beneficial roles in the same way that other phytochemicals may be beneficial.

Oxalates

The purpose of this section is to clarify what oxalates do and why this author believes that they are mostly a non-issue—just one more thing you shouldn't have to worry about when you are trying to enjoy your wild food meal.

Warnings about oxalates are typically nonspecific, giving the impression that they are in some way poisonous. One warning is specific: oxalates bind calcium in the digestive tract. The recommendations are typically "Don't eat too much" or "Don't eat more than one bowl." The consequence of these statements is to give novices one more reason to needlessly be intimidated by wild foods.

Let me first say that soluble oxalates are the topic of this section, not calcium oxalate crystals. Calcium oxalate crystals (Kingsbury, 1964; Kallas, 1997) are found in skunk cabbage (*Symplocarpus foetidus* [eastern] / *Lysichitum americanum* [western]), jack-in-the-pulpit (*Arisaema triphyllum*), and dumb cane (*Dieffenbachia seguine*); these present a real problem that is not discussed here.

What are oxalates?

Oxalates, also known as oxalic acids, are naturally occurring substances found in almost every living thing. They are soluble in water as sodium oxalate or potassium oxalate salts, and are typically found in greater quantities in members of the wood sorrel family (Oxalidaceae), the buckwheat family (Polygonaceae), the purslane family (Portulacaceae), and the goosefoot family (Chenopodiaceae).

Plants and foods known to have high concentrations of oxalates include, but are not limited to, the following:

DOMESTICATED	WILD
Spinach	Wild spinach
French sorrel	Sheep sorrel
Rhubarb	Wood sorrel
Swiss chard	Purslane
Beet leaves	Docks
Black tea	Japanese knotweed
Cocoa	Pokeweed

In green plants, higher concentrations of oxalates are often accompanied by higher concentrations of calcium.

Oxalates are a normal part of the human diet and are a normal part of human amino acid and ascorbic acid metabolism. You know a food like spinach is high in oxalates because your teeth get this funny sandpapery feel when you eat it. When this happens, the oxalates in the food are temporarily binding to the calcium of your teeth. This quickly resolves itself within a few minutes but is fun while it lasts.

Claims of a problem

One of the big problems in the field of wild foods is that misconceptions and misattributions are made regularly and then cited repeatedly in ensuing literature. They eventually become "truisms" that everybody believes, including professionals who cite these same misconceptions.

The misconception that soluble oxalates are a great concern to humans essentially began with John Kingsbury's classic 1964 book, *Poisonous Plants of the United States and Canada*. While his book was primarily a review of animal research combined with smatterings of human data, many writers interpreted the information as applicable to humans—falsely raising fears. Kingsbury himself warned readers that "Oxalate poisoning (even in animals) is fundamentally complex and poorly understood." Since Kingsbury's book, retrospective and targeted studies have been done to look directly at the oxalate issue—dismissing many of the fears.

There were claims during World War II that the cause of poisonings from people eating rhubarb leaves was the oxalates contained there. Unfortunately, the proponents of this logic did not know at the time that the stalks, which we do eat, have almost as much oxalates as the leaves. In fact, spinach leaves have about 30 percent more oxalates than rhubarb leaves. I do not see people in North America dropping like flies as they enjoy their spinach salad. Rhubarb leaves are poisonous for reasons that have nothing to do with oxalates.

In 1989, the first and only report of a human poisoning from oxalates was titled *Fatal Oxalic Acid Poisoning from Sorrel Soup* (Farre, 1989). The tabloid title really makes one think "Wow, am I lucky I haven't died from all those times I ate gobs of sorrel soup, spinach, and other oxalate-containing greens. How did I survive, as did millions of other people around the planet who eat oxalate-containing plants on a regular basis. We should all be dead—but wait! We aren't!"

Here's the problem: From what I've read, that report could have been more accurately titled "Fifty-three-year-old man dies of poor health, failing blood chemistry, liver, and kidneys due to a life of excessive drinking, smoking, and poorly managed insulin-dependent diabetes after enjoying several bowls of sorrel soup." It is not unreasonable to assume that this fellow's body was ready for catastrophic failure, and he only needed a catalyst to set death in motion. Calcium oxalate crystals were found in his kidneys because his abnormal blood chemistry did not prevent the crystals from forming. My normal digestive tract absorbs only a small fraction of dietary oxalates, and my normal blood pH does not allow oxalates to bind with calcium. Those crystals in his kidney were probably building over a long time from bad blood chemistry, not just from one meal as was the impression left by the report. So this fellow had lots of problems independent from sorrel soup.

To this day, I still hear from people afraid to eat oxalates for fear that they will be poisoned. This bad information gets repeated again and again, from book to book, and now it is all over the Web.

As early as 1973, the National Research Council of the National Academy of Sciences came up with some conclusions (Fassett, 1973) about oxalates in human metabolism, as stated in their report "Toxicants Occurring Naturally in Foods." What follows is my perspective on the oxalate issue based on information from that report and my general knowledge of human physiology.

The facts as I see them

Humans are not cattle or sheep in their dietary habits, their physiology, or even their number of stomachs. While I love rhubarb, I would not enjoy eating five pounds of it per day for a month at the exclusion of other foods. Like most humans, I enjoy a diverse diet; cattle and sheep do not have a diet that diverse. This focus on cattle and sheep data greatly affects the exaggerations about dietary calcium deficiencies and the idea of toxic intakes in humans. As far as I know, only the one case I just mentioned, concerning toxic intake of naturally occurring soluble oxalates, has ever been reported, and that case has nothing to do with normal humans.

Oxalates can bind with calcium and other minerals in the digestive tract, making both the calcium and the oxalates unavailable for absorption. This may be a natural protective effect that calcium provides to further decrease the amount of oxalates absorbed. In a normal healthy diet that has foods eaten by a normal healthy human, almost all dietary oxalates are excreted with the feces, with little being absorbed through the intestinal membranes. It is interesting to note that plants with high oxalate content are often high in calcium. So, dietarily, there would be no net loss of calcium; the plant supplies the calcium so that is not depleted in your diet.

Food and intestinal secretions in a typical digestive tract create a complex chemical environment in which calcium complexes and oxalate salts are in relatively small and dispersed amounts. So many other things can happen to calcium and so many other things can happen to oxalates within the total of stomach contents that it is difficult to justify the often-repeated and somewhat-absolute statement that oxalates "block" the absorption of calcium.

Since oxalates bond to calcium in the digestive tract, they may also bond to toxic metals like mercury, lead, and cadmium, helping to eliminate them from the body before they can be absorbed. In fact, the calcium oxalate compound itself may bond to toxic metals, so do not rule out a positive role for oxalates. The point I am making is that some things we think are bad turn out to have a more nuanced and potentially positive story in the context of a healthy diet.

Gut oxalates vs. blood oxalates

There is little scientific evidence that dietary oxalates promote the development of kidney stones or gallstones in healthy people. Oxalates have to transport from the gut into the bloodstream for that to happen. Since most is excreted in the feces, little dietary oxalate gets to the kidneys or the liver. People who develop kidney stones have a physiological abnormality that promotes excessive "creation" and deposition of oxalates within the body. Even so, many physicians think it is "prudent" to limit dietary oxalates for these people, "just in case."

If you are really heart-set on pumping your blood full of oxalates, take megadoses of vitamin C. Ascorbic acid is oxalate's "Trojan horse." Vitamin C is easily absorbed from the digestive tract into the bloodstream. In normal metabolism, humans convert excess ascorbic acid (vitamin C) into oxalates and other breakdown products that get filtered through the kidneys and end up in the urine. High intake of vitamin C results in much greater metabolic oxalate production than any healthy consumption of high oxalate vegetables. Those oxalates have to be excreted through the kidneys where the stones can form. Even oxalates that are in the blood do not bind with calcium in healthy individuals because our blood chemistry/pH will not allow it.

In summary, my understanding and opinion is that in the context of a normal, healthy, diverse diet, dietary oxalates are a nonissue for healthy people. Unfortunately, they still cause a lot of unnecessary fear in the wild food community. Consume sorrel, dock, purslane, and wild spinach without fear unless you are chronically malnourished, have complicated or unusual blood chemistry, or are counseled by your doctor not to.

If you have an abnormal physiological propensity for kidney stones or digestive issues, observe how your body reacts when you do eat high oxalate foods. If you have a sensitivity, then by all means heed those feelings and react accordingly. And always follow the directions of your physician.

THE TROJAN HORSE

While "Trojan horse" is thought of today as computer malware, its original meaning had to do with a tactic invented by Odysseus, a war hero in Greek mythology.

To end a long war, the Greeks left a giant wooden horse at the gates of Troy, the large fortified city they were battling against. The Greeks left the impression that they had abandoned the battle, so the Trojans brought the horse into the city as a sign of victory over the Greek army and as a symbolic gift to the gods. In the middle of the night while the city slept, Greek warriors led by Odysseus emerged from the horse, killed the sentries, opened the gates, and let in the rest of the Greek army.

In our example, the digestive tract (Trojan gatekeepers) will not let the oxalates (Greek warriors) in directly, but they will let in the innocent-looking ascorbic acid (Trojan horse) that is carrying the oxalates.

Nitrates

As you read through wild food literature, you often hear a warning that some plants are nitrate accumulators. You do not hear much beyond that—just a warning. So what does that mean from a practical standpoint? What should you do with that information? The following is my understanding of nitrate accumulators and nitrite physiology.

What are nitrates?

Nitrates are a class of substances containing nitrogen and other molecules.

In caring for a yard, a garden, or a farm, you should know that nitrogen is an important part of fertilizer. Plants use nitrogen for growth. Nitrates are building blocks for DNA, amino acids, and proteins. Without nitrates, growth comes to a halt in plants and humans.

Realistic perspective

Since the primary concern in the scientific literature of nitrate accumulation and toxicity is in the poisoning of livestock, this is where most of the research has been conducted. Humans and livestock are different physiologically and dietarily. Direct comparisons are difficult, so I will try to give you a more human point of view. Just looking at this from a consumption perspective, livestock often eat large amounts of the same food from the same land for days and weeks at a time. Humans have a more diverse diet, so any one substance found in a particular food gets diluted. Diversity in the diet is the best defense against small amounts of potentially toxic constituents in what we consider to be normal foods. Diversity includes both the types of foods you eat and the different lands from which they are harvested.

The actual risk

Overall, there appears to be no actual risk of nitrate toxicity to healthy human adults or even children over three months of age. I could find no incidence of recorded poisonings over three months of age. As far as I can tell, humans four months old and older have nothing to fear and can ignore warnings about nitrates.

There have been rare instances, only a handful in the last 100 years, of recorded poisonings of infants due to ingestion of high nitrate spinach that was puréed into baby food. I could find no instances of other plants being a problem, even though other plants accumulate nitrates. The rarity makes one think that the high concentrations of nitrates were an unlucky and rare combination of circumstances, that the infants were not given a diverse enough diet, and/or the infants already had compromised health. The point is that it is so rare that we should not worry about it. Being informed is better than worrying.

What happens in infants

In humans, nitrates are not toxic. Nitrates play a variety of roles in human physiology. It is the nitrites that are of concern, and that concern only applies to infants under four months of age. If infants are breast-fed, that would solve any nitrate accumulation problem and make this whole section a moot point.

But, if a parent were to make a purée of a nitrate-accumulating plant and feed it in enough quantity to an infant (this would be difficult to do), here is what would happen:

Once the infant had eaten the food, natural digestive bacteria would begin converting nitrates (useful) to nitrites (the bad guys). This does not happen in older humans (four months old and older) because their digestive tracts are more mature and their stomachs are more acidic, preventing the conversion. Nitrites in the infant stomach are absorbed and pass into the bloodstream.

Once in the blood, adult physiology converts nitrites

NITRATES OR NITRITES?

Reading this section might be confusing, particularly for those of us who miss small differences in spelling. Please note that much of this discussion is about the differences between nitrates (with an "a") and nitrites (with an "i").

back to nitrates. Infant physiology is not mature enough to do that yet, so nitrites stay nitrites. Since these kids are very young, about 80 percent of their hemoglobin is leftover fetal hemoglobin; that is, made by the fetus for fetal physiology. Only about 20 percent is new adult-style hemoglobin. Fetal hemoglobin has an affinity for nitrites that is much stronger than adult hemoglobin. So hemoglobin gets covered with nitrite molecules in infants. These nitrites block oxygen from attaching to the hemoglobin. Since oxygen has trouble attaching to hemoglobin, breathing brings in less oxygen, and the infant starts showing signs of oxygen deficiency. If enough nitrites are in the body, the infant eventually turns blue and can suffocate if not treated quickly. This condition of nitrite-surrounded hemoglobin is called methemoglobinemia. In contrast, adult hemoglobin can fend off whatever nitrites have survived in the blood up to that point.

Symptoms of nitrite poisoning

The first symptoms in low levels of methemoglobinemia in infants are a flushing of the face and extremities, headache, and stomach discomfort. This will pass shortly if the offending plant matter is no longer eaten. Higher, more dangerous levels can produce increasing levels of abdominal pain, nausea, vomiting, a bluish coloration of the skin, and eventual collapse.

Again, keep in mind that while methemoglobinemia is theoretically possible, dangerous levels have only been documented a few times in the last hundred years. It's so rare that I will not mention it in my plant chapters.

Plants that tend to accumulate nitrates

Here are a few plants considered to be nitrate accumulators; there are many more nitrate accumulators than those listed here. I just wanted to point out a few representative ones.

DOMESTICATED	WILD
Turnip greens	Purslane
Spinach	Wild spinach
Celery	Curly dock
Corn	Miner's lettuce

Making choices

For healthy humans over three months of age, there is no evidence that I can find to suggest any harm from eating plants high in nitrates in the context of a normal and diverse diet. Nitrates are a normal part of eating, and our bodies have the means for processing them.

I do not recommend feeding plants growing in uncontrolled conditions, nitrate accumulators or not, to infants. Even though the risk is probably very low, making baby food out of any plants, wild or cultivated, is unnecessary.

If you chose to feed puréed vegetables of any kind to infants under four months of age, keep these things in mind: This is a complex decision of which you can not have all the facts, particularly with wild plants growing in uncontrolled conditions. Without laboratory testing of the soil and of the plants growing in them, you cannot know the nitrate content of the parts you are feeding your infant. The risk outweighs the benefit, even though that risk is low. Diversity in a baby's diet is a good hedge against any one food causing a problem. So, as long as you don't feed homemade puréed vegetables to infants, nitrate accumulation is another non-issue that you do not have to worry about.

Chapter 23

Agriotrophytology

The Study of Wild Food Plants

When doing research on edible wild plants, I have to dive into many disciplines to find what I am looking for: ethnobotany, cultural foodways, nutrient content, nutritional biochemistry, nutritional toxicology, dendrology, chemical composition, pharmacognosy, economic botany, plant morphology, plant taxonomy, plant physiology, weed science—you name it. And while I mostly do my work outside of academia, I think it is appropriate that someone should at least propose an academic-style Greekified label for scholars doing research in this area.

After all, our ancestors all over the world have depended on wild foods since the beginning of human existence. Many people in Africa, South America, and the Mediterranean still get a substantial proportion of their diet from wild plants. The now-famous Mediterranean diet included most of the wild greens covered in this book. To this day, the inhabitants of small Greek villages eat plenty of wild foods.

In addition to defining edible wild plants in another part of this book, I propose the following label to describe the study of this field: *agriotrophytology*. It comes from my understanding of the Greek roots of words I extracted from other definitions in the *Compact Edition of the Oxford English Dictionary* (1971) and the English-Greek lexicon at www.kypros.org. Since I am not a professional lexicographer, it may need refining by someone who knows what they are doing. But I think it will work in its own esoteric way. Here are the roots of agriotrophytology:

AGRIO

Agrio is a Greek word meaning "wild." It is different from *agri*, a Latin word meaning "land," from which the word "agriculture" is constructed.

agrio means "wild" or "untamed," from the Greek word αγριο.

troph means "food" or "nutriment," from the Greek word τροπη.

phyto means "plant," from the Greek word πηψτο.

logy means "the treatment or discourse of a particular field," often called "the study of," from the Greek word λογια.

As name alternatives, I tried *agriotrophphytology*, including the extra "ph" and switched the terms around for *trophagriophytology*, but I was not pleased with either one.

Someone who studies wild food plants or its synonym phrase "edible wild plants" would be an *agriotrophytologist*.

Suggested Areas of Study

Historical agriotrophytology involves the study of the written record related to edible wild plants. Both scientific and lay literatures contribute information about wild food uses and foodways.

Nutritional agriotrophytology involves nutrient analysis of wild foods and the roles those nutrients and other chemicals play in human nutrition.

Ethnographic agriotrophytology involves the documentation of traditional wild foodways through observational and interview techniques. This describes in detail what is done by individuals or groups in the context of their situations and lives using established ethnographic methods.

Quantitative agriotrophytology involves the evaluation of the use and management of edible wild plant resources by individuals and groups. This examines the practices and dynamics involved to manage adequate sustainable harvests over time in different ecosystems. This can be for natural and intensified situations.

Experimental agriotrophytology involves testing procedures and methods for gathering, transporting, processing, preserving, and cooking wild foods. Those procedures and methods can be innovative (new/invented by the experimenter) or based on accurate or best-guess accounts of cultural foodways.

Botanical agriotrophytology involves the overlapping edibility between related species, as well as how morphology and physiology at different stages of growth affect edibility.

Culinary agriotrophytology involves the science and art of turning wild plants into food. This includes combining foods, managing flavors and textures, and inventing recipes.

Agricultural agriotrophytology involves the technology necessary to domesticate, grow, harvest and transport wild foods to markets.

Chapter 24

Crafting a Wild Paradise

Let's face it. Many of us just want to go out and gather wild food. It's a simple and uncomplicated idea. We gather because we thirst for the quest, the journey, the adventure, and we thrive on the finding, gathering, and eating. But, in addition to the quest, wouldn't it be great to have some of your favorite wild foods at whim, within reach, to have them more regularly and in abundance?

(facing) A tomato plant surrounded by edible weeds. The weeds closest to the tomato plant that would compete with it have been harvested. To prevent the soil from drying out, it's a good idea to mulch the base of the plant where the earth has been exposed.

Many of us who have more feral yards and neighborhoods are lucky enough to have lots of wild foods nearby. I might have pokeweed and miner's lettuce. A neighbor has a huge patch of chickweed. Down the street are massive amounts of wild spinach. Not everyone is so fortunate. Many people live in highly manicured areas—places where perfectly coiffed grass is exactingly trimmed along the sidewalks, and nary a weed is found under sculptured shrubbery.

To overcome society's inclination for order, one might engage in mischievousness by fostering desirable weeds. Yes, you heard me—promote weed growth in your own yard. There are two ways of doing this. Both require some effort each year.

The first, a Wild Garden, is simple and provides bountiful results—great for an annual taking of plants. The second, a Wild Landscape, provides more variety, greater quantity, and better quality over a longer period of time. The wild landscape is a long-term approach—more work up front, but more long-lasting benefits.

The Wild Garden

A wild garden is just that: a garden you manage differently from everyone else. Instead of grimacing, you cheer with joy as weed seedlings begin to sprout. Let's examine how this works.

As you would in a regular garden, turn over the soil in spring as soon as it is workable. Mix in compost and whatever other soil amendments you typically use. Plant tomatoes, peas, and peppers. Water generously, regularly,

Weed sprouts emerging from a late spring garden. Plants in this picture include wild spinach, green amaranth, wild mustard, borage, and mallow.

and wait for the magic to happen. Soon you will see thousands of seedlings begin to sprout. With the help of this book, you will begin to recognize some of the seedlings of the weeds you want to keep. Pull or pinch off all the rest. In many situations, grass may be your biggest foe—always pull out any grass you see. If you do not recognize some seedlings, let a few continue to grow and study them over time, recording the progress with a camera. Let some of the unknowns grow to maturity if that is what it takes for you to identify them. Once you know what you have, pull the undesirables and never let them go to seed.

The fast-growing leaves of young plants are often considered the choicest. So, as your weeds are growing gatherable leaves and stems, thin them and eat the thinnings— assuming, of course, that you know which ones are edible. Gourmets would consider these baby greens. Your take can be quite substantial. Make salads, cook them, use them any way you want. The thinning process allows the remaining weeds to flourish due to less competition. You'll see examples of these edible weeds at their prime for collecting as you read through the plant chapters of this book.

At the same time you are thinning in general, selectively harvest the weeds around the base of your domesticated plants. Harvest from the base outward. When your tomatoes are two feet tall, you should have harvested everything within about six inches of their bases. Cover that now-barren ground with mulch. When the tomatoes are three feet tall, you should have harvested everything within a foot of the base. These are rough amounts; someday someone will do a study to calculate exactly how much space to allow. In the meantime, try what I have suggested; you will get the hang of it. Your goal is to grow as much weed as you can without choking out the domestic plants. Just like the weeds, your tomato plants will do better with plenty of soil nutrition, water, and sunlight.

If you plant your domestics close together, your gradual weed-harvesting process will result in whole patches of the garden being weedless. This is fine—continue to mulch those areas if you want. It is better for the soil creatures and your domestic plants to have mulch. Take care not to harvest all the weeds. For year-to-year sustainable yields of edible weeds, you need to let a few of them go to seed. Once the seeds begin to drop, aid the process by spreading them throughout the garden. When you turn the soil the next spring, the seeds will get mixed into different depths. The ones near the surface will germinate when the conditions are right again.

The fully wild garden

You can, of course, take this all a step further and create a fully wild garden, planting no cultivars at all. I find I now prefer this type of garden since I do not really have great gardening skills or the time to develop them. Plus, I want more wild food. Accomplishing this requires turning over the soil at least once, often twice, or even three times a year and watering as if you had domesticated plants to nurture. I prefer adding soil amendments like organic compost, minerals, and lime so that the weeds will really perform. As you will see throughout this book, some of our prime annual weeds will grow to sizes you can only imagine. This produces better-quality food over a much longer season in much greater quantities.

Some people love weeds because of their legendary tenaciousness. They believe that weeds are strong, vital, and stubborn, and will grow regardless of your neglect. These people are correct, sort of. Refuse to water or nourish the soil in your garden, particularly after continual harvests that deplete the soil, and the weeds will be happy to show you how strong, stubborn, tiny, stringy, fibrous, leafless, and generally useless as a food they can get. Starving them gives you starved plants. They will mature rapidly into tiny beings and be past their prime (if you can call it a prime) in the blink of an eye. If nature provides you with enough rain, then you can just sit by and watch. But without some soil amendments over time, you will deplete your soil and the wild foods will be much less productive.

To keep my annual weeds thriving year after year, I remove the debris of old stems and branches in the autumn and turn over selective parts of the garden before winter arrives. This allows the weed seeds to wait in the soil under ideal conditions for the next growing season. Some sprout in the fall but stay small and relatively dormant until they can explode with growth in the spring. Others, the biennials, develop their roots so that they can finish out their life in the second year. Where the biennials have started, I do not turn over the soil. Perennials that have sprouted in convenient corners of the garden are left undisturbed so they can continue to produce for me year after year.

After some of my early spring plants have spent themselves, I turn over part of the garden again to stimulate a new set of seeds into germination for a whole new crop of young plants.

Here are some basic considerations for keeping the garden productive. They are not much different from things a domesticated garden needs:

WATER SUPPLY: If you do not water regularly, your plants will not produce as much as they could. They will be small and short-lived with sparse leafage.

SOIL AMENDMENTS: If you do not enrich the soil, the depleted ground will starve the weeds over time, causing them to be small and unproductive. They will still grow and survive, but not enough to feed you. Harvesting weeds depletes the soil just as harvesting domesticated plants does.

THINNING: If you do not harvest (thin out excess plants) regularly, the weeds will compete with each other, and you will not like the results. Either they will be short and stunted or they will bolt into tall stringy plants with fewer leaves. Having to keep up with the growth of your weeds can be fun because you get all this fresh food in rapid succession. Often you will have to freeze, can, or dry some of it because it will be just too much to eat. With the wrong attitude, keeping up with rapid growth may become a chore. But if you really love eating wild foods, and you want your garden to be the most productive it can be, you will have to can, freeze, or dry some of it. If you don't, the plants will go past their prime, and you will have lost the

Part of my 2006 wild garden. Other than some perennial asparagus, French sorrel, and irises along the fence, this is all wild. Plants in this image include pokeweed, wild spinach, wild mustard, dandelion, mallow, nipplewort, and sheep sorrel.

good stuff. If you are willing to do some of the basic things listed here, you will harvest more choice wild food than you could have imagined.

Even with successful crops of wild foods, you will find that some weeds will not be able to keep up with your insatiable hunger for them. If this is the case, try to go with the flow and take what your garden gives you. If you still want more, then go ahead and turn more of your yard into garden space and/or go foraging in your neighborhood.

Introducing wild seed into your garden or yard

There are many times over the years that I have wanted to expand the diversity of wild edible plants growing in my garden. Every time I move to a new home and landscape, I take the first year to assess which edible weeds are already in the soil. I decide which of my favorite plants are missing. Then I go on a quest in search of those plants. When I find them, I assess their form. Since each wild plant is an individual genetically, each can vary in how it grows. For example, a tall-stemmed wild spinach plant with few leaves will most likely produce the same kind of stemmed children. A plant crowded with large leaves will produce offspring that grow into plants crowded with large leaves. I wait till that preferred plant is going to seed, uproot it, and randomly spread the seed where I want it to grow. I've even transplanted immature plants into my backyard so they would eventually spread their seed where I wanted it.

If you are not careful, you will introduce bad seed (producing weeds with poor form) into your garden, and then you are stuck with its children for years.

The Wild Landscape

Landscaping is different from gardening. A landscape is more permanent than a garden and contains more perennials. It is usually located in areas around the perim-

Eastern Blue Violet (*Viola Sororia*). This edible plant makes an excellent ground cover.

eter of your yard, along sidewalks, and wherever grass is not intended.

Wild landscaping is what I have done around my house in addition to my wild garden. I did not go to the extent of replacing all the grass, but I did use the borders of the yard to foster a variety of mostly perennial wild foods. Anywhere that was available, I either let preexisting wild foods take over or brought in ones I wanted. Among others, I've introduced common blue violet (*Viola sororia*), sweet violet (*Viola odorata*), and miner's lettuce (*Claytonia perfoliata*). All three are doing well and carpeting certain areas. Pokeweed (*Phytolacca americana*), tawny daylily (*Hemerocallis fulva*), and lady fern (*Athyrium filix-femina*) were already here.

"Edible landscaping" is the practice of planting food-producing trees, shrubs, vines, and perennial herbs on your land as opposed to or in addition to nonedibles. So, beyond just wild food perennials, consider planting fruit trees, nut trees, and spice bushes. You can get a huge amount of food from your own yard over time.

Edible landscaping is more productive if you are disciplined. It is just as much work as conventionally landscaping your yard if you want tight control over its look and

Japanese knotweed shoots (*Polygonum cuspidatum*). While delicious, this plant can spread out of control.

productivity. If you do not care how wild it looks, it is a lot less work.

Care must be taken to understand and replicate the growing conditions for some of the more finicky annuals like miner's lettuce (*Claytonia perfoliata*) and chickweed (*Stellaria media*). Certain plants require very soft soil, others like hard soil, and still others grow no matter where they are. Certain ones thrive in full sun, others despise it, and others adapt to whatever they get. You may have to transplant some wild edibles, soil and all, in order to get them established.

Ideal growing conditions for a plant may not be ideal growing conditions for harvesting and eating. You have to plan for this when deciding what plants should go where. While dandelion (*Taraxacum officinale*), a perennial, can grow in highly shaded to full-sun conditions, it is better for eating and harvesting if it is growing in well-shaded, well-watered areas. Full sun and dry soil make dandelions intolerable to eat for most of the year.

If you are diligent in the first few years of setting up your landscape, you will reach a point where there is less and less maintenance. The weeds you want will thrive; the weeds you don't want will eventually have no seed left in the soil to grow. After a few years, I'm getting to the point now that whole areas of my yard are covered with only the plants I want. I can harvest at will from sustainable areas during their prime harvesting seasons.

There are edible weeds you may not want to allow in your yard or garden. Green amaranth (*Amaranthus retroflexus*), for instance, seems to outcompete all other weeds. Its roots are massive and spreading. It will choke out other weeds you want to thrive. Other examples of problem plants are mint (wild and domesticated varieties), henbit (*Lamium purpureum*), and Japanese knotweed (*Polygonum cuspidatum*). They spread underground and can stubbornly take over whole areas. Of course, you may actually want some plants to take over your yard.

Chapter 25

Feeding Yourself and Society

One day I was out on a u-pick farm, gathering cultivated marionberries. Surrounding the trellises that supported these plants were thousands and thousands of wild foods—mostly goosefoot and amaranth plants. There were rows and rows of them, vigorously growing anywhere the beds received water. In a few minutes, I had collected a bushel of the greens. As I was paying for the berries, I asked if there was any charge for the weeds I had gathered. After a perplexed look and sizing me up with some seriousness, she declared, "no charge." When she realized that I was not an escapee from an asylum and learned how I was going to use them, her expression changed. She said that I was more than welcome to take as much as I wanted. "Come back soon," she pleaded. "Take more!"

Another time I was on my friends' organic vegetable farm. Their intended crops, as usual, were invaded extensively by wild spinach, amaranth, sheep sorrel, and field mustard. Volume-wise, there were much more of these weeds then there were the lettuce and spinach they had planted. As usual, I gathered a bunch for my own use.

This story is repeated every time I visit a farm. Gobs of wild edibles all over the place. Every farm in the world has to contend with these plants. Farmers spend great amounts of time and resources trying to kill them. Whether mechanical (pulling or machining under) or chemical (herbicides), these behaviors are expensive, burning fossil fuels and polluting the soil and groundwater.

There is a huge resource here—lots of lushly growing free food waiting to be harvested alongside the intended crops. The question is, what can we do about it? Is there a way to rid the farmer of a problem and help ourselves and others in the process? Can something be done on a large scale?

I'd like to propose several holistic approaches to combating the problem. These approaches will work only if the farm is organic and allows some proportion of their beds to be hand-weeded.

Feed Yourself—Help the Farmer

Fresh edible weeds can be collected by individuals for their own use. Setting up this arrangement requires developing a relationship with a farmer. One cannot just trespass, thinking that since they are doing a good deed (pulling weeds) that it is okay to invade someone else's property unannounced. The individual will probably be allowed in the fields when others are either doing the same thing or when paid staff are pulling weeds. As a result of this book, and if there are enough people interested in this activity, clubs might form for just such a purpose and perhaps sponsor wild food dinners and other events from the foods collected.

In order for this to work, the farm would have to be open to coordinating days when outsiders can go into the fields—supervised or unsupervised. There would also have to be some sort of training mechanism to ensure that harvesters know the plants they are gathering, how to tell them from look-alikes, and how to work around the beds so that they do not damage them or any intended crops. Training could be done by farmers, the USDA's Cooperative Extension Service, Master Gardener programs, or local wild food clubs.

In the process of making it possible for organic farmers to succeed, what follows are some of the benefits of wild foods for farmers and the society in general.

Farmers—Turn a Liability into an Asset

Edible weeds compete with farmland crops. Since the plants covered in this book are wonderful contributors of flavors and nutrients, why not create a new market? These are, after all, now considered exotic foods. I've seen fine restaurants tout dishes that include wild foods. Wild mushrooms are most commonly used, but more and more "exotic" and "wild" greens are being offered—often at premium prices.

Creating new markets would accomplish many things. Harvesting wild foods would provide the following:

—Another tool would be added to the arsenal of integrated weed management. Many weeds would transform from a liability to an asset.

—A more diversified crop portfolio would be available; both planted crops and weeds would be sold, increasing the variety of offerings and decreasing dependence on just a few plants. If certain crops failed, others would survive, particularly hardy weeds.

—The farmer would benefit financially. The expense of hand-weeding would be offset by the income of harvested culinary weeds. Each plot could be harvested several times, bringing in additional income. Less money would be spent on killing or removing weeds.

—More farmhands could find work and spend their money to help stimulate our economy. The profits produced by selling the wild foods would cover payrolls and bring additional income to the farm.

—The population would benefit from an increase in the diversity of food supply. This would be true from both culinary and nutritional standpoints.

—Harvesting edible weeds would be good for the environment; there would be no need for herbicides that leach into the groundwater, remain as residue on plants, or affect farmworkers.

One strategic option that farmers could choose is to dedicate whole plots and farms to wild foods. This would be less complicated overall—easier to manage, easier to monitor, easier to harvest, etc. Weeds are often more disease-resistant and require less care. Weeds are often hearty and can survive unexpected conditions that would cause many "conventional" crop plants to die.

Marketing Wild Foods to the Public

The difficulties in introducing new foods to the public should not be understated. Developing venues for new products takes sophisticated marketing, education, support, and follow-through. You cannot just introduce new foods (okay, these are old foods being reintroduced as new) and expect them to fly off the shelves. Underdeveloped introduction of these foods into the market would result in financial strain for the people attempting it.

For introduction of a wild edible to be successful, the public has to be made aware that these new "desirable" foods exist, of the general health benefits of increasing the diversity of vegetables in the diet, and of any known nutrient data. Consumers need to know how these foods can be used in conventional ways, of the great flavor possibilities, and they need to be intrigued enough to start experimenting with them.

Farmhands weeding around tomato plants. Gleaners could harvest weeds from around cultivated plants to be used for a variety of food-related purposes.

Expectations must be positive, first experiences must be delightful (or at least comparable to conventional foods), consumers must be given access to easy starter recipes, and so on. Unless there is a grassroots movement driving the market, making wild foods a mainstream reality will require substantial up-front investments. I hope that this book will provide a user-friendly educational guide to help support at least some of this process.

In addition to consumer awareness, the management of these plants from germination to presentation in the marketplace needs to be worked out. Growth characteristics, optimal harvest times, mass-scale harvesting techniques, packing, transporting, shelf life, and shelf presentation all need to be established through testing and experience.

That being said, there is tremendous potential for many of the wild foods discussed in this book to become mainstream foods if managed properly.

Humanitarian Organizations— Fresh Food for the Poor

There are nonprofit groups that employ gleaners, who spread out over cropland that has already been harvested to collect any plants (broccoli, carrots, cabbage) that were missed or rejected for market. These foods are then delivered directly to the poor, given to humanitarian organizations, or served fresh or cooked in soup kitchens that serve the poor and homeless.

Gleaning for the remnants of a cultivated crop is limited to postharvest. For instance, gleaners have to wait until the cabbage has been harvested before they can go in to pick the leftover cabbage heads. Most leftovers are perfectly edible, just damaged or otherwise unattractive, and would not sell very well on the open market.

In contrast, wild food gleaners have the advantage of being able to harvest wild foods at their prime all season long. Wild foods grow in beds anytime the soil is turned and watered. Within weeks after any planting, a new crop

GLEANING

Today, gleaning is typically done by nonprofit organizations that gather food for the poor. Gleaning involves more than just gathering crop leftovers. Gleaning organizations receive donations from food manufacturers in the form of goods that may have been mislabeled or overproduced, from bakeries, and from supermarkets dumping nonperishable items that are not selling or are getting near their expiration dates.

of wild foods would be available. There are always weeds to pick.

For this to work, gleaners would have to be trained in the details of harvesting, packaging, and transporting these new foods. Food preparers would need to be trained in how to make best use of the plant matter they receive.

Wild foods represent a huge untapped resource that could, under the right circumstances, improve the food options of consumers, help the farmer, and improve the condition of many underprivileged people.

References

Allen, David E., and Gabrielle Hatfield. *Medicinal Plants in Folk Tradition: An Ethnobotany of Britain & Ireland.* Timber Press, Portland, OR, 2004.

Aliotta, Giovanni, and A. Pollio. "Vitamin A and C Contents in Some Edible Wild Plants in Italy." *Rivista Italiana* EPPOS 63 (1981): 47–48.

Andersson, Annica, et al. "Chemical Composition of the Potential New Oilseed Crops Barbarea vulgaris, Barbarea verna and Lepidium campestre." *Journal of the Science of Food and Agriculture* 79, no. 2 (1999): 179–86.

Angier, Bradford. *How to Stay Alive in the Woods.* New York, NY: The Macmillan Company, 1956.

Anonymous: "Quinoa: a Delicate Balancing Act." *Biodiversity International. 2006 Annual Report.* Publication 1253, 17–19. Online version copied 9/15/2009: http://www.bioversityinternational.org/fileadmin/bioversity/publications/pdfs/1253.pdf.

Bianco, V. V., et al. "Nutritional Value and Nitrate Content in Edible Wild Species Used in Southern Italy." *Acta Horticulturae* (ISHS) 467 (1998): 71–87.

Cheatham, Scooter, et al. *The Useful Wild Plants of Texas, the Southeastern and Southwestern United States, the Southern Plains, and Northern Mexico.* Volume 2. Austin, TX: Useful Wild Plants, Inc., 2000.

Chestnut, Victor K. *Plants Used by the Indians of Mendocino County, California. Contributions from the U.S. National Herbarium.* Washington DC: U.S. Department of Agriculture, Division of Botany 7, no. 3 (1902): 295–408; reprinted by Mendocino County Historical Society, 1974.

Compact Edition of the Oxford English Dictionary. New York, NY: Oxford University Press, 1971.

Coon, Nelson. *Using Wayside Plants.* New York, NY: Hearthside Press Inc., 1960.

Cowan, J. W., et al. "Composition of Edible Wild Plants of Lebanon." *Journal of the Science of Food and Agriculture* 14, no. 7 (July 1963): 484–88.

Davis, Donald R., et al. "Changes in USDA Food Composition Data for 43 Garden Crops, 1950 to 1999." *Journal of the American College of Nutrition* 23, no. 6 (2004): 669–82.

Drenowski, Adam, and Carmen Gomez-Carneros. "Bitter Taste, Phytonutrients, and the Consumer: a Review." *American Journal of Clinical Nutrition* 72, no. 6 (December 2000): 1424–35.

Duke, James. *Handbook of Edible Weeds*. Ann Arbor, MI: CRC Press, 1992.

Emerson, Ralph Waldo. *Fortune of the Republic: Lecture Delivered at the Old South Church, March 30, 1878*. Boston, MA: Houghton, Osgood and Company / The Riverside Press, Cambridge, 1878.

Farre, M., et al. "Fatal Oxalic Acid Poisoning from Sorrel Soup." Lancet 2 (8678–8679) (December 1989): 1524.

Fassett, David W. "Nitrates and Nitrites" / "Oxalates." In *Toxicants Occurring Naturally in Foods*. Washington, DC: National Academy of Sciences, Committee on Food Protection, Food and Nutrition Board, National Research Council, 1973, 7–25, 346–62.

Foster, Steven, and James Duke. *A Field Guide to Medicinal Plants*. Boston, MA: Houghton Mifflin Co., 1990.

Gail, Peter. *The Dandelion Celebration: A Guide to Unexpected Cuisine*. Cleveland, OH: Goosefoot Acres Press, 1994.

Gibbons, Euell. *Stalking the Healthful Herbs*. New York: David McKay Co. Inc., 1966, 271, 276–77.

———. *Stalking the Wild Asparagus*. New York, NY: David McKay Co. Inc., 1962.

Guil-Guerrero, José Luis, et al. "Lipids Classes, Fatty Acids and Carotenes of the Leaves of Six Edible Wild Plants." *European Food Research and Technology* 209, no.5 (1999a): 313–16.

———. "Nutritional Composition of Sonchus Species (S. Asper L., S. oleraceus L., and Stenerissimus L.)." *Journal of the Science of Food and Agriculture* 76, no. 4 (1998): 628–32.

———. "Nutritional Composition of Wild Edible Crucifer Species." *Journal of Food Biochemistry* 23, no. 3 (1999b): 283–94.

Hall, Allan. *The Wild Food Trailguide.* New York, NY: Holt, Rinehart and Winston, 1973.

Harlan, Jack. *Crops and Man.* 2nd Edition. Madison, WI: American Society of Agronomy-Crop Science Society, 1992.

Harrington, Harold D. *Edible Native Plants of the Rocky Mountains.* Albuquerque, NM: University of New Mexico Press, 1967.

Harris, Ben Charles. *Eat the Weeds.* Barre, MA: Barre Publishers, 1961.

Hu, Chun, et al. "Luteolin and Luteolin-7-O-Glucoside from Dandelion Flower Suppress iNOS and COX-2 in RAW264.7 Cells." *Molecular and Cellular Biochemistry* 265, no. 1–2 (2004): 107–13.

Kallas, John N. "Skunk Cabbage . . Lives Up to Its Name." *Wild Food Adventurer* 2, no.1 (1997): 1.

Kansas State University. *Practical Cookery.* New York, NY: John Wiley & Sons, Inc., 1975.

Keys, Ancel, ed. "Coronary Heart Disease in Seven Countries." *Circulation* 41 (suppl) (1970):1–211.

Keys, Ancel. *Seven Countries: A Multivariate Analysis of Diet and Coronary Heart Disease.* Cambridge and London: Harvard University Press, 1980.

Kingsbury, John M. *Poisonous Plants of the United States and Canada.* Englewood Cliffs, NJ: Prentice-Hall, Inc., 1964.

Kochilas, Diane. *The Glorious Foods of Greece: Traditional Recipes from the Islands, Cities, and Villages.* New York City: HarperCollins Publishers (William Morrow Cookbooks), 2001.

Leichsenring, Jane M., et al. "Many Wild Greens Have Food Value." *Minnesota Farm and Home Science* 4, no. 3 (1947): 4–5.

Louv, Richard. *Last Child in the Woods: Saving Our Children from Nature-Deficit Disorder.* New York, NY: Algonquin Books, 2005.

Mattson, Fred H. "Potential Toxicity of Food Lipids." In *Toxicants Occurring Naturally in Foods*. Washington, DC: National Academy of Sciences, Committee on Food Protection, Food and Nutrition Board, National Research Council, 1973, 189–209.

Mayer, Anne-Marie. "Historical Changes in the Mineral Content of Fruits and Vegetables." *British Food Journal* 99, no. 6 (1997): 207–11.

Mercadante, Adriana, et al. "Carotenoid Composition and Vitamin A Value of Some Native Brazilian Green Leafy Vegetables." *International Journal of Food Science & Technology* 25, no. 2 (1990): 213–19.

Murray, Hazel C., and Robert Stratton. "Vitamin C Content of Wild Greens." *Journal of Nutrition* 28, no. 6 (1944): 427–30.

Pieroni, Andrea, et al. "*In Vitro* Antioxidant Activity of Non-Cultivated Vegetables of Ethnic Albanians in Southern Italy." *Phytotherapy Research* 16, no. 5 (2002): 467–73.

Raju, Marisiddaiah, et al. "Carotenoid Composition and Vitamin A Activity of Medicinally Important Green Leafy Vegetables." *Food Chemistry* 101, no. 4 (2007): 1598–1605.

Rombauer Becker, Marion., et al. *The 1997 Joy of Cooking*. New York, NY: Simon & Schuster, Inc., 1997.

Royer, France, and Richard Dickinson. *Weeds of the Northern U.S. and Canada*. Renton, WA: Lone Pine Publishing, 1999.

Schuddeboom, L. J. *Nitrates and Nitrites in Foodstuffs*. Report of the Committee of Experts on Health Control of Foodstuffs. Strasbourg, France: Council of Europe Press, 1993. Online version copied 9/15/09: http://www.coe.int/t/e/social_cohesion/soc-sp/public_health/food_contact/NITR-E.pdf.

Schütz, Katrin, et al. "Characterization of Phenolic Acids and Flavonoids in Dandelion (Taraxacum officinale WEB. ex WIGG.) Root and Herb by High-Performance Liquid Chromatography/Electrospray Ionization Mass Spectrometry." *Rapid Communications in Mass Spectrometry* 19, no. 2 (2005): 179–86.

Sengupta, S. R., and B. Pal. "Composition of Edible Wild Greens." *Journal of the Science of Food and Agriculture* 21, no. 4 (1970): 215.

Simopoulos, Artemis P., et al. "Common Purslane: A Source of Omega-3 Fatty Acids and Antioxidants." *Journal of the American College of Nutrition* 11, no. 4 (1992): 374–82.

———. "Purslane in Human Nutrition and Its Potential for World Agriculture." In *Plants in Human Health and Nutrition Policy* 77. Series by *World Review of Nutrition and Dietetics*. Edited by A. P. Simopoulos. Basel, CH: Karger, 1995, 47–74.

Simopoulos, Artemis P. "Omega-3 Fatty Acids and Antioxidants in Edible Wild Plants." *Biology Research* 37, no. 2 (2004): 263–77.

Smith, Chef Michael: http://www.chefmichaelsmith.ca/en/home/default.aspx. Online version copied 9/15/09. Search for "Homemade Mustard" within a Honey Cured Salmon recipe.

Stein, Sara. *My Weeds: A Gardener's Botany*. New York, NY: Harper & Row, Publishers, 1988.

Su, Q., et al. "Identification and Quantitation of Major Carotenoids in Selected Components of the Mediterranean Diet: Green Leafy Vegetables, Figs, and Olive Oil." *European Journal of Clinical Nutrition* 56, no. 11 (2002): 1149–54.

Supreme Scientific Health Council. "Dietary Guidelines for Adults in Greece." *Archives of Hellenic Medicine* 16 no. 5 (1999): 516–24. Online version copied 8/25/09: http://www.nut.uoa.gr/english/GreekGuid.htm.

Strauss, Judi, and Peter Gail. *The Great Dandelion Cookbook: Recipes from the National Dandelion Cookoffs & Then Some*. Cleveland, OH: Goosefoot Acres Press, 1997.

Trichopoulou, Antonia. "Components of the Mediterranean Diet." In *International Conference on Health*

Benefits of Mediterranean Diet: Highlights on Cancer & Cardiovascular Diseases, 2003, 13–14.

———, et al. "Nutritional Composition and Flavonoid Content of Edible Wild Greens and Green Pies: A Potential Rich Source of Antioxidant Nutrients in the Mediterranean Diet." *Food Chemistry* 70, no. 3 (2000b): 319–23.

U.S. Department of Agriculture, Agricultural Research Service, USDA National Nutrient Database for Standard Reference Release 18: http://www.nal.usda.gov/fnic/foodcomp.

Valadon, L. R. G., and R. S. Mummery. "Carotenoids of Certain Compositae Flowers." *Phytochemistry* 6, no. 7 (1967): 983–88.

Vardavasa, C. I., et al. "The Antioxidant and Phylloquinone Content of Wildly Grown Greens in Crete." *Food Chemistry* 99, no. 4 (2006): 813–21.

———. "Lipid Concentrations of Wild Edible Greens in Crete." *Food Chemistry* 99, no. 4 (2006): 822–34.

Wiese, B., et al. "Chemical Composition of Rumex crispus L. Seed." *Journal of the American Oil Chemists' Society* 72, no. 9 (1995): 1077–78.

Yıldırım, Ali, et al. "Determination of Antioxidant and Antimicrobial Activities of Rumex crispus L. Extracts." *Journal of Agricultural and Food Chemistry* 49, no. 8 (2001): 4083–89.

Zeghichi, Sabrina, et al. "Nutritional Composition of Selected Wild Plants in the Diet of Crete." In *Plants in Human Health and Nutrition Policy* 91. Series by *World Review of Nutrition and Dietetics)* 91. Edited by A. P. Simopoulos and C. Gopalan. Basel, CH: Karger, 2003, 22–40.

Zennie, Thomas M., and Dwayne Ogzewalla. "Ascorbic Acid and Vitamin A Content of Edible Wild Plants of Ohio and Kentucky." *Economic Botany* 31, no. 1 (January 1977): 76–79.

Index

Z